CHIEF e-LEARNING OFFICER

IN THE ERA OF SPEED

YOUR GUIDE TO SECURING CXO ROLE BEYOND BEING AN E-LEARNING STRATEGIST

CHIEF e-LEARNING OFFICER

IN THE ERA OF SPEED

Digital Learning Strategies to Speed Up Workforce Performance

Dr Raman K. Attri

A Publication of Speed To Proficiency Research: S2Pro©

Copyrights © 2021 Raman K Attri and Speed To Proficiency Research: S2Pro©

All rights reserved. No part of this publication may be reproduced, distributed, or transmitted in any form or by any means, including photocopying, recording, or other electronic or mechanical methods, without the prior written permission of the author and publisher, except in the case of brief quotations embodied in critical reviews and certain other noncommercial uses permitted by copyright law.

ISBN: 978-981-18-7079-8 (e-book)
ISBN: 978-981-18-7080-4 (paperback)
ISBN: 978-981-18-7081-1 (hardcover)

Published in Singapore
Printed in the United States of America / Australia / UK

https://www.speedtoproficiency.com
info@speedtoproficiency.com

National Library Board, Singapore Cataloguing in Publication Data

Name(s): Attri, Raman K., 1973-
Title: Chief e-learning officer in the era of speed : digital learning strategies to speed up workforce performance / Dr Raman K. Attri.
Description: Singapore : Speed To Proficiency Research, [2023] | Includes bibliographic references and index.
Identifier(s): ISBN 978-981-18-7080-4 (paperback) | 978-981-18-7081-1 (hardback) | 978-981-18-7079-8 (epub)
Subject(s): LCSH: Employees—Training of—Computer-assisted instruction. | Organizational learning.
Classification: DDC 658.31240285—dc23

Editor: (Ms.) Farheen Malik, Pakistan

*To James Keller, an incredible mentor,
supportive colleague, great e-learning strategist,
and training program manager*

AUTHOR

Dr. Raman K. Attri is a sought-after *coach to the futuristic chief learning officers* who are ready to stay ahead of their competition. Dr. Attri is the world's leading authority on the "science of speed" in professional learning and performance, with over two decades of research in performance science. His outstanding achievements have earned him recognition as a Brainz Global 500 leader alongside other stellar personalities such as Oprah Winfrey, Gary Vee, Jim Kwik, and Jim Shetty.

He is multifaceted personality with a range of talents, including being a scientist, author, speaker, L&D leader, and artist. Despite being permanently disabled since childhood, Dr. Attri is known as a powerhouse of positivity and inspiration. He has transformed his inability to walk into a unique expertise in teaching people how to walk faster in their professional world.

He is the creator of a time-tested, proven system that can help leaders and organizations to speed up the path to mastery and leadership in any domain by two folds. His most recent project is the GetThereFaster portal, a comprehensive resource for anyone seeking to learn the secrets of learning better and faster.

Dr. Attri is a professional speaker who shares research-based insights at leading international conferences with top business executives, helping them to master speed in business, shorten workforce time-to-proficiency, and accelerate employee development.

He is also a global training thought leader at a Fortune 500 technology corporation, managing one of the world's top 10 Hall-of-Fame training organizations.

As a prolific author of 50 multi-genre books, Dr. Attri writes books and articles on various topics ranging from business and leadership to performance and expertise, as well as training and development to HR and workforce development.

Passionate about continuous learning, Dr. Attri has earned two doctorates in learning, over 100 international educational credentials, several degrees and diplomas, and some of the highest certifications. He is an authentic accelerated learning business coach who practices what he preaches.

Featured in over 125 articles, interviews, and shows, Dr. Attri was awarded as one of the Most Admired Global Indians of 2022. He is a highly sought-after expert whose remarkable achievements continue to inspire everyone he touches to strive for true excellence in their personal and professional lives.

You may contact @DrRamanKAttri on Facebook, LinkedIn, YouTube, Twitter, Instagram, and Tiktok, among other social media platforms. Or visit **https://get-there-faster.com**.

PREFACE

In 2018, I conducted a large-scale study. I interviewed 85 world-class leaders and gathered 66 project cases from over 70 word-class learning organizations spanning 42 industries. The participants hailed from various business segments, job types, and skills. Thus, the study has a reasonably broad coverage of contexts and settings.

My goal was to explore how organizations have increased the slope of the proficiency curve. The research revealed powerful insights for the first time regarding how organizations shortened time-to-proficiency.

While my research question was about overall strategies to shorten time-to-proficiency, I found that several organizations used a range of e-Learning and technology-based training solutions as one of the critical practices to shorten time-to-proficiency.

My research generated many breakthrough strategies. However, the findings were ahead of time, as most organizations did not have a culture of "speed" in employee development. At best, most organizations emphasized mad rush, putting aggressive timelines on employee deliverables. That's how far they could go to institute a 'fake speed culture' in which doing things faster is deemed as 'speed.' But in reality, they did not attain any competitive edge with a sustainable speed over their competitors.

Then things began to explore differently during the pandemic of COVID-19. The pandemic questioned every traditional mode of working. That's where organizations looked for solutions to improve employee skills quickly. Pandemic restrictions washed out those who did not find the way.

This pandemic has opened up executive eyes to how badly they needed e-Learning, online learning, and other technology-based learning solutions. At the same time, the world is changing now for good at the onset of Industry 4.0 and the highly accelerated digital revolution.

More than ever, most organizations now need robust, speedier e-learning, remote learning, and online learning solutions. You also might have been given the same challenge to create effective e-Learning solutions that could speed up employee development rapidly. Ironically, most designers have not trained on how to design robust e-learning for faster development of employee skills and prepare them for the era of speed.

In this book, I will share some breakthrough strategies and frameworks based on my research and the implementations I drove during the pandemic technological revolution. I focus on teaching you how to use an e-learning strategy that positively contributes to accelerating learning and acquiring new skills to the desired mastery level.

Let's get there faster together!

Dr Raman K Attri

June 2023

Disclaimer:

Brands, technologies, and companies mentioned in this book are for the sake of illustration and example. It should not be construed as any recommendation or sponsorship. Readers are advised to use discretion before adopting or using any stated technologies.

Apps and platforms mentioned in this book, along with URLs, are correct and accessible at the time of writing the book. As new technologies continue to erase previous technologies faster than one can imagine, readers are advised to do due research on contemporary technologies built on stated principles.

Contents

1.
E-LEARNING AND THE DIGITAL REVOLUTION

TRENDS IN E-LEARNING 5
CLASSIFICATION OF E-LEARNING 7
EMERGENCE OF REVOLUTIONARY E-LEARNING 19
STRATEGIZE E-LEARNING FOR ACCELERATED EMPLOYEE
DEVELOPMENT 26
E-LEARNING SUCCESS GUIDELINES 30
REFLECTION TIME 32
YOUR LEARNING JOURNEY 34

2.
EMERGING ROLE OF A CHIEF E-LEARNING OFFICER

EMERGENCE OF A NEW ROLE 39
WHY CHIEF E-LEARNING OFFICER? 42
RESPONSIBILITIES OF A CeLO 45
WHY DEVELOP YOURSELF AS A CeLO? 46
HOW TO BE A DIFFERENTIATED CeLO 47
E-LEARNING LEADERSHIP 49
E-LEARNING STRATEGIC THINKING 52
THE SPEED OF EMPLOYEE DEVELOPMENT IS THE REAL KPI 55
YOUR SUCCESS GUIDELINES 63
REFLECTION TIME 65
YOUR LEARNING JOURNEY 67

3.
SPEED OF EMPLOYEE DEVELOPMENT AS E-LEARNING KPIS

MEASURING EMPLOYEE DEVELOPMENT 74
HOW LONG IS TTP? 79

MARKET PRESSURES FOR SPEED	80
BENEFITS OF SHORTENING TTP	85
TIME-TO-PROFICIENCY GUIDELINES	88
REFLECTION TIME	89
YOUR LEARNING JOURNEY	91

4.
STRATEGIC E-LEARNING DESIGN FOR SPEED

3 ELEMENTS OF E-LEARNING DESIGN	97
5 E-LEARNING STRATEGIES	98
E-LEARNING STRATEGY GUIDELINES	103
REFLECTION TIME	105
YOUR LEARNING JOURNEY	107

5.
SCENARIO-BASED E-LEARNING

CONTEXTUALIZATION	113
PRINCIPLES OF CONTEXTUALIZATION	114
CONTEXTUALIZING E-LEARNING TRENDS	119
DESIGNING CONTEXTUALIZATION FOR ACCELERATION	127
REFLECTION TIME	137
YOUR LEARNING JOURNEY	139

6.
TIME-SPACED MICROLEARNING CONTENT

DEBUNKING ATTENTION SPAN MYTH 146
PRINCIPLES OF MICROLEARNING 147
DESIGNING MICROLEARNING FOR ACCELERATION 151
REFLECTION TIME 160
YOUR LEARNING JOURNEY 162

7.
OPTIMALLY SEQUENCED E-LEARNING PATH

CONCEPT OF E-LEARNING PATH 167
PRINCIPLES OF OPTIMALLY SEQUENCED E-LEARNING PATH 169
OPTIMIZING E-LEARNING PATH FOR ACCELERATION 173
REFLECTION TIME 183
YOUR LEARNING JOURNEY 185

8. ON-DEMAND PERFORMANCE SUPPORT SYSTEMS

LEVERAGING PSS FOR ACCELERATION..209
REFLECTION TIME..217
YOUR LEARNING JOURNEY 219

9. EXPERIENCE-RICH MULTI-TECHNOLOGY MIX

RISE OF BLENDED LEARNING...225
PRINCIPLES OF MULTI-CHANNEL LEARNING................................227
MIXING CHANNELS FOR ACCELERATION.....................................235
REFLECTION TIME..242
YOUR LEARNING JOURNEY 244

10. SPEED-ENABLING E-LEARNING SYSTEMS APPROACH

THINKING E-LEARNING OUT-OF-THE-BOX 249
OUTCOME-DRIVEN DESIGN 250
5 GUIDE QUESTIONS TO DESIGN E-LEARNING 252
5 CORE GUIDING FORCES 254
HOLISTIC IMPLEMENTATION OF E-LEARNING 257
THINKING AHEAD 266

11.
SUMMARY OF E-LEARNING DESIGN GUIDELINES FOR SPEED

SELF-GUIDED E-LEARNING GUIDELINES (PRE-ILT PHASE) 273
VIRTUAL OR REMOTE E-LEARNING GUIDELINES (ILT PHASE) 275
ON-THE-JOB E-LEARNING GUIDELINES (POST-ILT PHASE) 277
E-LEARNING GUIDELINES FOR PROFICIENCY MAINTENANCE
(SUSTENANCE PHASE) 279
TAKING IT FORWARD 281

12.
EMERGING E-LEARNING REVOLUTIONS

EMERGING LEARNING TECHNOLOGIES 289
EMERGING SOCIAL TECHNOLOGIES 293

EMERGING AI-BASED E-LEARNING 300
EMERGING WORKFORCE ANALYTICS 305
THINKING AHEAD 311

CAREER ACCELERATION RESOURCES

LEARN FROM POWER-PACKED BOOKS... 315
ENROLL IN ONLINE TRAINING COURSES 317
GET CERTIFIED IN THE SCIENCE OF SPEED.................................... 319

REFERENCES

INDEX

Chapter 1
E-LEARNING AND DIGITAL REVOLUTION

Chapter 2
A ROLE OF CHIEF E-LEARNING OFFICER

Chapter 3
SPEED OF EMPLOYEE DEVELOPMENT AS E-LEARNING KPIs

Chapter 4
STRATEGIC E-LEARNING FOR SPEED

Chapter 5
SCENARIO-BASED E-LEARNING

Chapter 6
TIME-SPACED MICROLEARNING CONTENT

Chapter 7
OPTIMALLY SEQUENCED E-LEARNING PATH

Chapter 8
ON-DEMAND PERFORMANCE SUPPORT SYSTEMS

Chapter 9
EXPERIENCE-RICH MULTI-TECHNOLOGY MIX

Chapter 10
SPEED-ENABLING E-LEARNING SYSTEMS APPRAOCH

Chapter 11
SUMMARY OF E-LEARNING DESIGN GUIDELINES FOR SPEED

Chapter 12
EMERGING E-LEARNING REVOLUTIONS

1
E-LEARNING AND THE DIGITAL REVOLUTION

During the COVID-19 pandemic, organizational leadership expected new solutions within a few days during lockdowns. Among such new solutions, e-learning emerged as a lifesaver for many organizations. Designing e-learning programs that positively accelerate the acquisition of new skills in the new norm has become necessary. This chapter drives a point that with the increasing pace of business, e-learning can act as a pivotal catalyst to speed up employee development. However, it does require specific strategies.

TRENDS IN E-LEARNING

A survey by E-learningindustry.com in 2014 reported that over 47% of the Fortune 500 companies then used some form of educational technology. Corporations value e-learning as the second most valuable training method, saving businesses at least 50% of the cost when traditional classroom training is replaced with e-learning (Pappas 2013).

According to the ASTD (2014) State of the Industry Report, 38% of the training was delivered using technology-based solutions. This report also cited an IBM report stating that companies employing e-learning have the potential to boost productivity by 50%. According to their estimates, every $1 spent on e-learning results in a $30 increase in productivity.

A decade following these observations, e-learning has certainly made big waves nowadays. The global e-learning market was estimated to be worth $144 billion in 2019 and is projected to reach $374.3 billion by 2026[1]. However, the recent COVID-19 pandemic from 2019 to 2022 has fueled e-learning growth far beyond those estimates. The overall

---

[1] Facts and Factors 2021

organizational reliance on e-learning has gone beyond bounds. It has emerged as one of the most attractive and cost-effective solutions with the flexibility to support self-paced learning that can be delivered geographically anywhere. According to a 2023 report by Research and Markets[2], the global e-Learning market stands at $149.31 billion in 2022, projected to reach $588.63 billion by 2030, at a CAGR of 18.70% during the forecast period.

From a business standpoint, e-learning scores everything like saving money, scalability, and efficiency. But not all online learning enjoys the effectiveness as it should, and certainly, not all online training designs can lead to accelerating skill acquisition. Therefore, most e-learning programs have both pros and cons. There is a particular appeal to e-learning or online training solutions in various organizations.

In the recent pandemic, technology-driven e-learning has even become the best bet. It has become every executive's favorite transformation strategy. E-learning and digital learning allow learners to access course materials at their own pace and schedule, making it an ideal option for people with busy schedules or those who prefer self-directed learning. It allows learners to access education regardless of their location as it can be accessed from anywhere in the world.

E-learning is efficient as it can be instantly delivered all across the world at no cost. It also offers scalability as many people can be trained online on a large scale with minimal infrastructure investment. It can be more cost-effective than traditional learning methods as it eliminates the need for physical classrooms and textbooks. It leads to massive cost savings on account of face-to-face training and travel. This reason is probably the single most significant factor that has been pushing online learning in business.

---

[2] eLearning Market Intelligence Report - Global Forecast 2023-2030.
https://www.researchandmarkets.com/reports/5623863/elearning-market-intelligence-report-global

CH 1 – E-LEARNING AND THE DIGITAL REVOLUTION

CLASSIFICATION OF E-LEARNING

Categorizing e-learning can be challenging because of its different methods of delivery and diverse learning objectives. Before we understand e-learning's advantages, disadvantages, and strategies, we need to be cognizant of its context. There are four different taxonomies, as shown in Figure 1.1, for categorizing e-learning based on the following factors:

Figure 1.1: Various anchors for e-learning classification

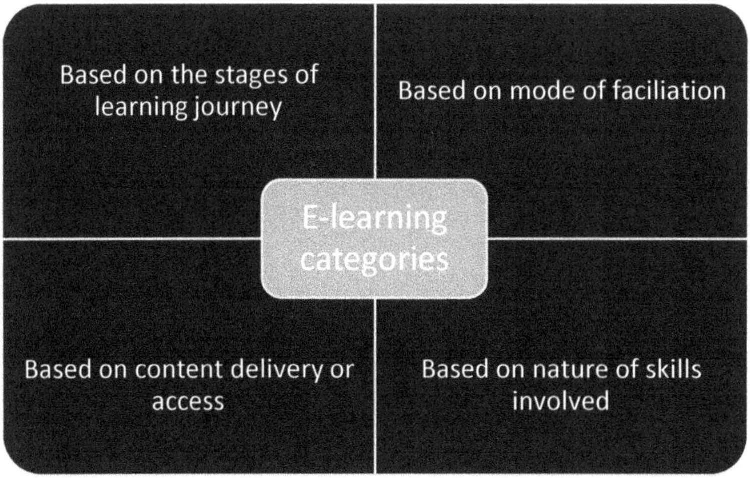

Based on the stages of learning journey	Based on mode of faciliation
Based on content delivery or access	Based on nature of skills involved

E-learning categories

1. MODE OF FACILITATION

At a high level, three types of e-learning come under this taxonomy, as shown in Figure 1.2:

Self-Paced e-learning: This mode refers to content that allows learners to progress through material at their own pace. This also includes an 'asynchronous' e-learning content that enables learners to access and review materials anytime without real-time participation requirements. Examples are recorded lectures and assignments.

Instructor-driven e-learning: This is content driven or facilitated by the instructor in real time. It usually requires learners to participate in real-time activities, such as virtual meetings and discussions.

Group e-learning: This includes the content that encourages or requires learners to work together in groups to complete assignments and projects. Such content can be a supplement to self-paced or instructor-driven e-learning.

Figure 1.2: Types of e-learning by mode of facilitation

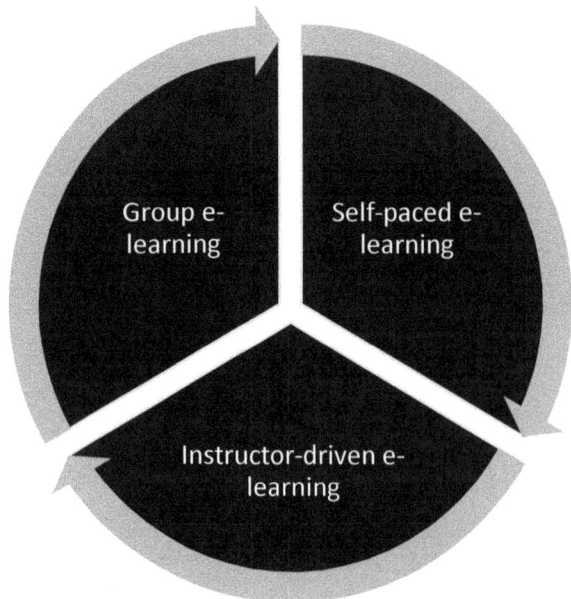

2. NATURE OF SKILLS

E-learning differs based on the nature of the intended skills. Though not many designers think about such segmentation, this is critical to acquire skills faster. There are four main categories of e-learning based on this taxonomy, as shown in Figure 1.3:

Informational skills: E-learning for imparting informational content includes self-paced material, video tutorials, eBooks, and text-based content. Suh content is designed for learners to access and complete at their own pace. Often this content is straightforward to inform or make them aware of some information, concepts, facts, or guidelines. Usually, content does not require higher-order thinking. It may include video tutorials demonstrating how to complete specific tasks or use specific tools. Or it can be written materials such as eBooks, guides, and manuals for learners to read and use for self-guided learning.

Complex thinking-based skills: This e-learning content caters to engaging and developing higher-order thinking skills. It usually involves scenario-based learning, simulations, gamification etc. Scenario-based learning presents learners with real-life scenarios, challenging them to use complex thinking skills to solve problems. Simulations simulate real-world environments, allowing learners to practice applying complex thinking skills in a risk-free setting. Gamification uses game elements, such as points and leaderboards, to engage learners in complex thinking activities.

Intensive hands-on skills: This e-learning content focuses on teaching or triggering intensive hands-on skills. It may involve gamified or immersive virtual labs environment to practice hands-on skills. Some content uses interactive elements like quizzes and assessments to allow learners to practice hands-on skills, interactive learning, and Augmented Reality (AR) or Virtual Reality (VR). AR and VR technologies provide learners with immersive, hands-on experiences.

On-the-Job workplace skills: This is a special type of content developed to let learners learn and apply the skills on-the-job directly. This content revolves around using performance support systems like job aids and reference materials to help them complete tasks. It also includes content that can be downloaded or accessed during the workflow while performing certain tasks, allowing learners to apply skills and knowledge in real time. Some e-learning is geared explicitly toward creating checklists or assessments to provide ongoing coaching and mentoring support to help develop skills and succeed in their jobs.

Figure 1.3: Types of e-learning by the nature of skills

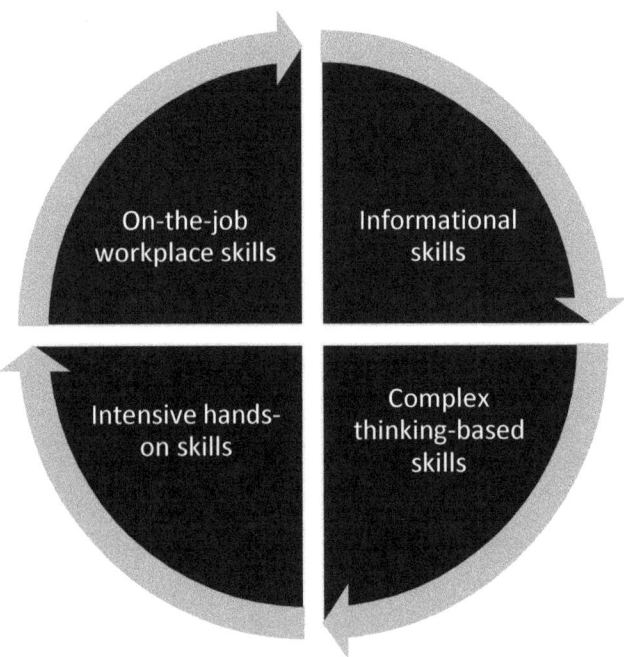

3. CONTENT DELIVERY OR ACCESS

The nature and strategies of e-learning differ based on how learners access the content or how it is delivered. There are four categories of e-learning based on content delivery or access modes, as shown in Figure 1.4:

Instructor-facilitated e-learning delivery: More complex jobs invariably require some form of instructor-facilitated e-learning. This includes live virtual sessions, online seminars, webinars, and discussion forums where instructors and experts teach and interact with learners in real-time. Coach-driven or mentor-driven sessions need appropriate material to teach or coach employees in the field or post-ILT (instructor-led training) sessions. They are also a form of e-learning that must be designed beforehand.

On-Demand e-learning delivery: This bucket of e-learning includes a range of resources or materials that learners can access when they need it, either while doing the job or during the task workflow. Pre-recorded video tutorials or self-paced online courses are a popular form of on-demand e-learning. In addition to that, static or need-based written materials, such as manuals and guides from central documentation repositories, allow learners to access and search for specific information related to their job tasks.

Workflow-based e-learning delivery: Some e-learning content can be made available via performance support systems or workflow tools like chat assistants, remote assists, AR models, and on-screen software help, among other means. This e-learning content, in the form of job aids or decision-support, allows learners to perform a task efficiently without spending time learning the information or content.

Pushed e-learning delivery: This type of e-learning relates to the content which is not required to be learned upfront but is more meaningful when the time comes. It is pushed onto user mobiles, laptops, or accounts based on user subscription or job requirements. Such content can be text messages, video links, summary documents, newsletters, field bulletins, safety notices, acknowledgments of reading the document, or quick snapshots or summaries of desired content, ensuring that learners stay up-to-date with compliance requirements related to their job. For instance, mobile quizzes allow learners to receive questions related to specific topics and test their knowledge on-the-go. Others are mobile reminders that remind learners to complete specific tasks or review specific content related to their job.

Figure 1.4: Types of e-learning by the content delivery or access

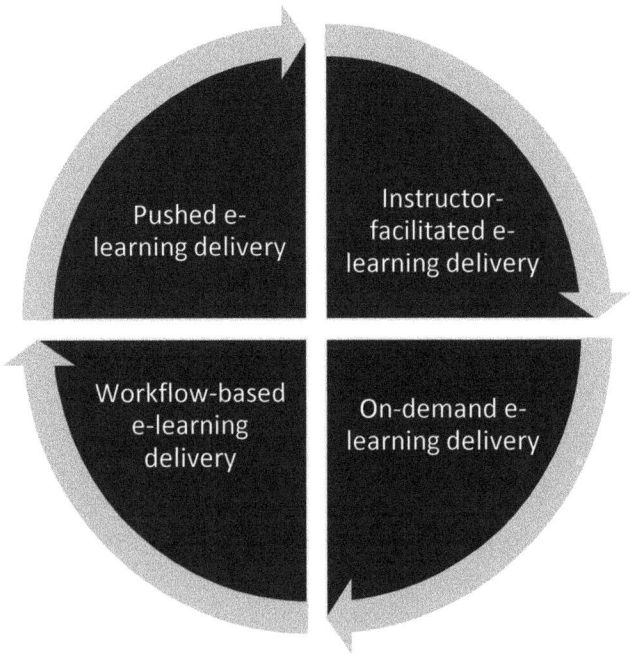

CH 1 – E-LEARNING AND THE DIGITAL REVOLUTION

4. STAGES OF THE LEARNING JOURNEY

A learner goes through several stages as he is being made ready for the job. Most jobs require learners to attain proficiency. Attending formal ILT is one essential part of such a journey. Based on that, one goes through four typical training stages, as shown in Figure 1.5:

Self-guided e-learning before an ILT session: These preparatory e-learning modules are designed to prepare learners for an upcoming instructor-led training session. Some form of foundational e-learning content is also included, providing learners with a basic understanding of the concepts or skills they will study in the ILT session. The content at this stage varies from video-based tutorials, self-learning texts, watching recorded lectures, and completing assessments or assignments.

Instructor-driven virtual or remote e-learning: The goal of all the e-learning avenues at this stage is to impart complex thinking skills and critical hands-on skills which otherwise are impossible to deliver in self-paced content. This stage includes interactive learning through a live, virtual, or remote session via platforms like Zoom. These sessions can be facilitated via other platforms, such as Blackboard, in educational settings. Supplemental e-learning provides additional information, assignments, quizzes, and resources to reinforce learning. It can be instructor-driven chats, discussions, or assignments via Blackboard. The sessions may include a range of e-learning resources like simulators, scenarios, AR/VRs, gaming, and others.

Post-ILT on-the-job e-learning: After ILT sessions, e-learning given to the learners includes applied learning content designed to use the skills and knowledge learned during the ILT session in real-world situations. The goal of all these e-learning avenues in unison is to enable learners to reach the stage of independent proficiency. At this stage, e-learning also provides coaching and mentoring aids like checklists, assessments, and on-the-job training (OJT) trackers to help reinforce learning and develop skills further. Examples are e-learning accesses via performance support systems, on-demand resources, and in-workflow tools.

E-learning for proficiency maintenance: Once learners have attained the required proficiency, they need continuous reinforcement and refresher learning to maintain their proficiency. For that, e-learning content is distributed to them occasionally to reinforce their previous learning. Such content may include videos, bulletins, notices, reminders, and new content on procedure changes and up-to-date information. Some content is pushed on-the-go, while others are available on-demand. Performance support systems and workflow tools are key delivery vehicles at this stage which aims to maintain skills over time to ensure ongoing proficiency.

Figure 1.5: Types of e-learning based on stages of the learning journey

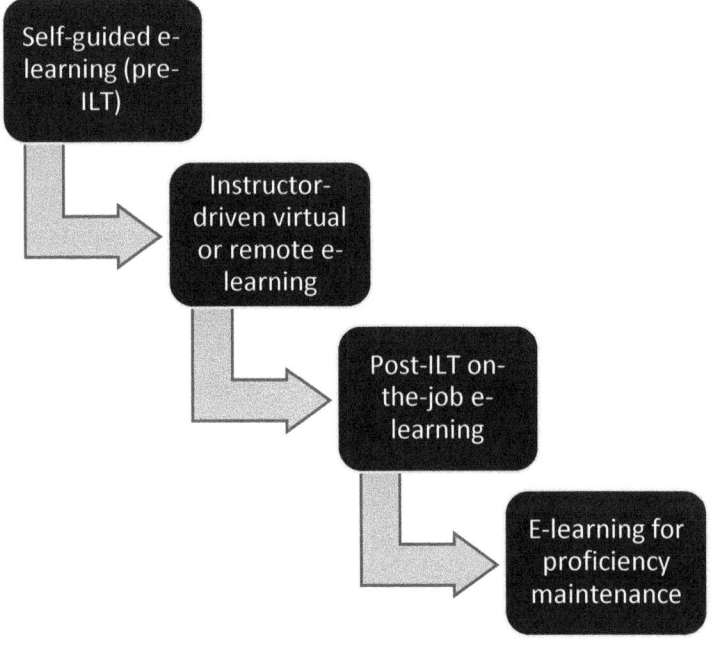

The guidelines presented in this book are described in relation to these four stages. Therefore, it is imperative to set grounds here. Figure 1.6 shows four phases of the learning journey represented in terms of proficiency acquisition. The vertical axis represents a hypothetical improvement in proficiency, while the horizontal axis represents time. The two sets of piece-wise lines show a simplified depiction of how learners acquire proficiency over time depending upon how e-learning is structured and used to support their learning journey. How e-learning is designed determines how fast learners can attain proficiency. We will come back to this proficiency-time chart in subsequent chapters.

Figure 1.6: e-learning during various phases of proficiency acquisition

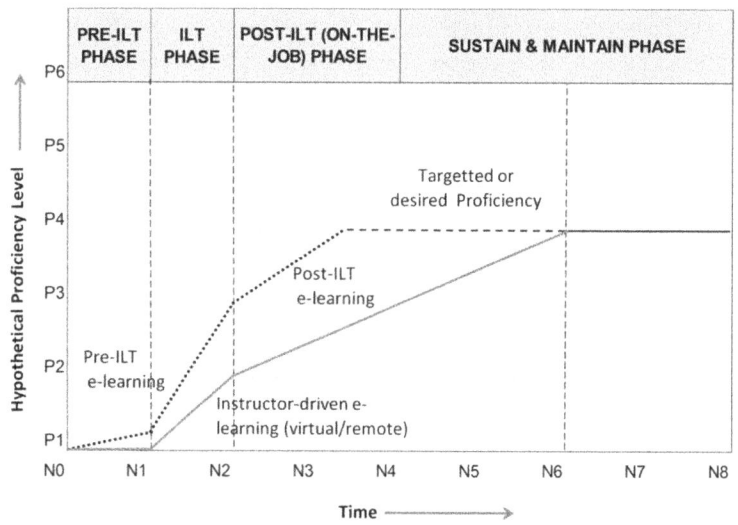

HOLISTIC PICTURE OF E-LEARNING CLASSIFICATION

As you can see, multiple elements can come under the e-learning umbrella. The issue is that this classification is dynamic and overlapping. The boundaries between classroom versus off-class activities are diffusing as technologies converge. Before the COVID-era, most in-person training sessions already employed computer-based, web-based, or AR/VR-based e-learning to deliver some content. In the post-COVID era, we have already seen the hybrid classroom trend, which eliminates the boundary between in-person and remote learning.

While e-learning is categorized in various ways, you, as an e-learning strategist, must classify e-learning avenues appropriately. You need to set the grounds to define what falls under your job role and what does not. If you don't do so, several activities, whether e-learning in nature or not, will fall under your responsibility.

Further, such an agreed terminology that you will use across the organization also has some impact on the application of strategies while designing e-learning to speed up employee development.

Since the subsequent book is focused on employee development and proficiency journey, it makes perfect sense to take stages of learner's proficiency as the main anchor to drive discussions and implementation.

Table 1-1 is a representative categorization of e-learning based on various variables anchored to stages of proficiency. Remember that this classification map is not fully exhaustive, and there is much overlap between them. However, this can act as your guide to setting the taxonomy right in your organization.

Table 1-1: Categorization of e-learning channels and avenues

Stages of the Learning Journey	Modes of Facilitation	Nature of Skills	Content Delivery or Access	Representative Examples
Self-guided e-learning before an ILT session	Self-paced e-learning Group e-learning	Informational skills	On-Demand e-learning delivery	• Pre-recorded video tutorials • Self-paced online courses • Written materials • Self-learning texts • Procedures and manuals • Informational content • Presentation slides • Group assignment
Instructor-driven virtual or remote e-learning	Instructor-driven e-learning Group e-learning	Complex thinking-based skills Intensive hands-on skills	Instructor-facilitated e-learning delivery	• Live virtual sessions • Remote training sessions • Interactive learning • Simulators • Scenarios and games • AR/VR • Assignments and quizzes • Chats and discussions • Coaching sessions • Group assignments
Post-ILT on-the-job e-learning	On-the-Job workplace skills	Intensive hands-on skills On-the-Job workplace skills	Workflow-based e-learning delivery	• Performance support systems • On-demand resources • In-workflow tools

CHIEF E-LEARNING OFFICER

	Informational skills	On-the-Job workplace skills	Pushed e-learning
Group e-learning	• On-screen contextual help • Coaching and mentoring aids • Checklists and checksheets • Assessments • Proficiency tests • Procedures and manuals • Group assignments • Forum-based e-learning content		• Updated videos • Field bulletins • Newsletters • Safety notices • Web-based training • Compliance acknowledgments • Summary of procedures • Task reminders • Refresher content • Procedure change notifications • On-the-go mobile quizzes • Performance support systems • Workflow tools • Checklists and checksheets
Self-paced e-learning			
E-learning for maintenance of proficiency			

EMERGENCE OF REVOLUTIONARY E-LEARNING

In the earlier days, computer-based training was deemed as e-learning, while in most recent times, VR is considered a new face of e-learning. The definition of e-learning changes with the endless possibilities every new electronic technology brings (Kahiigi et al. 2008).

The last two decades have significantly changed how we learn and access education. E-learning and digital learning have evolved since the early 2000s, with new technologies and platforms constantly emerging. It has become a popular alternative to traditional learning methods, offering flexible and accessible options for learners of all ages and backgrounds.

2000-2010: THE EMERGENCE OF E-LEARNING

The first decade of the 21st century saw the emergence of e-learning as a viable and popular alternative to traditional classroom-based learning. In the early 2000s, e-learning platforms were primarily used by universities and other higher education institutions to offer online courses and distance learning programs. One of the earliest and most well-known e-learning platforms of that time was Blackboard, founded in 1997.

Revolutionary Web 2.0-based Learning Platforms

In the mid-2000s, the emergence of Web 2.0 technologies led to the development of new e-learning tools and platforms that allowed more interactive and collaborative learning experiences. One such platform was Moodle, an open-source learning management system (LMS) first released in 2002. Moodle allowed the creation of online courses and provided various tools for communication, collaboration, and assessment.

Massive Open Online Courses (MOOCs)

Another notable development in the e-learning industry during this decade was the emergence of MOOCs. MOOCs were first introduced in 2008 with the launch of a course on artificial intelligence (AI) by Stanford University. They offered free online courses that anyone with an internet connection could access, and they quickly gained popularity among learners worldwide. Some of the most popular MOOC platforms included Coursera, Udacity, and edX. Lately, platforms like LinkedIn Learning, Khan Academy etc., have emerged that offer courses and training in various subjects, including business, technology, and creative skills.

However, in the early days, e-learning was mostly text-based and lacked multimedia content because it was difficult to deliver due to low-speed internet.

2010-2019: THE RISE OF DIGITAL LEARNING

The second decade of the 21st century saw significant growth and development in the e-learning industry, with new technologies and platforms emerging rapidly.

On-the-go Mobile Learning

One of the most significant developments during this time was the widespread adoption of mobile devices which led to the development of mobile learning or m-learning. M-learning allowed learners to access course materials and participate in online courses using their smartphones and tablets, making learning more flexible and accessible.

A report by FinancesOnline[3] in 2023 stated that mobile learning had reached maturity by the end of 2019, and since then, it is continuously offering flexibility and accessibility. As mobile learning continues to evolve, we expect to see compatibility and responsiveness advancements to improve the overall user experience[4].

Gamified Learning

Another notable development during this decade was the emergence of gamification in e-learning. Gamification involves using game design elements in non-game contexts, such as education, to engage learners and motivate them to learn. One of the most well-known examples of gamified learning is Duolingo, a language learning platform that uses game-like activities to make learning fun and engaging.

Adaptive Learning

The emergence of adaptive learning technologies is another significant development during this decade. These technologies use data analytics and machine learning algorithms to personalize the learning pathways or experiences for individual learners based on their preferences and performance. One example of an adaptive learning platform is Knewton.

Rise of Blended Learning

The rise of mobile learning and self-learning on-demand resources evolved into blended learning whereby organizations mixed ILT with on-demand learning resources. The on-demand portion of such an approach led to more flexibility and accessibility, and it made learners best use their time waiting for the next instructor-led event.

---

[3] 11 New Elearning Trends & Predictions for 2023. https://financesonline.com/elearning-trends/
[4] eLearning Trends: Top 8 L&D Trends to Watch Out For In 2023.
https://elearningindustry.com/elearning-trends-top-ld-trends-to-watch-out-for-in-2023

2019-2022: THE DIGITAL EXPLOSION

The COVID-19 pandemic has significantly impacted education, with many schools, colleges, and universities starting online or e-learning.

Shift to remote and virtual learning

This has led to an explosion in e-learning as educators and learners have to adapt new ways of teaching and learning. Most corporations had to shift to remote, virtual, and online learning. One such example is the use of video conferencing tools such as Zoom and Microsoft Teams.

Zoom has been widely adopted for remote teaching and learning during the COVID-19 pandemic. It allows teachers and learners to connect in real-time, even when they are physically distant from each other. According to Statista[5], 70% of organizations in 2020 suggested that they are investing in virtual learning delivery systems. However, the definition includes the latest virtual means like AR, VR, metaverse, etc.

Hybrid Learning As Expected Channel

With the success of remote learning during the COVID-19 pandemic, followed by eased cross-border restrictions among some countries, hybrid learning emerged as a powerful learning mechanism that allowed mixing onsite and remote learners to leverage mixtures of multiple technologies. Boston.com's 2020 surveys suggested that 80% of the students chose the hybrid learning mode over the traditional one. Most organizations replaced instructor-led events with remote or virtual training sessions by leveraging their previously mastered blended learning models. This allowed the flexibility of virtual learning and the intensity of in-person learning into one. However, there are several

---

[5] 10 eLearning Software Trends for 2022/2023. https://financesonline.com/elearning-software-trends/

technological challenges to make it work, which became taxing for the facilitators.

Adoption of Microlearning

Another notable development during this decade is the increased focus on microlearning. Microlearning involves breaking down learning content into small, bite-sized modules that can be accessed and completed quickly. This approach is particularly well-suited to the needs of busy professionals with limited learning time. The E-learning Industry reported in 2021 that among L&D professionals, 94% prefer microlearning compared to other tools.

The Emergence of VR/AR

Another emerging trend is using VR/AR technologies to create immersive e-learning experiences. VR/AR can simulate real-world environments and provide learners with hands-on, immersive, and interactive learning experiences. This technology is particularly well-suited to training and education in fields such as healthcare and engineering. Various companies have begun developing VR/AR technologies to create immersive learning experiences. For example, Microsoft has developed HoloLens, which is an AR headset used to simulate real-world scenarios in fields such as healthcare and engineering. These technologies have become more accessible and affordable, making them increasingly popular in digital learning.

Innovation in AI

We are also seeing the continued development and adoption of AI and machine learning (ML) in e-learning. For example, AI-powered chatbots can be used to provide learners with instant support and assistance. AI is a trend that has the potential to revolutionize digital learning. It can be used to personalize learning, provide real-time feedback, and automate administrative tasks.

2023 – 2030: THE PARALLEL WORLD

The e-learning industry has undergone significant growth and development over the past two decades, and the ongoing COVID-19 pandemic has accelerated the adoption of digital learning solutions worldwide. E-learning is expected to become even more prominent in the future with the emergence of new technologies and trends. As we look ahead to the next decade, several trends and technologies will likely shape the future of e-learning.

Increased Use of AI and ML

One of the most significant forecasts for the e-learning industry in the next decade is the increased use of AI and ML. These technologies can help to identify learners' individual learning needs and preferences and tailor learning experiences accordingly. For example, AI-powered chatbots can provide instant support and assistance to learners, while intelligent tutoring systems can provide personalized feedback and guidance. These technologies can also automate tasks such as grading and assessment, freeing educators' time to focus on more complex tasks.

Widespread Adoption of VR/AR

Another significant forecast for the e-learning industry is the increased adoption of VR/AR) technologies. These technologies can be used to create immersive learning experiences that simulate real-world scenarios and provide hands-on, interactive learning opportunities. For example, VR/AR can be used in medical or engineering education to simulate surgical procedures or provide virtual simulations of equipment and machinery, respectively. This technology can also be used to create interactive virtual classrooms where learners can collaborate and interact with each other in a virtual environment.

CH 1 – E-LEARNING AND THE DIGITAL REVOLUTION

Continued Growth of Microlearning into Nano-Learning

As the world is becoming fast-paced and the younger generation's attention span shorter, microlearning is shifting toward bite-sized modules that can be absorbed on-the-go via mobiles. This approach is particularly well-suited to the needs of busy professionals with limited learning time. Nano-learning can be delivered through a range of platforms and devices, including smartphones and tablets, and can be used to provide just-in-time learning opportunities. This approach can help improve learners' retention and engagement and make learning more accessible and flexible.

Increased Focus on Soft Skills

In addition to technical skills, there is likely to be an increased focus on soft skills in the next decade, such as communication, collaboration, and problem-solving. These skills are becoming increasingly important in the modern workplace, where teamwork and adaptability are essential. E-learning can be an effective way to develop these skills through the use of collaborative learning activities and simulations. For example, virtual team projects can allow learners to develop communication and collaboration skills in a safe and supportive environment.

Greater Integration of Social Media

Social media is likely to become increasingly integrated into e-learning platforms and tools in the next decade. According to Thinkific's *Digital Learning Trends 2023 report*[6], the world is expected to see the rise of community-first digital learning. While digital communities have traditionally been an add-on to existing courses or learning products, there's an undeniable move toward communities as the main play to building e-learning.

---

[6] https://www.thinkific.com/elearning-trends/

Social media can be used to support collaborative learning and provide opportunities for learners to connect and engage with each other. For example, social media can facilitate peer feedback and discussion and give learners access to a broader network of professionals and experts. Social media can also be used to provide personalized learning recommendations based on learners' interests and activities.

As we look ahead to the next decade, it is clear that e-learning will continue to play a significant role in education and training. By embracing new technologies and platforms and focusing on the development of soft skills and technical skills, e-learning has the potential to revolutionize the way we learn and work in the years to come. As the world continues to evolve and the demand for remote and flexible learning solutions grows, e-learning is likely to become an increasingly important part of education and training.

STRATEGIZE E-LEARNING FOR ACCELERATED EMPLOYEE DEVELOPMENT

A real corporate challenge is that most jobs are becoming complex. The problems employees encounter are non-routine and non-linear, requiring their proficiency in complex skills like decision-making, problem-solving, and troubleshooting.

E-learning has shown great potential in enabling employees with the skills to solve routine or predictable problems. However, a question often arises whether it is a plausible medium to deliver complex cognitive skills or not. It also gets questioned about its 'stickiness' or effectiveness in transferring skills to the workplace, particularly for complex skills. Sims et al. (2008) stated that "In fact, a common criticism of e-learning is that face-to-face courses are directly transferred to an electronic format with the assumption that these courses will be equally effective and accepted by trainees."

Complex skills indicate the need to approach the learning of complex and simple skills differently. For example, learning simple skills profits from an 'increase in load' whereas learning complex skills requires a 'reduction in load.' The point here is that e-learning targeted at developing highly complex cognitive skills needs a different set of strategies.

In general, it is believed that learners are at a loss due to e-learning, mainly because of the following four reasons:

Lack of Social Learning

Social learning is the biggest multiplier of learning during face-to-face settings. People can work with each other, ask each other, and seek out help, feedback in-person, and instant performance changes. That part is taken away by online training. You could add many interactions among learners, but it does not compensate for that face-to-face social encoding of learning.

Longer Time-to-Proficiency (TTP)

Though e-learning solutions are efficient from the angle that they are available timely to the employees, that doesn't mean employees will learn faster when the social part of learning is already subtracted from it.

My research found out that TTP using e-learning solutions tends to go longer. It probably has something to do with poor design. Some organizations simply record their very long face-to-face lectures or presentations and make them digitally available in the name of e-learning.

A couple of years back, I signed up for an expensive 18-month training program that was supposed to be delivered face-to-face. Due to COVID-19, that training organization simply converted their 8 hours of videos to an e-learning course. I learned very little from that poor e-learning design. Such poor designs are ineffective because they are designed around the content, not around the learners. The result is a drastically long TTP for learners.

Shallow Depth of Skill Acquisition

Another issue with e-learning is that the depth of skills goes shallow. People need to experiment, observe, reflect, or think about something. They need personal or social interactions. Much of such multi-sensory processing goes into encoding the skill deeply inside one's personality. That part tends to suffer in typical e-learning design.

It appears that e-learning fails to deliver results when designers get into the trap of using principles meant for simpler skills to design for complex skills. In reality, principles derived from the study of simple skills do not generalize to complex skill learning (Wulf & Shea 2002).

Only a few research studies provide evidence or guidelines to design e-learning that could accelerate expertise or TTP. Some industry figures substantiate the fact that e-learning holds the potential to accelerate proficiency. According to E-learningindustry.com, e-learning cuts instruction time by 60%, and information retention rates increase by 60%. Compared to classroom learning, e-learning students are reported to have a 60% faster learning curve (Pappas 2013).

Despite the lack of studies, the value of e-learning technologies, platforms, or methods cannot be denied in regard to their ability to cut down training length and allow self-paced learning and reinforcement to traditional training methods (Clark & Mayer 2011; Zhang 2005).

The COVID-19 pandemic has highlighted the importance of flexible and adaptive learning systems that can withstand disruptions and ensure continuity in education delivery. As the demand for remote and flexible learning solutions grows, the complexity level of e-learning technologies is growing too. At the same time, most technologies are becoming expensive and capital-intensive due to the sheer size of implementation. The organizational structures and typical e-learning tech roles no longer suffice to survive and thrive in the fast-paced world that is upon us.

Then what is the solution?

The solution is to institute a highly strategic role of *Chief e-learning Officer (CeLO),* who has a seat on the table alongside CLOs, CFOs, CTOs, and CHROs. The next chapter explores the emergence and need for such a role and discusses what it takes to be a strategic CeLO.

E-LEARNING SUCCESS GUIDELINES

☞ Embrace a growth mindset and continuous learning: Stay up-to-date with industry developments, research, and best practices to ensure you can adapt and grow with the rapidly evolving e-learning landscape.

☞ Invest in upskilling and reskilling: Encourage your team members to participate in professional development opportunities, such as online courses, workshops, and conferences, to stay current with the latest e-learning tools and techniques.

☞ Prioritize user experience and accessibility: Ensure your e-learning content is engaging, easy to navigate, and accessible to users with varying abilities and learning styles.

☞ Leverage data and analytics for informed decision-making: The digital revolution has made it easier than ever to collect and analyze data related to e-learning. Regularly assess your e-learning programs' key performance indicators (KPIs) to optimize the learning experience.

CH 1 - E-LEARNING AND THE DIGITAL REVOLUTION

 Foster a culture of innovation and experimentation: Encourage your team members to explore new technologies, pedagogical approaches, and learning strategies to identify what works best for your learners. Be open to trying new things, learn from failures, and iterate on your e-learning programs to ensure they remain relevant, effective, and engaging in the face of the digital revolution.

REFLECTION TIME

If, somehow, you could design e-learning so effectively that it could accelerate employees' rate of proficiency acquisition, organizations would be able to derive massive financial and competitive benefits. Hence, it is essential for you, as a leader and designer, to figure out the best e-learning design strategies to help you achieve better employee performance in a shorter time.

Use the space below to reflect upon and note down your major takeaways to this point. *Are you on top of the latest and greatest e-learning development like apps, software, platforms, and methods? If not, this is the time to get ahead of the curve.*

> *Question to think ahead!*
>
> *What can you do to stay ahead of the curve by getting involved in e-learning pilots and experimentation at the source or ahead of the other organizations? How do you cut short the bureaucratic approval process to shorten time-to-implementation?*

Reflections

YOUR LEARNING JOURNEY

Through a brief account of the emergence of the digital revolution, you learned in this chapter a viewpoint that implementing e-learning strategies is far more strategic and far more complex than what it was years ago. Thus, there is a need for a strategic and specialized role to lead e-learning initiatives at the CXO level to stay ahead in organizational competitiveness.

In the next chapter, we will discuss the role of a CeLO and what it will take for you to be one.

Chapter 1
E-LEARNING AND DIGITAL REVOLUTION

**Chapter 2
A ROLE OF CHIEF E-LEARNING OFFICER**

Chapter 3
SPEED OF EMPLOYEE DEVELOPMENT AS E-LEARNING KPIs

Chapter 4
STRATEGIC E-LEARNING FOR SPEED

Chapter 5
SCENARIO-BASED E-LEARNING

Chapter 6
TIME-SPACED MICROLEARNING CONTENT

Chapter 7
OPTIMALLY SEQUENCED E-LEARNING PATH

Chapter 8
ON-DEMAND PERFORMANCE SUPPORT SYSTEMS

Chapter 9
EXPERIENCE-RICH MULTI-TECHNOLOGY MIX

Chapter 10
SPEED-ENABLING E-LEARNING SYSTEMS APPRAOCH

Chapter 11
SUMMARY OF E-LEARNING DESIGN GUIDELINES FOR SPEED

Chapter 12
EMERGING E-LEARNING REVOLUTIONS

2
EMERGING ROLE OF A CHIEF E-LEARNING OFFICER

CH 2 – EMERGING ROLE OF A CHIEF E-LEARNING OFFICER

The end goal of any e-learning strategy, program, or technology is to improve knowledge retention, enhance employee engagement, and increase skill development. In the previous chapter, you observed that such a goal now has multiple aspects to it.

With the advent of technologies such as AI, ML, and adaptive learning, the scope of e-learning is becoming more complex, diverse, and cross-functional. Increased globalization, borderless working, and remote working have resulted in scalability challenges.

Most technologies continue to be cloud-hosted, sharing infrastructure with other competing organizations while also being concerned about data security and safety. Thus, the e-learning space is no longer straightforward. There is a complex mesh of options across software, platforms, apps, and solutions that need to be evaluated to deliver highly efficient and cost-effective e-learning.

As the e-learning industry continued to evolve and grow, organizations recognized the importance of dedicated professionals overseeing their learning technologies. In this chapter, I will highlight why we need to revisit those roles.

EMERGENCE OF A NEW ROLE

During the recent pandemic, we saw several organizations thriving and making revenues at an unimaginable rate that was never possible before the pandemic. But at the same time, we saw the fall of thousands of great businesses. As I analyzed, the single thing that differentiated successful from shut-down businesses is the ability to leverage a range of e-learning flexibly to keep employees in the field even during the lockdowns. That was the fundamental reason how and why some organizations thrived at a rapid rate, and others did not.

On top of that, the pandemic fueled technological innovations at a rate never seen before. That emerged as another factor that the organizations which deployed learning technologies and technology-based e-learning thrived faster through the pandemic with flying colors, beating their competition far behind.

The key was how they strategically deployed and leveraged e-learning to increase employee development speed, which in turn accelerated innovative solutions into the market.

The technology-driven and technology-backed success of thriving organizations during the pandemic has proven one thing for sure. First, you can't deem e-learning as an 'add-on' or 'nice-to-have' capability within a learning organization. Second, you can't treat e-learning strategists as second-to-learning function heads.

Although CLOs and learning heads stood out as the hero of the story in regards to how they leveraged e-learning in offering and deploying innovative training solutions to employees locked up in the field, the real heroes behind the scenes were the e-learning strategists. However, why they are not inside the boardroom because many organizations still continue to treat e-learning as a support function inside the realm of a larger learning organization or business unit.

That treatment is subduing in the changing landscape during the pandemic, and several organizations have begun to recognize e-learning as a standalone business unit. As you progress in the book, you will be convinced that the e-learning space is so wide and deep that it requires an organization of its own.

Ironically, most organizations miss the point and continue to stack e-learning groups inside the mainstream training department. The organization design, however, needs major updates in larger organizations. The reason is that e-learning is a cross-cut between organizational technologies and learning and development. From that

CH 2 - EMERGING ROLE OF A CHIEF E-LEARNING OFFICER

angle, it requires its own space, authority, and KPIs. Now, traditional corporate training and e-learning can co-exist within the same organization.

That could work well for most business units and operations. However, the learning and training function is altogether a different beast. Without knowing how learning processes work and how technologies are effective or hindrance for certain aspects, one cannot implement technologies that could certainly ensure speed of employee learning and development.

We now live in a different world that requires strategic technological thinking. Frontline managers and even the department heads are not developed or groomed to that level of strategic thinking. In the current era, selection, testing, implementation, obsolescence, and upgrade of workplace and e-learning require higher-order strategic thinking where the person could rub shoulders with C-suit executives to push the innovations.

As the e-learning industry continues to evolve and grow, organizations recognize the importance of a dedicated professional overseeing their e-learning strategies and initiatives. To address this need, a new role has emerged in many organizations - the Chief e-learning Officer (CeLO).

A Chief e-learning Officer is vital for an organization that wants to stay up-to-date with the latest e-learning technologies and strategies, improve learning outcomes, reduce costs, increase engagement and retention, and support ongoing learning and development.

WHY CHIEF E-LEARNING OFFICER?

If an organization wants strategic success and to stay competitive in the fast-paced world, it needs to start inducting a new dedicated leadership role of the Chief e-learning Officer (CeLO) and then develop its brilliant e-learning technologists for that role.

As a global learning leader, I view a CeLO as being vital for an organization that wants to stay up-to-date with the latest learning technologies and e-learning strategies, improve learning outcomes, reduce costs, and increase engagement and retention. Thus, a well-accounted role of a CeLO is an essential aspect of your strategic leadership as technology continues to transform the way organizations learn and work.

By leveraging the latest learning technologies and collaborating with other learning and development professionals, a CeLO can help organizations stay ahead of the curve and ensure that their learning initiatives are effective, efficient, and aligned with their strategic objectives.

Some pressing reasons why an organization needs a CeLO are summarized in Figure 2.1.

CH 2 - EMERGING ROLE OF A CHIEF E-LEARNING OFFICER

Figure 2.1: Emerging role of a Chief E-learning Officer

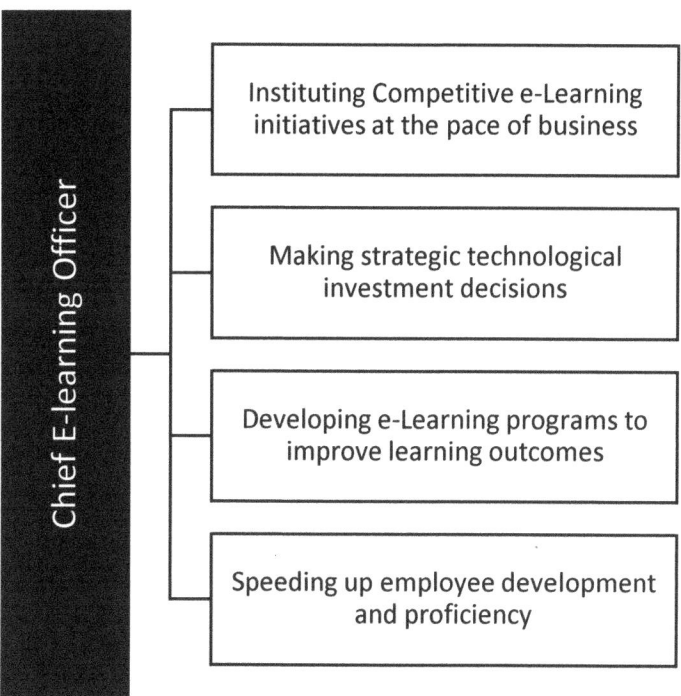

Instituting Competitive e-Learning Initiatives at the Pace of Business

A CeLO is pivotal to instituting and overseeing competitive e-learning initiatives that could position an organization ahead of the competition. Traditional e-learning initiatives get swayed from their main strategic goals in an attempt to look technologically "cool" or ahead of peers. The CeLO's role is to ensure that any new e-learning initiative is strategic in nature for its actual value and not for its grandeur.

CHIEF E-LEARNING OFFICER

Making Strategic Technological Investment

Technology is rapidly evolving, and e-learning is becoming an increasingly important part of employee training and development. Traditionally, technology projects are led by someone from the company's IT department. Such leadership underserves the learning department because IT specialists are not training experts. The CeLO's role is to stay up-to-date with the latest e-learning technologies and strategies, ensuring that technologies are implemented to ensure that e-learning programs meet business goals. A CeLO needs to ensure the most cost-effective e-learning solutions while ensuring the organization gets the most value from its investment in e-learning.

Developing E-Learning Programs to Improve Learning Outcomes

A CeLO can help an organization improve learning outcomes by developing and implementing effective e-learning strategies. By identifying the skills and knowledge employees need, a CeLO can develop e-learning programs and resources that support these objectives and help employees achieve their full potential. This can allow employees to acquire new skills and knowledge throughout their careers, improving employee retention and supporting the organization's long-term goals and objectives. By investing in a CeLO role, an organization can ensure its employees can access the most effective and engaging e-learning experiences. Above all, a CeLO can help ensure that an organization's learning technology and e-learning approaches are truly strategic and built for the speed of employee development.

Speeding up Employee Development and Proficiency

Most e-learning professionals try their best to focus on developing e-learning programs that are engaging, interactive, and tailored to the needs of different learners, increasing engagement and retention rates. Traditionally developed e-learning programs fail to accelerate the employee learning curve because designers keep chasing 'aesthetics' and 'trendiness' in such programs. However, a CeLO's role is not to make such programs look good to the audience or the executives. The real reason why organizations need CeLO who is a specialist who focuses entirely on how to speed up employee development, performance, and proficiency through e-learning programs.

RESPONSIBILITIES OF A CELO

The role of a CeLO is becoming increasingly important as organizations recognize the value of e-learning in achieving their goals and objectives. As a CeLO, some of the key responsibilities would be:

Develop and Implement an E-Learning Strategy

Your primary responsibility is developing and implementing an e-learning strategy that aligns with the organization's goals and objectives. This involves conducting a demand-analysis to determine the organization's e-learning needs, developing a plan for delivering the solutions to those needs, and then overseeing their implementation.

Stay Up-to-Date on E-Learning Trends and Technologies

You are responsible for staying up-to-date on the latest e-learning trends and technologies. This includes attending industry conferences and events, monitoring industry publications and blogs, and networking with other e-learning professionals. By doing so, you can ensure that the organization's e-learning strategies are cutting-edge and effective.

Manage E-Learning Programs and Projects

You are responsible for managing e-learning programs and projects from conception to completion. This involves developing project plans, identifying and managing resources, monitoring progress, and ensuring that projects are completed on time and within budget.

Provide Leadership and Guidance to E-Learning Team

You are responsible for providing leadership and guidance to the organization's e-learning team. This includes hiring and training staff, setting performance goals, and providing ongoing feedback and support. This is how you can ensure that the organization's e-learning initiatives are successful.

Evaluate and Measure the Effectiveness of E-Learning Programs

You are responsible for evaluating and measuring the effectiveness of the organization's e-learning programs. This involves developing evaluation criteria, collecting and analyzing data, and making recommendations for improvement. This is how you can ensure that the organization's e-learning initiatives are meeting its goals and objectives.

WHY DEVELOP YOURSELF AS A CELO?

It is not an understatement that a CeLO role will soon emerge as the right hand of a Chief Learning Officer (CLO).

While the CLO and CeLO share similar responsibilities, a CLO focuses on learning and development broadly, and a CeLO specifically focuses on e-learning and digital learning. At a high level, the CeLO role is more marketable because he can rise as a CLO. It is not always the case that a CLO could make more strategic technology decisions like a CeLO.

A CLO's primary focus is developing and managing an organization's overall learning and development strategy. He is responsible for ensuring that employees have all the skills and knowledge they need to be successful in their jobs. This includes developing training programs, managing talent development programs, and overseeing learning initiatives that support the organization's goals and objectives.

As a CeLO, on the other hand, you are focused specifically on e-learning and digital learning initiatives within an organization. Your primary focus is on developing and implementing e-learning strategies that support the organization's goals and objectives. This includes identifying the appropriate e-learning technologies and platforms, developing e-learning content, and managing e-learning programs and projects.

Another key difference between the two roles is the level of technology expertise required. You, as a CeLO, need deep expertise in e-learning technologies and platforms. At the same time, the CLO may have a more general understanding of technology and its application to learning and development.

No organizational or corporate learning is feasible without strategically thought-out e-learning programs and technologies. How fast the organizational learning stays in sync with the market is highly dependent upon how you lead the show.

Thus, stay in your niche but stop thinking of yourself as a support or add-on staff. Rather, you have to continue making a bigger presence for upward movement. You must demand a seat at the board table.

HOW TO BE A DIFFERENTIATED CELO

Becoming a successful CeLO requires a combination of skills and expertise in several areas. Following are some of the critical skills that you would need to develop in order to be successful:

CHIEF E-LEARNING OFFICER

Strong Leadership Skills

As a leader of the e-learning team, you must possess strong leadership skills. You must be able to inspire and motivate your team, set clear goals and objectives, and provide guidance and support as needed.

Business Acumen

You must have a strong understanding of the organization's business objectives and how e-learning can support those objectives. You must be able to communicate the benefits of e-learning to key stakeholders and build buy-in for e-learning initiatives across the organization.

Technical Expertise

You must have a deep understanding of e-learning technologies and platforms and the ability to evaluate new technologies and determine their suitability for the organization. You must also be able to manage e-learning projects and programs effectively, which requires a strong understanding of project management methodologies and tools.

Analytical and Strategic Thinking

You must be able to think critically and strategically about e-learning initiatives. You must be able to analyze data and metrics to evaluate the effectiveness of e-learning programs, identify areas for improvement, and make strategic recommendations for future initiatives.

Communication Skills

You must possess strong communication skills, both written and verbal. You must be able to communicate effectively the benefits of e-learning to key stakeholders and their e-learning teams.

Creativity and Innovation

You must be able to think creatively and innovatively about e-learning solutions. You must be able to identify new and innovative ways to use e-learning technologies and platforms to support the organization's goals and objectives.

Collaboration and Teamwork

You must be able to collaborate effectively with other departments and stakeholders across the organization. You must be able to work effectively as part of a team, build consensus, and navigate complex organizational structures to achieve their goals.

While other competencies continue to be in line with any other senior roles in an organization, leadership practices, and strategic thinking skills are the ones that would make you stand out from the rest of the executives. Let's explore these two competencies in detail.

E-LEARNING LEADERSHIP

As a leader in the e-learning space, your leadership practices as a CeLO will differ in several ways from others. Here are some key areas in how you need to practice your leadership differently:

Change Management

Some learners and even leaders hesitate to use new technologies or platforms, and some stakeholders may resist investing in them. It is not always about the technology. It's about the frustrating unstable, or less-than-pleasant experience that comes with any new technology. If you do not demonstrate a perfect change management regime for any new changes, you will continue to experience this challenge.

Thus, your utmost focus will be on change management, which is unavoidable given your technological space. Unlike other leadership roles, your role requires faster and more profound change management.

How well can you communicate the benefits of e-learning to stakeholders across the organization and build buy-in for e-learning initiatives, even in the face of resistance or skepticism? This single most critical factor will make or break your success as a CeLO leader.

Agile and Adaptable

While other leaders talk about being agile, you have to live it day and night. Agility and speed are your life. The critical thing about agility is how, as a CeLO, you stay focused on the speed of innovation and human resources development in your organization. Among other metrics, TTP will be your core metric to impact. You will be able to quickly pivot and adjust e-learning strategies and initiatives based on changing needs or new technologies.

Focus on Continuous Improvement

Continuous improvement will be the first on your agenda because the shelf life of technologies is condensing. While you are testing one technology, the market may have already moved to the next one. The time-to-market for most new revolutionary technologies is down to three months post-COVID. In the AI era, the time-to-market is squeezing down to a few weeks.

How fast can you implement your technologies and stay on top of improving them at the pace of innovation? You need to focus your leadership on unconventional, high-speed, continuous improvement. You will regularly evaluate the effectiveness of e-learning initiatives and make necessary adjustments to ensure that learners are getting the most out of their e-learning experiences.

Focus on Learning Outcomes

You will be less concerned with traditional measures of success, such as profits or revenue, and more focused on ensuring that learners achieve their objectives and acquire the skills they need to succeed. By keeping your leadership practices revolving around learning outcomes, your initiatives and programs will never go wrong, and you'll stand a chance of always being able to defend your budgets and plan to your executives.

E-Learning Expertise

You will deeply understand e-learning technologies, platforms, and best practices, unlike other leaders. Your leadership practices will be characterized by a deep understanding of learning technologies, their capabilities, and their potential impact on learning outcomes. You will be able to provide leadership in selecting, implementing, and integrating learning technologies into the organization's learning initiatives. You will make informed decisions about e-learning initiatives and strategies. While all leaders must be technically strong in their functional areas, you have to remember that one organization would have only one CeLO. That also means you are unique in your role. So, what you have is unique to you. You can't be average in what you are known for.

Instilling a Learning Culture

Learning is an undeniable foundation of corporate innovation. In fact, a large part of your time will be spent on building this culture. Unlike other leaders who may focus primarily on business objectives, your primary focus will be on the learning and development of the organization's employees. As a result, your leadership practices will emphasize the importance of creating a learning culture within the organization. You will do anything within your power and means to ensure that learners have access to the resources and support they need to succeed and that the organization values and prioritizes ongoing learning and development.

Emphasis on Collaboration

One of the biggest challenges you may face is a lack of understanding and support from other organizational stakeholders. As I said, your technological and learning expertise is unique in the organization, and you could be one of a kind across an organization. Thus, there may be no equivalent expertise in your domain across your organization. Some stakeholders may not immediately understand the benefits of the learning technologies you propose. Or others may be resistant to change, and you may face limited resources such as funding, staff, or technology, making it challenging to implement effective technologies and initiatives.

Thus, your leadership practices will emphasize collaboration and teamwork. You will work closely with other departments and stakeholders across the organization to ensure that e-learning initiatives are aligned with the organization's goals and objectives. Your leadership will be far different from others in this domain simply because your e-learning programs will have far-reaching impacts across business units and the company. Due to your boundaryless influence, you need far more developed skills in seeking and establishing cross-functional collaboration.

E-LEARNING STRATEGIC THINKING

I can't emphasize enough how strategic thinking is essential to your success. It is more applicable to dynamic roles, far more impactful across the organization, and has far-reaching long-term roadmaps. To be more strategic in your position, here are a few competencies you need to acquire:

CH 2 - EMERGING ROLE OF A CHIEF E-LEARNING OFFICER

Master the Science of Speed in the Organization

Historically speaking, nothing has proliferated and impacted as fast as e-learning has. In other words, the need for speed has fueled the growth of e-learning innovations. Therefore, as a CeLO, the first thing you need to master is the science of speed. Unless you are fully educated on the strategies for measuring and ensuring speed in organizations, your job is half done.

Thus, as the most critical strategic thinker, you need to master the metrics and science behind organizational speed. Above all, you need to learn how to measure your workforce's TTP metrics (see next chapters) and how your learning technologies are impacting to improve them.

Measure and Report KPIs That Matter

To be more strategic, a CeLO should measure and report on the outcomes of e-learning initiatives. This involves identifying KPIs for e-learning, collecting and analyzing data, and using this data to make strategic decisions about future e-learning initiatives. Among others, the most critical metrics in today's fast-paced world are related to speed, such as TTP, time-to-first success, and time-to-market. Unless you keep yourself up to speed on how to impact these KPIs with e-learning, you will continue to have challenges making your mark.

Develop a Long-Term Vision for E-Learning

To be more strategic, you should develop an organization's long-term vision for e-learning. This involves looking beyond the organization's immediate needs and identifying how e-learning can support its future goals and objectives. This is beyond doubt the most important thing because the shelf-life of most technologies is compressing. That also means the rate of obsolescence is going up.

Often CeLOs are always in firefighting mode because they have not counted these obsolescences, sustenance, and upgrades of technology into their roadmaps and budgets. More and more technologies are capital-intensive. Hence, obsolescence needs to be computed in depreciation from a financial angle. On top of that, you also need to look at how fast you can upgrade and replace the technologies if the vendor declares the end of the support. Thus, you have to be highly strategic about the impact replacement of technology can cause. This also means fresh logistics, financial and leadership investment in change management.

Monitor Industry Trends and Best Practices

More CeLOs waste much energy convincing their upper management about the value of something which has not proliferated the market fully but has been tried successfully in some places. Staying on top of the research through forums, conferences, and research reports can build strategic thinking. To be more strategic, you must stay up-to-date on industry trends and best practices in e-learning.

This involves monitoring industry publications, attending conferences and events, and networking with other e-learning professionals. This allows you to look beyond your horizon and anticipate changes and the evolution of technologies. Often, CeLOs build a roadmap that looks glorious to their executives. But they hide the bitter truth about what is coming and how soon it needs to be integrated into mainstream operations. You can be preemptive in building roadmaps to stay ready for those changes.

Evaluate Emerging E-Learning Technologies

To be more strategic, stay up-to-date on emerging e-learning technologies and evaluate their potential to support the organization's e-learning goals. This involves looking beyond the currently available technologies and identifying new and innovative ways to use technology. This can be a tough area as reading reports, or best-known methods alone would not give you confidence that what works in another organization could indeed work in yours. You have to do a pilot and test the integration with other infrastructural elements of the company. This does invite massive investment.

However, more executives want to know the Return on Investment (ROI) of experimental investments. There is no easy answer. You have to be able to conduct your experimentation inside or outside your organization. Being a part of a research body or a group of university researchers or start-ups is a great way to execute such evaluations flawlessly. You can explore how to set up tie-offs with emerging start-ups to give them fair play to test out their technology while you focus on how their technology can help you achieve your organizational goals.

Align E-Learning Strategy with Overall Business Strategy

To be more strategic, you should conduct regular needs assessments to determine the organization's e-learning needs. This involves identifying the skills and knowledge that learners need to acquire to be successful and any gaps in the organization's current e-learning offerings. Then you need to ensure that your strategy aligns with the organization's overall business strategy.

THE SPEED OF EMPLOYEE DEVELOPMENT IS THE REAL KPI

While the role of the CeLO is becoming increasingly important in organizations, you may still face some challenges to become highly influential in the organizations.

CHIEF E-LEARNING OFFICER

CHALLENGES DETERMINING E-LEARNING ROI

Now, let me relate it to the real challenge you will face as a CeLO. The biggest challenge you will face is making defendable proposals to introduce new e-learning technologies and transformations. However, your upper management would always want you to compute the ROI of such initiatives and investments before it is implemented. And then, they want you to justify your ROI after the implementation. The core of ROI practiced in most organizations is always this equation: "We have put a certain X amount of dollars into a program. Did we get business results worth, say, five times those dollars?"

The only difference between an effortless, highly strategic, influential, and successful CeLO vs. a business-as-usual CeLO is the ability to nail down the ROI conversation with higher-level executives. Therefore, beyond doubt, this one survival skill should be your core focus.

Let me highlight first why measuring ROI for e-learning initiatives can be challenging. In my research, I observed that executives are asking CeLOs to demonstrate ROI on the things for which, in the first place, executives, HR leaders, and department heads have done nothing to institute metrics.

The Complexity of Impact Caused by Learning

Learning is an abstract process, and it can be very complex and difficult to measure its effectiveness. Though there are measurement frameworks like Kirkpatrick and even my framework for technical training, it can be difficult to isolate the business impact caused by learning alone.

Any business benefits achieved in the field result from multiple initiatives and programs working to enhance certain aspects of the job. It can be a statistical nightmare to do factor analysis in such situations.

You can conduct controlled studies to isolate the impact of e-learning initiatives on learning outcomes. By comparing learners who have participated in e-learning initiatives with those who have not, E-learning strategists can identify the specific effect of e-learning on learning outcomes. This indeed gives you something to present but may not dollarize the returns.

Limited Data Analytics

Even if you think of doing an ambitious project to do complex statistical analysis, you may not have the right analytics to measure ROI. Learning analytics can provide insights into how learners are engaging with e-learning content and identify areas where improvements can be made. However, even before that, you may not have the correct data in the first place, and your organization may not even have a system to collect the required data. You could leverage technology to collect and analyze data on e-learning initiatives. That includes LMSs and Customer Relationship Management (CRM) systems, among others.

Lack of Standardized Metrics

Even if you have the right data collection platforms and the right data analytics, most organizations do not have a standard set of metrics for measuring the effectiveness of e-learning initiatives. You should work with other stakeholders in the organization to develop clear metrics for measuring the ROI. Even within the same organization, different departments may use different metrics, making it challenging to compare the effectiveness of e-learning initiatives across different departments.

So, what's the way around for a CeLO to survive this challenge?

The most serious difficulty in measuring and demonstrating is establishing the right metrics, collecting the right data, and leveraging the right framework to compute effectiveness scores or ROI.

CHIEF E-LEARNING OFFICER

THE REAL ROI THAT SHOULD MATTER

First, let's recalibrate.

As a CeLO, why would you exist in an organization? What is that single thing you will be required to deliver?

The answer might be shocking to you. It is not the technology implementation. It's not e-learning implementation. It's neither the effectiveness of your e-learning programs nor student feedback. It's also not the complicated data tables showing trends in improving learning scores.

You exist for one reason:

To accelerate the speed of employee development.

Your single most important and perhaps the only KPI that should matter is how fast employees are developing by implementing or leveraging a specific learning technology. If your employees are not learning fast enough, not developing fast enough, not attaining desired proficiency at a faster rate, and not able to gain experience fast enough to deliver their outcomes, there is no point in having the world's most innovative learning technologies in your organization.

If a CeLO cannot deliver the speed of employee development at the speed of business, the existence of this role is questionable.

Now, let's think for a moment.

Why would you want to implement powerful e-learning programs or technologies in your organization? When I ask this question to e-learning technologists or leaders, most of them mention reasons related to efficiency, effectiveness, automation, cost-effectiveness, and

CH 2 - EMERGING ROLE OF A CHIEF E-LEARNING OFFICER

scalability of their learning programs. Some even mention 'looking cool' or 'trendy' over competitors as the driving reasons.

As a general trend, the argument of cost saving comes number one, while the argument of scalability comes next, and then comes the argument of accelerated learning. For decades, they have tried convincing executives with the first or the second argument.

When the first two arguments do not work, they start using student feedback, impression scores, and improvement in paper-pen exams and similar metrics in an attempt to show how it *accelerates learners' performance*.

In my book "*Accelerated Proficiency in Accelerated Times*," I showed how training-related metrics misrepresent the real performance of employees. How great learners perceive an e-learning program - is in no way an indication of the speed with which they learn from such programs. On the contrary, my research showed that poorly implemented e-learning could actually be the biggest hindrance that could slow down employee development.

But I can tell you that most e-learning strategists and learning technologists would not admit that observation. Many of them know that traditional e-learning does not accelerate learning. All it does is provide employees with the basic readiness for the job, not the competitive edge.

Therefore, e-learning professionals tend to use pretty basic metrics to prove the applicability or effectiveness of e-learning strategies. They find a shortcut in using metrics like training durations and associated costs to prove that they are doing a great job. Their best fall back is to use surveys or qualitative 'feel' of users. This over-reliance on measures of likeability, efficiency, or effectiveness does nothing good for developing employees at a faster rate.

As I said, if an e-learning program, initiative, design, or infrastructure cannot justify or show it has accelerated the speed of employee development, all the efficiency improvement in the organization is not going to speed up employee performance.

Most e-learning programs, if not designed correctly, do not speed up employee development. Hence, they refrain from powerful metrics, like true TTP, which are the real metrics to measure the speed of employee development. They avoid such metrics as the basis of their proposals or ROI presentations because those metrics are either hard to measure or do not paint a rosy picture of e-learning effectiveness.

PRESENTING IRRUFUTABLE ROI

Most of the e-learning leaders are not too successful in demonstrating a good ROI. The reason is that they use irrelevant metrics to do so. Without clearly impactful metrics to demonstrate the value of e-learning, it can be challenging to build buy-in and support for future learning and technology projects.

When you are an out-of-the-box CeLO, you might take a shot at presenting data or metrics that shows how e-learning programs resulted in changes in the on-the-job behaviors of the employees. However, it is easier said than done simply because of the difficulty of isolating the factors. Nevertheless, this does not convince executives enough.

The speed with which teams are developed is far more critical now to meet the challenges of complex next-generation projects amidst a fast-paced business environment. The workforce needs to acquire next-generation skills and master never-seen-before technologies or products. Technologies are now the first line of defense to impact how employees learn, develop, and perform at the workplace. The real speed that matters from competitiveness from the market standpoint is how fast your employees develop that desired proficiency, where they can produce far more revolutionary products faster than your competition.

Think about this for a moment. If somehow you can demonstrate that your new technology implementation can cut one month of learning or development time for one employee, you can right away translate it to dollars saving over 2000 employees and then compound it to over five years for the influx of people who will benefit from those programs. However, most learning tech leaders are not taught this revolutionary approach which is so irrefutable that even the best of the best CEOs can't argue your numbers.

However, not all e-learning leaders are fully educated about how to measure the speed of employee development and then bring appropriate e-learning or technological infrastructure focused on increasing that speed.

The core goal of any program in an organization is to develop employees faster, handle new projects or solutions quicker and stay competitive. The TTP metrics represent the speed with which your workforce is developing. Thus, when you use TTP metrics as the main anchor for anything you do from an e-learning standpoint, you instantly get undeniable, undefeatable, and unquestionable ROI.

If I am to simplify this goal, the ability to demonstrate this ROI is what you, as a CeLO, will draw from this book. In the following chapters, you will learn how the metrics associated with the speed of employee learning and development and rate of performance improvement are your life savers to make you a CeLO with an unmatchable ability to present an irrefutable ROI of e-learning technologies.

You can win the game of ROI if you base your calculations on three indisputable numbers:

1) Historical trends of the influx of people or your user base, which typically is a solid number.

2) Historical TTP of that userbase.

3) An estimate of per day reduction in TTP.

The result is a projected saving, cost avoidance, and returns on any program for a defined set of users.

In the next chapter, you will learn deeply about these metrics to measure and track employee development speed and how those are relevant to your e-learning programs. At this junction, I recommend reading my other book "*Speed Matters*" which details TTP metrics across various jobs and industries and its implications from a measurement standpoint.

YOUR SUCCESS GUIDELINES

👉 Build buy-in for e-learning initiatives: Communicate the benefits of e-learning to key stakeholders across the organization and work to overcome resistance or skepticism.

👉 Stay current with e-learning technologies and platforms: Evaluate new technologies and determine their suitability for the organization while managing e-learning projects effectively using project management methodologies and tools.

👉 Analyze data and metrics to improve e-learning initiatives: Evaluate the effectiveness of e-learning programs, identify areas for improvement, and make strategic recommendations for future initiatives.

👉 Emphasize collaboration and teamwork: Work closely with other departments and stakeholders to align e-learning initiatives with the organization's goals and objectives.

👉 Foster a culture of learning: Prioritize ongoing learning and development within the organization, and ensure that learners have access to the resources and support they need to succeed.

CHIEF E-LEARNING OFFICER

☞ Master the science of speed: Understand the strategies for measuring and ensuring speed in organizations, focus on TTP metrics and their impact on e-learning programs.

☞ Develop a long-term vision for e-learning: Look beyond immediate needs and identify how e-learning can support the organization's future goals and objectives while considering technology obsolescence and replacement.

☞ Monitor industry trends and best practices: Stay up-to-date on e-learning trends by attending conferences, networking with professionals, and reading industry publications.

☞ Align e-learning strategy with overall business strategy: Conduct regular needs assessments to determine the organization's e-learning needs, identify skill and knowledge gaps, and ensure that the e-learning strategy supports the organization's overall business objectives.

CH 2 – EMERGING ROLE OF A CHIEF E-LEARNING OFFICER

REFLECTION TIME

To succeed as a CeLO in the era of speed, you need to master the science of organizational speed first. You need to understand how you can use speed as an anchor to propose transformations and build a differentiated career successfully. Besides that, your leadership needs to reflect how you display change management, agility, adaptability, and continuous improvement. While focusing on learning outcomes, you need to use your e-learning expertise to instill a learning culture. Above all, you need strategic thinking for measuring and reporting KPIs that matter. You need to get started by developing a long-term vision for e-learning, monitoring industry trends and best practices, and evaluating emerging e-learning technologies.

Use the space below to reflect upon and note down your major takeaways to this point. *Are you honing your leadership and strategic skills to become a differentiated chief e-learning leader? If not, this is your time.*

> **Question to think ahead!**
>
> *Where do you stand on leadership and strategic thinking to become successful as a CeLO? How would you master the science of organizational speed?*

Reflections

CH 2 – EMERGING ROLE OF A CHIEF E-LEARNING OFFICER

YOUR LEARNING JOURNEY

In this chapter, you learned how the e-learning space has evolved at a greater pace. Unless organizations create a role of CeLO equivalent to CLO, it will soon become a key factor affecting organizational competitiveness. The chapter culminated with the philosophical stand that the biggest challenge for a CeLO is presenting, defending, and measuring the ROI of capital-intensive e-learning programs, technologies, and transformations.

In the next chapter, we will discuss the speed of employee development and the associated metrics as a way to represent the ROI of e-learning initiatives. You will learn how these metrics should be considered while implementing e-learning technologies and new e-learning programs. You will learn how mastering the science of this KPI will guide the transformation of your e-learning design approaches.

- Chapter 1
  E-LEARNING AND DIGITAL REVOLUTION
- Chapter 2
  A ROLE OF CHIEF E-LEARNING OFFICER
- **Chapter 3
  SPEED OF EMPLOYEE DEVELOPMENT AS E-LEARNING KPIs**
- Chapter 4
  STRATEGIC E-LEARNING FOR SPEED
- Chapter 5
  SCENARIO-BASED E-LEARNING
- Chapter 6
  TIME-SPACED MICROLEARNING CONTENT
- Chapter 7
  OPTIMALLY SEQUENCED E-LEARNING PATH
- Chapter 8
  ON-DEMAND PERFORMANCE SUPPORT SYSTEMS
- Chapter 9
  EXPERIENCE-RICH MULTI-TECHNOLOGY MIX
- Chapter 10
  SPEED-ENABLING E-LEARNING SYSTEMS APPRAOCH
- Chapter 11
  SUMMARY OF E-LEARNING DESIGN GUIDELINES FOR SPEED
- Chapter 12
  EMERGING E-LEARNING REVOLUTIONS

3

SPEED OF EMPLOYEE DEVELOPMENT AS E-LEARNING KPIs

CH 3 - SPEED OF EMPLOYEE DEVELOPMENT AS E-LEARNING KPIs

According to a study, workforce composition is not the sole differentiator among organizations, as they all have access to almost the same pool of talent, resources, and markets. The real differentiator in the era of speed is the 'speed of employee development' or the speed with which they learn. The speed with which employees are developed is far more critical now to meet the challenges of complex next-generation projects amidst a fast-paced business environment. The workforce needs to acquire next-generation skills and master never-seen-before technologies or products.

On top of that, jobs are becoming increasingly complex in the workplace. A task as simple as 'calling a customer' has now become over-complex with considerations such as the ability to hold the client's attention; cultural and situational sensitivity to a customer's surroundings; ability to connect and relate with a customer's needs, not just in the business sense but in a socio-cultural sense too; ability to think through options and be able to research certain information for the customer.

This changing nature of the workplace and the ecosystem requires non-routine cognitive skills (Karoly & Panis 2004). The complexity of skills in the newer world, in turn, makes the development of proficiency a longer journey.

As seen in research, jobs involving complex cognitive skills require a different kind of design or approach. Face-to-face instructor-led and on-the-job mentored training has proven its potential in developing complex skills in the workplace as well as in educational or training provider's settings. However, e-learning's ability to deliver and accelerate highly complex cognitive skills has been debated extensively.

Despite that debate, e-learning has emerged as the first line of dependence in corporate training. How e-learning design is conducted has a major impact on how employees learn, develop, and perform at the workplace. However, traditional e-learning design does not always enable accelerated learning. Thus, most e-learning programs, while being efficient and cost-effective, fail to increase the speed of employee development.

MEASURING EMPLOYEE DEVELOPMENT

When an employee takes up a new role or job, we provide orientation or onboarding interventions, formal training, or coaching; then, we give them on-the-job support and tools. We do all sorts of things to accelerate their path, as shown in Figure 3.1.

The question is: What is the end goal of that path?

MEANING OF PROFICIENCY

We aim to make them fully proficient in their jobs as soon as possible. So, what does proficiency really mean?

Every job has some performance measures or KPIs. We want employees to deliver those KPIs as soon as possible. For instance, a salesperson's performance measure is sales of 1 million dollars per month; then proficiency is generating a minimum of that much every month. But just being one time hit wonder is not proficiency. We need to measure over a period of time, say three months. That steady state is called proficiency or proficient performance.

When employees reach a certain level of proficiency, they become fully prepared to produce the best possible business results in every possible situation. Thus, proficiency is a state of performance at which performers consistently produce business outcomes or deliverables to the set performance thresholds expected from a given job role. It refers to achieving and maintaining one pre-established performance level and does not imply progression through different stages or levels of performance. It is not an individual's performance demonstrated on a task or skill. Rather, it refers to the business performance of the job role.

Figure 3.1: Employee development journey

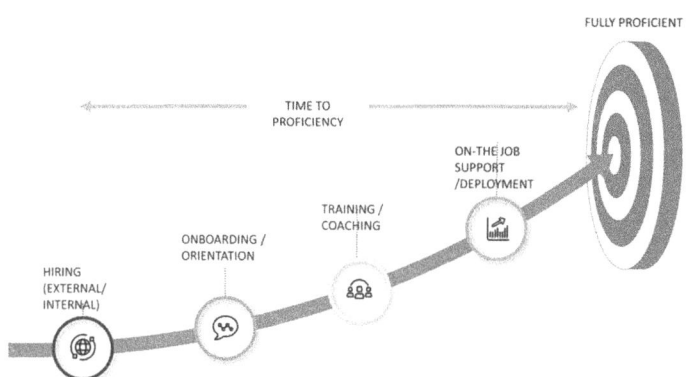

At this proficient performance stage, your teams deliver at least to the agreed threshold defined for their job roles. They provide a repeatable performance that you can be sure of it. Their outcomes are reliable, and you can depend upon them. They deliver consistently and are independently productive, so they don't need much supervision.

TIME-TO-PROFICIENCY (TTP) METRICS

Let me use a visual graph to make a point.

Figure 3.2 is a hypothetical proficiency-time chart. It is a simplistic representation of an employee's proficiency growth over time. The dotted horizontal line is the target proficiency you want your employees to reach. For instance, it could be $1 million in sales.

If you don't put in deliberate efforts, they will go off their own following the 'normal proficiency curve.' They will reach the target proficiency in a certain time. We call it time-to-proficiency (TTP). It's usually measured from the start of a job role or the date of hire to reach the point of being independently productive. If you don't do anything, employees might reach the desired proficiency level in time T1.

Figure3.2: Proficiency-Time Graph

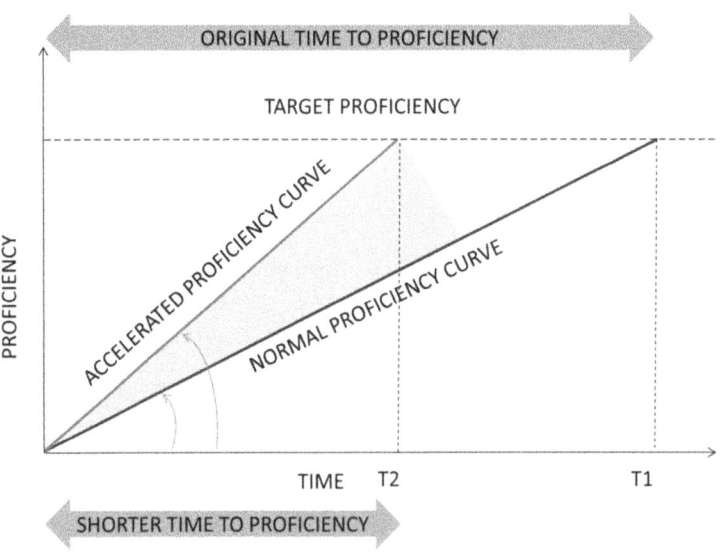

You have recently experienced during the pandemic that you could not wait for employees to take a natural path. You needed them to master new technologies, working methods, and skills in almost no time.

Perhaps that was the first time you wondered if there were ways to lift up that slope of the proficiency curve in a way that employees could follow an 'accelerated proficiency curve' as shown in Figure 1.2. The employees are likely to attain the same desired proficiency in a shorter time T2.

Employees' TTP metrics in any job tell us how slow or fast they are going compared to the market baseline. Employees, irrespective of their job role, require a certain amount of time to reach the level of proficiency desired by the organization they are associated with. The whole idea of speeding up employee performance is to measure and shorten TTP metrics.

A few clarifications about TTP are needed at this point.

- TTP does not apply only to newly hired employees. It equally applies to employees transferred from one job role to another.
- It does not always mean the onboarding time.
- It is not measured based on just a single activity; rather, it involves the collective time required for several activities such as onboarding, formal or informal training, on-the-job training, projects, and other activities to gain experience on specific tasks or skills required to do the work.
- It is not measured just for one employee but for the entire job role and is usually averaged across all employees serving the job role.
- It is not equal to the time taken to get trained on basic skills to start the job.
- It indicates the real time taken to produce the job outcomes consistently and independently.

DISTINCTION AMONG SIMILAR TERMS

There are other equivalent terms used to denote time-to-proficiency, but there are some notable differences. *'Time to complete training'* is wrongly called *'time-to-proficiency'* as it simply conveys the time taken by an individual to finish a training program. A shorter time to complete training indicates that the employee has been taught the necessary skills. It doesn't convey if they have attained the target proficiency.

Literature uses terms like *'time to first success,'* which measures the time from the beginning of a training program to the first instance of success, such as completing a task or project without assistance. It is an indication of the effectiveness of training programs and also indicative of their time to competence.

'Time to Competence' measures the time it takes for an individual to demonstrate competence in their role, as measured against predefined performance standards or benchmarks. Typically delivering performance or competence once is not an indication of proficiency until it is repeatable, reliable, and consistent for a fairly long period of time.

Organizations often use the *'time to full productivity'* term, which measures the time taken by an employee to reach his full potential in his role, contributing at the highest possible level of productivity. In most cases, it denotes proficiency if productivity is measured to define proficiency in the first place.

Another similar term is *'time to mastery,'* which measures the time it takes for an individual to achieve a level of expertise or mastery in their role, which is typically demonstrated by consistently high performance. Usually, mastery and expertise convey elite status far beyond standard proficiency, which is generally expected from employees. In a large population of employees, there is only a handful of experts or masters.

CH 3 – SPEED OF EMPLOYEE DEVELOPMENT AS E-LEARNING KPIs

HOW LONG IS TTP?

We need to understand why TTP metrics are so important in an organizational context. There are two aspects: First, the magnitude of TTP durations that make it worrisome for leaders. Second, the business drivers force leaders to think about the importance of these metrics.

TTP is usually so long that it has an adverse effect on employee competitiveness. I conducted a research study across 66 project cases across several job functions. As seen in Table 3.1, the magnitude of TTP was seen to be an upside of three years. For instance, TTP in technical jobs spanned two months to several years, depending on the industry. In scientific or R&D jobs, people take anywhere between 6 months to three years to become proficient.

Also, note that TTP was several folds compared to the time to train the employees. As a matter of fact, the function of training is no more than providing basic skills to get started. No amount of training can ensure building proficiency to the desired level. Employees need to get engaged in several experience-building activities to become consistent in their performance.

Table 3.1: Magnitude of TTP across different primary job types

Primary Job Nature	Count of Cases	Time to Training	Time-to-proficiency
Technical or engineering	16	5 to 18 weeks	2 months to several years
Sales - non-technical	5	1 to 10 weeks	3 months to 1.5 years

Scientific or development	4	No data	6 months to 3 years
Customer service helpdesk	4	4 to 12 weeks	1.5 months to 1 year
Sales - technical	3	No data	Unknown to 1.5 years
Managerial, supervisory	3	4 to 13 weeks	1 month to 14 months
Strategic management, leadership	3	No data	1 year to very long#
Medical, healthcare	3		3 months to 1 year
Production, manufacturing	3		1 month to 5 months*
Financial services	2	15 weeks	5 months to 3 years
Training or education	1	No data	1-2 years
Assembly, repair	1		1 week

Exceptions: Some rare events that happen once in 10-20 years (e.g., managers having to handle declining gold prices)

*Exceptions: Some rare events that happen once in 8–10 years events (e.g., miners dealing with underground fires)

MARKET PRESSURES FOR SPEED

There is a consensus that the time to achieve a higher level of proficiency to do any job consistently and reliably with a high degree of repeatability is generally very long. Organizations do not have that much time. Market pressure, particularly over the last decade, has warranted accelerating the expertise cycle as a necessity. Unpredicted disasters like the Covid-19 pandemic have opened the eyes of most L&D leaders.

Leaders now associate market competitiveness as a function of how fast the workforce can learn new skills to face future challenges. They have realized that the traditional approach of preparing employees for predictable situations is no longer a recipe for a competitive edge. The future is unpredictable and ambiguous. Employees need to quickly master the skills to the desired level in a much shorter time to handle unpredictable challenges.

When an employee takes longer to become proficient, it has repercussions on the business. Several market forces collectively drive the need for a shorter TTP in the workplace, such as time-to-market competitiveness; constant obsolescence of skills; the increasing complexity of jobs and skills; attrition of senior or aging workforce constantly getting replaced.

The magnitude and scale show us its impact on the business. The larger the magnitude and scale of the TTP, the more significant is the business impact. So, there is a larger push for organizations to think about shortening TTP. This impact manifests significantly as one or more of these four business drivers: time-related pressures, speed-related competitiveness, skill-related deficiencies, and cost/financial implications. These four drivers are summarized in Table 3.2 in terms of the nature of factors that push organizations to do something about the long TTP of employees.

Table 3.2: Definition of business drivers

Drivers	Definition	Examples
Time-related pressures	The drivers in which operational metrics were consciously measured in the unit of time.	The time required to launch a product, The actual length of TTP longer training duration
Speed-related competitiveness	The operational metrics in which speed was	Customer pressures to deliver fast;

	perceived as a measure of success.	market urgencies to produce fast;
		business ramp-up speed;
		The speed of launch of a new product, service, or business;
		The need for rapid operational readiness;
		Rapid hiring sprints
Skill-related deficiencies	The needs arise because of a lack of workforce skills or a lack of a qualified workforce.	Attrition and retirement;
		New hires replacing expert workforce;
		Performance issues due to a lack of skills and obsolete skills
Cost or financial implications	The factors and impacts were measured in the unit of money.	The cost of training, the cost of someone not being proficient;
		Errors and mistakes;
		The cost of opportunity lost while someone was not proficient;
		Regulatory pressures that cost the company severely if not observed, such as safety

Time and Speed-Related Drivers

Time and speed-related drivers relate to market urgencies such as time-to-market pressures, competitiveness, and business pressures, among other factors. With the pace of technology, time-to-market pressure on the workforce is increasing to acquire complex skills at a faster pace. Naturally, organizations that can develop employees at a faster rate would stand out in the competition.

As an organization, you need your employees to design products, solutions, and technologies at the rate of customers' demand. If somehow you could accelerate their learning, they can innovate faster by coming up to speed with newer technologies. In turn, it would allow you to shorten the time-to-market of your products or services and meet customer expectations at a faster rate. That's the key to staying ahead of the competition.

Skill Deficiency-Related Drivers

Third drivers relate to skill-deficiency-related business drivers, which include challenges like the retiring workforce, the complexity of jobs, and changing nature of work. These are the most foundational drivers. That means, even if everything has a dollar value, the capabilities and speed with which you develop employees is the most fundamental driver to think about while attempting to shorten TTP. Once you close the skill gaps faster or prepare the workforce at a higher speed, the chain reaction is a better time and speed advantage, better time-to-market performance, and better cost-efficiency.

You have to see skill deficiency in the context of the environment. According to a study by Deloitte (2017), the half-life of any skill in 2017 was shrinking to 1.5 years. Now in 2023, we expect it to be even further. That means any skill you acquire today would be obsolete within 2-3 years. You and your learners have no choice but to learn and master new skills much faster to stay relevant and productive. The shelf life of skills during the pandemic is seen to be roughly about three to six months, which will squeeze down further in the post-COVID era. And the time-to-market of products or services is close to 3 months for new products and services.

The more concerning thing is the time to master new skills or solutions, which is a rough upside of one year. It is a catch-22 that leads to two challenges. The first is how to hire fast, and the second is how to develop them quickly after hiring. Thus, there is a strong business case for speeding up learning at the workplace.

However, several non-financial reasons, such as the impact of non-proficiency in critical professions, are also equally important. For example, a study involving firefighting commanders established that firefighters could not wish for real events to happen to gain more experience because such events can lead to undesirable effects and endanger life and property. When such an event indeed happens, it requires proficient people to handle such catastrophic events. They needed to find ways to develop proficiency much faster than offered by exposing them to natural events. Along the same lines, businesses have a pressing need to accelerate the speed-to-proficiency of their employees in almost every job. Businesses simply can't wish for bad times to occur to expose their employee to such difficult events to build their proficiency. Such apparent deficiency in the skills to handle those events, if and when they happen, is an important driver toward shortening TTP.

Cost-related Drivers

Several studies indicated substantial financial or cost benefits of shorter training duration and faster workforce readiness from the reduction of TTP. Imagine an employee working for you takes one year to become good at his job. That's a massive amount of cost and opportunity lost. This is a foundational reason why we need accelerated workplace learning. If you prepare learners or employees at a faster rate, it will make them make fewer mistakes. Ultimately, you'll save a considerable sum of money that otherwise would be incurred to address those mistakes. This also means saving on account of costly retraining.

BENEFITS OF SHORTENING TTP

In my book titled *"Speed Matters,"* I explained how speed has become essential in ensuring that employees can learn new skills faster and become proficient in delivering business outcomes.

Fred Charles, the father of the term *'speed-to-proficiency,'* makes a compelling argument in his book Breakaway (2002, p. 16): "Speed to proficiency is more than a theoretical advantage. It is the most devastating competitive weapon in the world where the competitive forces of scale, automation, and capital are subordinate to the power of proficient workforce." The efforts to accelerate TTP thus lead to the faster readiness of the workforce, cost savings, and increased competitiveness in the market.

Irrespective of the actual length of TTP, if we agree that it indeed is unacceptable, shortening it. It must be recognized that the TTP business problem is too big for organizations to ignore. They must address this challenge because of its impact on the workforce, business metrics, profitability, and market competitiveness.

Sometimes, leaders would associate the length of training or overall TTP directly with the potential cost saving or the financial gains they can get by reducing it. While this is an undebatable relationship, I observed that the projects starting with the goal of saving costs for employee development might not result in overall better competitiveness. However, cost savings and financial gains are invariably achieved when projects are initiated to gain competitive advantages or skill efficiencies.

Leading workplace learning expert Jay Cross once stated: "The faster a worker becomes proficient, the more profitable the firm." Similarly, in their book *"Learning Paths,"* leading business consultants Rosenbaum & Williams stressed the importance of identifying the point at which desired performance is delivered: "You need to know the level of performance required to do the job and how long it takes to get there.... when you can get employees up-to speed in far less time, productivity rises at far less expense."

The faster employees learn the skills required to do the job up to set performance standards, the faster they are able to handle new customer needs, meet new market needs, perform to new expectations, and deliver new technologies or adopt new changes. Every business leader needs to consider how to shorten that TTP. When you shorten that time, you gain benefits shown by the gray area in Figure 3.2, representing dollars saved, improved productivity, and other business benefits. In my research study, I found four types of business benefits of shorter TTP. The ingredients are shown in Table 3.3.

Table 3.3: Nature of business benefits of shorter TTP

Benefit	Benefits seen by 50 organizations
Business gains	Increased market share, Shorter sales cycle, increased profit or revenue, Competitiveness, The readiness of staff, Improved sales, Higher customer satisfaction
Improvement in operational metrics	An increase in staff retention, Need for fewer staff, High training capacity Shorter courses, Improvement in skill scores

Improvement in productivity	An improvement in processing rate,
	Reduction in errors,
	Improved output,
	Availability of staff,
	Efficiency and saving of time
Cost savings	Shorter TTP,
	Shorter training duration
	Less travel is required,
	Cost savings aggregated on a larger population

In this era of speed, TTP is becoming one of the most important business metrics for fast-paced technological organizations. Accordingly, organizations worldwide are striving to figure out interventions, systems, and strategies to shorten the TTP of employees.

The big question is how such benefits can be drawn. The answer is simple: it depends on how a CeLO institutes TTP metrics as a system rather than as another measurement tool. In the following chapter, you will learn about the ingredients of such a strategic framework.

TIME-TO-PROFICIENCY GUIDELINES

☞ Establish clear and crisp measures of proficiency for each job role. One must know whether the targeted employee group is at the desired proficiency or not. Different job roles require different definitions, metrics, and measurements.

☞ Measure the TTP of the targeted group in terms of defined metrics. TTP measurement depends upon the definition of proficiency: Managers or leaders usually either do not measure TTP for critical roles or cannot do because proficiency for those roles is not defined clearly.

☞ Establish a baseline of the historical average across all the employees serving a given job role. You can measure it for individual employees or average across all employees or top employees in a job role, or it could be across the organization, depending on the goals of the employee development programs.

☞ Educate your leaders and stakeholders about the TTP impact. The leaders need to know where their employees are on the proficiency curve, what it means to stay ahead in the market, and the associated risks.

CH 3 – SPEED OF EMPLOYEE DEVELOPMENT AS E-LEARNING KPIs

REFLECTION TIME

In the era of the technological and digital revolution, at the onset of Industry 4.0, naturally, e-learning is viewed as the first line of defense for organizations to accelerate employee learning, development, and performance. We need to design learning, whether traditional or e-learning, not simply for knowledge delivery or skill teaching but to help our learners attain professional proficiency as fast as possible.

Use the space below to reflect upon and note down your major takeaways to this point. *Is 'speed of employee development' your number one priority? If not, then this is the time you start thinking about how to use it as an anchor to build a competitive workforce via your e-learning initiatives.*

> ***Question to think ahead!***
>
> *What is your organizational strategy to measure, baseline, and reduce the TTP metrics of your workforce across all critical job roles?*

Reflections

YOUR LEARNING JOURNEY

In this chapter, you learned why employee development speed is the most devastating competitive weapon in a fast-paced world. You realized that as a CeLO, you need to take a strategic stance, which involves implementing technologies to shorten TTP of the workforce.

In the following chapter, you will learn the ingredients of that strategic leadership for e-learning implementation.

- Chapter 1
  E-LEARNING AND DIGITAL REVOLUTION
- Chapter 2
  A ROLE OF CHIEF E-LEARNING OFFICER
- Chapter 3
  SPEED OF EMPLOYEE DEVELOPMENT AS E-LEARNING KPIs
- **Chapter 4**
  STRATEGIC E-LEARNING FOR SPEED
- Chapter 5
  SCENARIO-BASED E-LEARNING
- Chapter 6
  TIME-SPACED MICROLEARNING CONTENT
- Chapter 7
  OPTIMALLY SEQUENCED E-LEARNING PATH
- Chapter 8
  ON-DEMAND PERFORMANCE SUPPORT SYSTEMS
- Chapter 9
  EXPERIENCE-RICH MULTI-TECHNOLOGY MIX
- Chapter 10
  SPEED-ENABLING E-LEARNING SYSTEMS APPRAOCH
- Chapter 11
  SUMMARY OF E-LEARNING DESIGN GUIDELINES FOR SPEED
- Chapter 12
  EMERGING E-LEARNING REVOLUTIONS

4

STRATEGIC E-LEARNING DESIGN FOR SPEED

CH 4 – STRATEGIC E-LEARNING DESIGN FOR SPEED

3 ELEMENTS OF E-LEARNING DESIGN

In my other books (see the back pages), I have laid out the detailed results of my decade-long research with 85 best of the best organizations across seven countries.

We often tend to focus only on the design or delivery strategies, forgetting about the learner's experience. I found that you must first design the learning for an effective e-learning or online training design. Then you need to create the experience that a learner would get and then design the delivery as it is also a part of the design.

We tend to gear online training toward imparting content, knowledge, and information. And we go thin on real skill transfer. When the goal is to design online learning to transfer skills, you need to think away from content, and you need a massive shift in your design practices.

So, there are three critical elements of an e-learning design, as shown in Figure 4.1. These are: 1) design the learning, 2) design the experience, and 3) design the delivery.

There are five e-learning strategies that most organizations use to drive an acceleration of employee development through their online, virtual, and e-learning programs.

1) Design the learning

- Scenario-based contextualization of e-learning
- Time-spaced microlearning content

2) Design the experience

- Optimally sequenced e-learning path

3) Design the delivery

- On-demand electronics performance support systems
- Experience-rich and multi-technology mix

Figure 4.1: Three elements of e-learning design

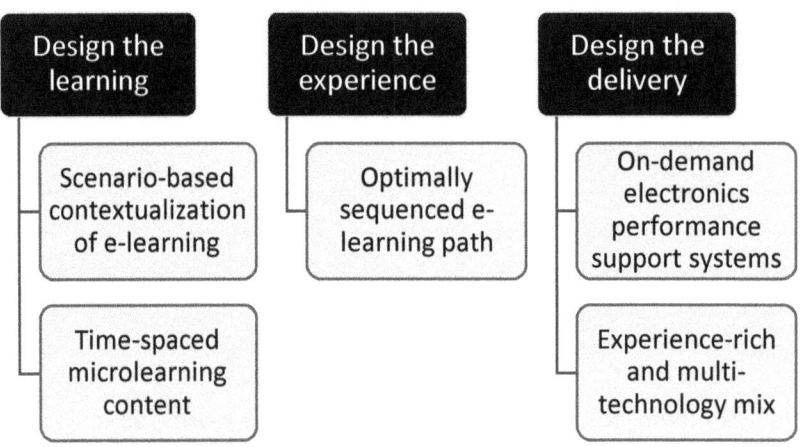

5 E-LEARNING STRATEGIES

I observed that TTP of employees could be shortened if organizations develop a shorter chunk of content; contextualize it with real-world problems relevant to the workplace; sequence and organize the chunks in an optimally designed learning path; deliver each chunk virtually or online using several technologies and making it available through electronic performance systems.

CH 4 – STRATEGIC E-LEARNING DESIGN FOR SPEED

At a high level, there are five strategies to design e-learning for speed. Each of these five strategies is indeed powerful in its own sense. However, one needs to implement these as a system to accelerate skill acquisition. These strategies are tied to each other in a closed-loop and interact with each other seamlessly to accelerate proficiency in an integrated fashion. The way one strategy is implemented can significantly impact the effectiveness of the other strategies by supplementing or complementing each other. Interestingly, there is a cyclic relationship among them, and in addition to this, each of these strategies had a dependency on the other four. The bi-directional arrows in Figure 4.2 show such interactions among them.

Figure 4.2: Conceptual model of e-learning for accelerated proficiency

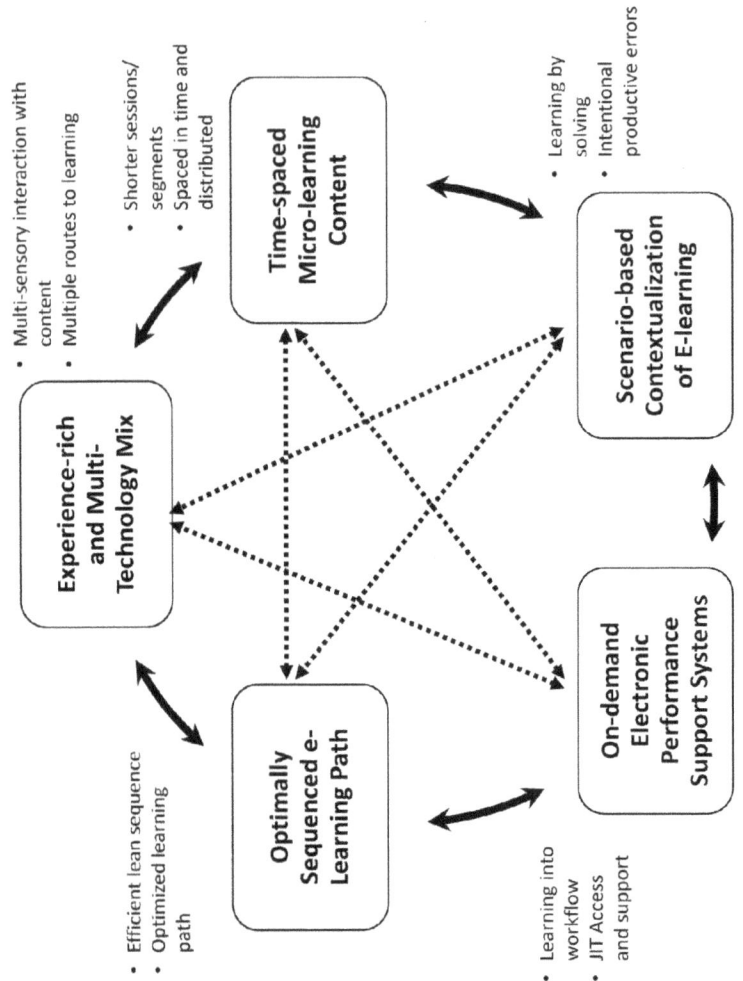

CH 4 – STRATEGIC E-LEARNING DESIGN FOR SPEED

1. SCENARIO-BASED LEARNING

You start by asking a guide question: Which tasks require more in-depth thinking and solving a range of problems to achieve business outcomes?

In this strategy, you start with the mindset to develop learning through intense thinking and problem-solving. You build intentional bugs into cases, scenarios, or problems and present them to learners to ensure appropriate emotional loading.

2. TIME-SPACED MICROLEARNING

Next, you ask: Which skills can be packed in shorter e-learning units that can be applied immediately at the job? In this strategy, you look at how to chunk these scenarios into smaller segments that could be spaced out. Then you look for additional practice and reflection exercises that must be interleaved between two chunked segments.

3. OPTIMALLY SEQUENCED E-LEARNING PATH

The following guide question is: Which e-learning activities can make someone reach proficiency quickly, and which cannot? In this strategy, you start looking at the overall learning path for learners. You map out the activities, chunk segments, and other tasks in a sequence and optimize to remove the irrelevant or wasteful activity. This gives you start-to-end the journey of a learner and additional insights into what can be taken out of the path.

4. ON-DEMAND PERFORMANCE SUPPORT SYSTEMS (PSS)

Then you explore: Which skills can be delivered through PSSs to provide just-in-time support at the moment of need? In this strategy, you look at which part of the scenarios or learning chunks could be delivered nearer to the point of need using PSS. You look into how some of the information content could simply be made available as a search engine instead of having learners spend their time learning it.

5. EXPERIENCE-RICH AND MULTI-TECHNOLOGY MIX

Here you ask: Which e-learning channel or technology can deliver the intended skill to provide enriched experience and deeper learning?

In this strategy, you look at the best mechanisms to deliver scenarios, chunked segments, or other activities. You employ multi-sensory interactions and use different technologies for different learning bits.

Then you look at the cyclic relationship in terms of how the designed scenarios are converted into chunks, spaced out, and delivered using different experience-rich delivery mechanisms, how these mechanisms reflect on the total learning path, and how learners leverage various PSSs to accelerate their learning.

The following chapters describe the essence and examples of each strategy in detail.

CH 4 - STRATEGIC E-LEARNING DESIGN FOR SPEED

E-LEARNING STRATEGY GUIDELINES

☞ Utilize scenario-based learning: Focus on developing learning through real-world problem-solving and in-depth thinking. Present learners with scenarios that require critical thinking and decision-making skills to achieve desired business outcomes.

☞ Implement time-spaced microlearning: Break down complex skills into smaller, manageable e-learning units that can be applied immediately on the job. Include practice and reflection exercises between these units to reinforce learning and facilitate skill acquisition.

☞ Develop optimally sequenced e-learning paths: Map out the sequence of learning activities, tasks, and chunks to eliminate irrelevant or wasteful content.

☞ Offer on-demand performance support systems: Provide learners with just-in-time support through PSS at their moment of need. Utilize search engines and other tools to make relevant information easily accessible to learners, reducing the time spent on learning extraneous content.

☞ Leverage experience-rich and multi-technology mix: Employ various e-learning channels and technologies to deliver different learning bits, creating a multi-sensory and engaging learning experience. Adapt the delivery mechanisms based on the content and learners' needs to optimize learning outcomes.

CH 4 – STRATEGIC E-LEARNING DESIGN FOR SPEED

REFLECTION TIME

The e-learning space is flooded with several designs and pedagogical theories and strategies. However, all those strategies mainly aim to make e-learning effective or give users a good experience. When you get stuck into operational metrics, you stand lesser chances of being a differentiated CeLO. Thus, be wary that none of the e-learning strategies in the literature precisely target shortening TTP and speeding up employee development. You need a more strategic and big-picture approach to tackle the issue as big as shortening TTP. Therefore, you need to expand your horizon of focus beyond e-learning programs and instead shift it to the overall competitiveness of the workforce.

Use the space below to reflect upon and note down your major takeaways to this point. *Are you focusing on the impact-making metrics that determine and ensure the speed of employee development? If not, then start focusing on those metrics.*

> *Question to think ahead!*
>
> *How can you avoid daily operational metrics that undermine the power of e-learning initiatives and focus on impacting your organization's competitive metrics, such as TTP, through next-generational e-learning programs or platforms?*

Reflections

CH 4 – STRATEGIC E-LEARNING DESIGN FOR SPEED

YOUR LEARNING JOURNEY

In this chapter, you learned three elements of successful e-learning design that can make your e-learning programs highly effective in shortening TTP. You learned five strategies that are foundational to achieving that goal.

In the following chapter, you will learn the first strategy to design scenario-based e-learning courses and programs, which significantly accelerates employee performance.

Chapter 1
E-LEARNING AND DIGITAL REVOLUTION

Chapter 2
A ROLE OF CHIEF E-LEARNING OFFICER

Chapter 3
SPEED OF EMPLOYEE DEVELOPMENT AS E-LEARNING KPIs

Chapter 4
STRATEGIC E-LEARNING FOR SPEED

Chapter 5
SCENARIO-BASED E-LEARNING

Chapter 6
TIME-SPACED MICROLEARNING CONTENT

Chapter 7
OPTIMALLY SEQUENCED E-LEARNING PATH

Chapter 8
ON-DEMAND PERFORMANCE SUPPORT SYSTEMS

Chapter 9
EXPERIENCE-RICH MULTI-TECHNOLOGY MIX

Chapter 10
SPEED-ENABLING E-LEARNING SYSTEMS APPRAOCH

Chapter 11
SUMMARY OF E-LEARNING DESIGN GUIDELINES FOR SPEED

Chapter 12
EMERGING E-LEARNING REVOLUTIONS

5
SCENARIO-BASED E-LEARNING

In day-to-day life, in order to solve problems, employees need to think of the solutions first and then handle the problem or a certain challenge. This requires higher-order thinking and problem-solving skills. So, these skills need to be embedded as scenarios, problems, cases, simulations, or games in online training.

Designing e-learning around real job challenges can accelerate proficiency in highly complex skills. Such an approach is called 'contextualization' (Clark & Mayer 2013), which means linking the task at hand to the realist job environment and challenges. If e-learning is designed around scenarios, it enhances cognitively complex learning.

CONTEXTUALIZATION

Contextualization strategies are the top online training design strategies today. Contextualizing e-learning with real-world cases or scenarios could accelerate expertise (Gott & Lesgold 2000; Clark & Mayer 2013).

Several names exist for the methods used to achieve contextualization, such as: case-based curriculum, problem-based e-learning, scenario-based simulation, simulated scenarios, gaming or gamification, strategic rehearsal, and variations. The basic premise of these methods is that if they apply that knowledge in a scenario, they are more likely to remember because they are actively using their knowledge, and secondly, it's now tied to the context of use.

The most crucial approach to accelerate proficiency is to design e-learning around cases or scenarios to provide a rich context for learning. A case or scenario could be factual or fabricated cases from real life. Gone are the days when online training was about imparting content, information, or slides. Instead, you can try various ways to build a context in e-learning: drive learners to analyze a real-life scenario; solve the stated problem; describe the root cause; recommend a solution; make decisions; and explore an option.

Such methods enable learners to solve real-world problems by triggering higher-order thinking instead of memorizing abstract concepts. The short or large scenarios employ the power of story-telling and bring context into play. This approach triggers deep thinking, introduces a great amount of emotional loading, and creates pressure and emotional involvement. It makes learning very active because it is immediately relevant to the job. Employees are more likely to remember when they apply it in the context of problems.

PRINCIPLES OF CONTEXTUALIZATION

Every organization in my research used contextualization as the first line of defense. Regardless of the method or modality, the basic idea of contextualization is to introduce intentional errors, obstacles, hardships, and challenges into the scenarios in a non-linear fashion that a learner would encounter in real life. These deliberate difficulties must be realistic, not just for the sake of making learning challenging. When you add a series of obstacles that may lead learners to possible failures, their learning actually gets accelerated tremendously.

Among many different variations of contextualization, four elements, as shown in Figure 5.1, are the most important to ensure that the e-learning you design has the potential to shorten TTP:

1. *Compress or pack experience in a shorter time*
2. *Increase emotional loading*
3. *Ensure active involvement*
4. *Incorporate active processing*

CH 5 – SCENARIO-BASED E-LEARNING

Figure 5.1: Principles of scenario-based e-learning

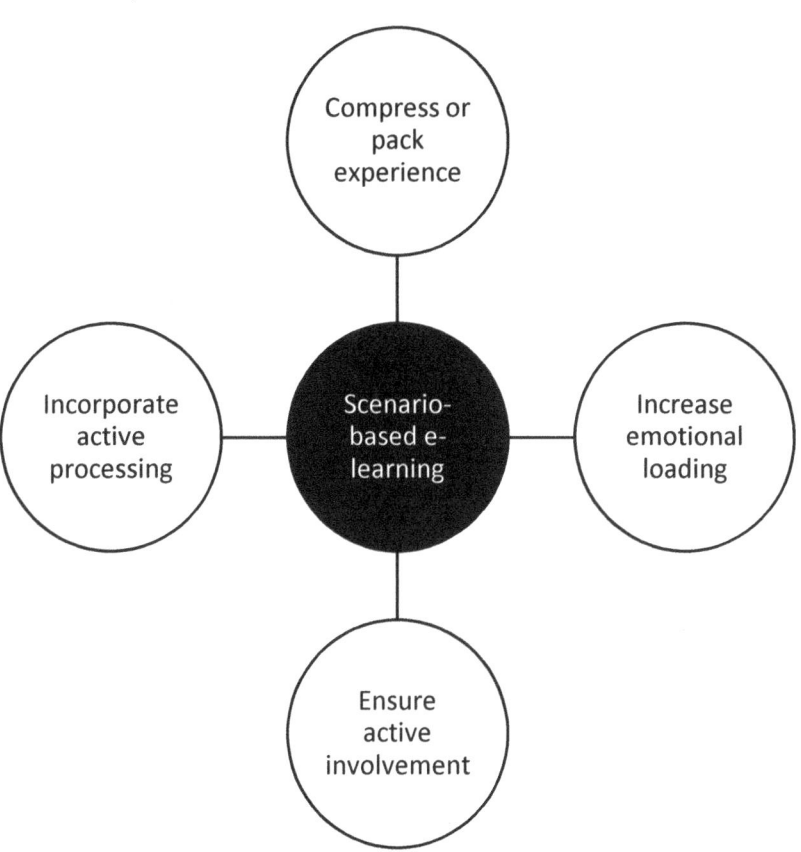

1. COMPRESS OR PACK EXPERIENCE

Instead of designing a few cases or scenarios, designing a sequence of cases can result in rapid skill acquisition. By working through a series of job scenarios in e-learning, designers can compress the equivalent real-world experience in a shorter time, which otherwise could take months or years to experience. One case study showed that exposing learners to a well-defined sequence of cases through e-learning developed financial professionals' expertise in a much shorter time (Arnold & Collier 2013).

In essence, scenario-based e-learning is a job experience in a box, designed to be unpackaged and stored in the learner's memory. Such scenarios can let designers train the learner's experience in a specific sequence and structure of events to guide learning in a controlled manner (Clark & Mayer 2013).

2. INCREASE EMOTIONAL LOADING

Transfer of skills to the job and reduction in TTP appears to have some link with emotional involvement and stakes during learning.

Several researchers have recognized the role of emotions in online learning (Dirkx; Hara & Kling 2000; Shen, Wang, & Shen 2009; Värlander 2008). Most recently, studies have demonstrated some positive relationship between emotions and learning effectiveness (Trigwell, Ellis, & Han 2012; Schuwirth, 2013).

Emotions automatically get escalated in each task employees do when there are consequences of not achieving the desired quality. As I suggested in the book *"Accelerated Proficiency for Accelerated Times,"* this causes a phenomenon of 'emotional loading' among employees. This emotional loading comes due to extreme emotional involvement when something crucial is at stake. It appears to impact their speed-to-proficiency in the workplace.

Emotional involvement and loading are seen to play a significant role in the effectiveness of online learning (Arnold & Collier 2013). The higher levels of emotional response are the key to embedding learning permanently in human brains because emotions play a huge role in how we learn (DiBello, Missildine & Struttman 2009; Bjork 2013; Clark & Mayer 2013).

However, historically and traditionally, 'emotions' have been kept out of the so-called 'dry and formal' education system.

How to achieve constructive emotional loading without making it a stressful experience? Real-life scenarios appear to trigger emotional loading and involvement in learners due to their immediate relevance to the job and the consequences of it. They also trigger active learning in which learners are fully involved. The emotional loading experienced by learners while solving real-life scenarios helps accelerate proficiency.

3. ENSURE ACTIVE INVOLVEMENT

Higher-order complex cognitive skills are typically non-linear, i.e., the problem space and approaches could be fuzzy and structured rules may not always be applicable. Hence, one-way static e-learning may not work effectively. Thus, active participation is the key to accelerating learning in complex skill acquisition.

There is compelling evidence from research that active processing via active involvement and non-linear thinking accelerates proficiency in face-to-face settings (Fadde & Klein 2012; Hinterberger, 2010; Klein, Hintze, & Saab 2013; Phillips, Klein, & Sieck 2004). You can achieve similar even in e-learning to increase active processing, involvement, and non-linear thinking even in e-learning by using correct contextualization.

One such technique is introducing possibilities of errors, failures, bugs, or hurdles in e-learning. E-learning sessions are designed around scenarios that present carefully crafted failures or obstacles to the learners, thus increasing active involvement. It triggers deeper thinking.

When learners struggle with something while solving a tough problem in which their chances of succeeding are low, their learning becomes permanent. That makes up for the time they lost while trying to solve the problem. This approach has seen the highest potential to shorten TTP while learning a complex skill.

Two variations of this approach are incorporating 'desirable errors,' the ones that can enhance learning (Bjork & Linn 2006; Bjork 2013) and exposing learners to rapid failure cycles in compressed time (DiBello, Missildine, & Struttman 2009). Both of these approaches not only keep learners emotionally involved but also increase the stakes in learning by integrating time pressure.

Part of my research in the book *"Modeling Accelerated Proficiency in Organizations"* suggested that exposing learners to a series of failures in online learning adds specific pressures and generates emotional involvement, which appears to accelerate the speed toward proficiency.

4. INCORPORATE ACTIVE PROCESSING

Another key strategy for contextualization is to trigger 'active processing' among learners. Clark and Mayer emphasized 'active processing' as the most critical strategy for acquiring complex skills. They stated, "People learn by actively processing information, which includes constructing mental models of learned information" (Clark & Mayer 2011, p. 65). Active processing involves actively solving a problem. Problem-based learning is an approach to expose learners to apply their skills in solving physical problems and troubleshooting issues (Hinterberger 2011).

Studies reported that you could increase active processing in e-learning through 'challenging interactions' that require the learners to take an active role in training and learning experience (Dror, Schmidt &

O'connor 2011, p. 293). Some examples include medical and computer science training.

CONTEXTUALIZING E-LEARNING TRENDS

As technologies are evolving, several new methods of contextualizing e-learning are emerging. Technologies are converging so that boundaries among these methods are becoming fuzzy. Largely, four approaches to contextualizing e-learning have demonstrated their value in shortening TTP.

COMPUTER-BASED ONLINE SCENARIOS

The first set of examples is computer-based online scenarios. The simplest version you might have seen is the good old days of text-based cases requiring you to choose the right path. Those things work equally well as long as they are tied to the job.

Several studies provided examples of how some disciplines like medicine, engineering, business studies, sales, clinical, equipment maintenance, electronics, software, and aviation design a curriculum with a simulation of intentional errors, bugs, and failures to drive deeper thinking in learners. During these activities, whether self-paced or instructor-led, learners are engaged actively in tasks such as computing, processing, transforming etc., as opposed to just reading the content.

Some latest examples of accelerating learning through computer-based online scenarios are:

Financial training: A financial organization used an expert system with a web interface that held a repository of previous company cases. The cases were progressively presented to the new financial analysts, which they were required to solve. They could rapidly prepare these employees in a much shorter time.

Language learning: Duolingo, a language learning platform, uses gamification to teach users new languages. It provides computer-based scenarios that simulate real-life situations, making it easier for users to learn and practice new vocabulary and grammar. The platform also adapts to users' skill levels, providing personalized learning experiences. A study by the City University of New York found that students who used Duolingo performed significantly better on a standardized language proficiency test than those who used traditional language learning methods.

Coding training: Codecademy[7], an online learning platform, teaches users how to code through interactive exercises, quizzes, and real-world projects that help users develop practical coding skills. Users can work at their own pace and receive instant feedback, making the learning process more efficient.

Medical training: Virtual simulations have become increasingly popular in medical training. A medical services company used computer-based scenarios to teach learners step-by-step emergency CPR to a patient. In such scenarios, learners needed to choose the correct option. Companies like Simbionix[8] offers computer-based scenarios that simulate surgeries and medical procedures, allowing medical students to practice clinical skills and decision-making in a safe and controlled environment before entering the surgery room.

---

[7] https://www.codecademy.com/
[8] https://simbionix.com/

Safety training: Safety training simulations have become popular in industries where safety is a top priority, such as manufacturing and construction. Companies like UL PureSafety[9] use computer-based scenarios that simulate hazardous situations, allowing workers to practice safety protocols and procedures before encountering real-life situations.

SIMULATED GAMES

The use of computer-based simulated games is one of the highly talked about e-learning strategies holding the potential to accelerate proficiency. It has shown great potential in accelerating the development of complex knowledge and skills in cell biology, aviation, transportation, military, and business management (Higgins 2015).

Simulated games offer a safe, controlled environment for learners to practice and improve their skills. These simulations can be customized to specific industries and scenarios, making them a valuable tool for accelerating learning and improving performance. In a research study, 20% higher confidence of learners was reported after using computer-based simulated games, compared to classroom instruction, which resulted in a higher transfer of knowledge and skills to the workplace (Sitzmann 2010).

Some recent examples include:

Aviation training: Commercial or public flight simulators have been used for decades to train pilots and other aviation professionals. These simulators replicate real-life scenarios, allowing pilots to practice procedures and techniques in a safe, controlled environment. A study found that pilots trained in simulators were better equipped to handle

---

[9] https://www.ul.com/software/puresafety

emergencies and had fewer accidents than those who only received traditional classroom training (Hays et al. 1992). One example of a computer-based simulator is Microsoft Flight Simulator, allowing learners greater flexibility at no cost. 85% of the new pilot expressed using MS Flight simulator to maintain proficiency (Beckman 2013).

Management training: Business simulations are used to teach management skills and decision-making in a simulated business environment. For example, the Everest Leadership simulator, developed by Harvard Business School, places participants in the role of a mountaineering team. Participants must make decisions about how to allocate resources and manage risks while climbing the mountain. They found that participants who completed the simulation had improved decision-making skills and could better apply what they learned to real-life situations (Roberto & Edmondson 2008).

Military training: The military uses simulations to train soldiers in a range of scenarios, from basic training to combat situations. The early studies by Gott & Lesgold (2000) in military settings showed that 25 hours of scenario-based simulation on the computer accelerated the expertise of 2 years of technicians in diagnosing electrical faults in aircraft as equivalent to those holding ten years of experience. For example, the US Army developed a simulation called Virtual Battlespace 2 and 3, which allows soldiers to practice tactics and techniques in a virtual environment. A study found that soldiers trained with the simulation improved performance and decision-making skills in real-world situations (Whitney, Temby & Stephens 2013).

Medical training: Early experiments showed the value of gaming in the medical domain as an e-learning strategy to accelerate the learning of complex skills on how to cope with unexpected events (Dror, Schmidt & O'connor 2011).

GAMIFICATION

Gamification has emerged as one of the recent advances in e-learning, strongly believed in building and accelerating the experience in complex skills which otherwise are hard to encounter or not feasible to simulate or practice in real-life (Higgins 2015). The idea is to gamify real-world scenarios. Scenarios can be real or fabricated but need to be something likely to happen on the job. A simple example of gamification is the Yousician[10] music learning app that uses gamification to motivate users to practice by providing instant feedback, rewarding progress, and allowing users to compete with friends.

Among other examples of creating gamification are interactive leaderboards used in businesses to encourage employees to improve by making them aware that the rest of the team can see their progress.

On those lines, Salesforce's Trailhead gamified the onboarding process for employees, where users earn badges and points for completing training modules.

Some platforms can now use microlearning with gamification, which involves learning in short bursts, with gamification elements to engage users and increase their participation. Some examples of gamification include:

Firefighter training: It includes developing or accelerating skills of firefighters to fight fire in a real fire incident or of underground miners to respond to emergency protocols in an actual event. Such situations may require higher-order complex cognitive skills like problem-solving, decision-making, or troubleshooting (Slootmaker et al. 2014).

Virtual immersive universes: Simply speaking, this approach is like creating strategy games with immersive interfaces. Combining the

---

[10] https://yousician.com/lp/yousician

power of computers and gaming, designers build a gamified 'virtual world' on computers. The entire ecosystem around a situation is created. These gaming scenarios give employees sensory experience and feedback while solving realistic situations. Metaverse[11] is growing its attention following this approach. However, well-established virtual world-based games as e-learning tools are already available.

For instance, an underground mine company built the entire underground mine virtually to train their employees in different hazardous conditions that may occur. One can navigate with virtual world with headsets. The virtual world is equipped with additional features like smoke or heat-emitting devices to give the feel to the participants of handling an underground fire situation. One cannot wait for a real-life fire to occur to practiceObviously, you would not want to train them in the actual event but prepare them through immersive technologies to handle those unpleasant hazardous situations. . That's where simulated virtual worlds have huge value.

Motivation building in e-learning mode: Classcraft[12], an educational role-playing game, helps students develop skills such as collaboration, critical thinking, and problem-solving. In this game, students create avatars and work together in teams to complete quests and challenges. The game also includes a reward system where students earn points and unlock new abilities as they progress. A research study observed that such platforms could efficiently create optimal gamification learning processes that can positively influence learning achievement and motivation (Zhang, Yu & Yu 2021).

Gamified Assessment: Kahoot!, a game-based learning platform, allows teachers to create quizzes and other interactive activities for their students. It uses a competitive format where students can earn points and see their rankings on a leaderboard. In a study, the researchers

---

[11] https://about.meta.com/metaverse/
[12] https://www.classcraft.com/

found that students actively engaged in scientific or technical material positively impacted their learning (Jones et al. 2019).

Scientific problem-solving: Foldit[13], an online puzzle game, challenges players to solve complex protein folding problems. The game uses a crowdsourcing model where players worldwide work together and find solutions to real-world scientific problems. Foldit has been used in various research studies, including one where players solved a protein-folding problem that had stumped scientists for over a decade (Cooper 2010).

AR/VR-BASED IMMERSION

Technological advances have evolved into "mixed reality (MR)," combining VR and AR elements to create a more immersive experience. MR can be used for gaming, education, and training. This gamification is far more real and immersive than experiencing it on the computer. AR and VR technologies can be used to create enhanced online training simulations that completely immerse learners in a virtual situation, eliminating distractions and providing a more engaging and effective learning experience.

It can simulate real-life scenarios, enabling students to do the impossible, such as exploring far-off lands or diving deep beneath the ocean surface without leaving the classroom. One can build simulations of complex phenomena such as natural disasters, medical procedures, and scientific experiments inside AR, VR, or a combination of both, allowing students to experience and comprehend the information first-hand, deepening their engagement and understanding. Some AR and VR technologies are being used to create serious games featuring memorable characters and immersive storylines that enable employees

---

[13] https://fold.it/

to use all the resources at their disposal to overcome challenges. Feedback is provided that highlights their mistakes, along with tips to improve their performance.

Some new innovations have stretched the possibilities of deep immersion and gamification even further:

Haptic Feedback: This technology provides physical feedback to the user, such as vibration or pressure, to enhance the immersive experience.

Insightful Analytics: AR and VR technologies can feature detailed analytics to track every move of online learners, including their emotional state and level of alertness, via sensors, providing instructors with valuable feedback to improve their teaching methods.

If you are able to use these technologies strategically, you may be able to speed up employee learning and shorten TTP drastically. Some possibilities are listed below:

Medical training: Medical professionals are using VR simulations to train for complex procedures and surgeries. For example, companies like VirtaMed[14] use VR to equip medical students with realistic surgery skills before performing actual surgery. Osso VR[15] has developed a VR platform that allows surgeons to practice procedures and receive feedback in a safe environment. This VR platform immerses healthcare professionals into repeated practice on critical complex workflows while its analytics monitor their proficiency until they achieve the desired precision. Their trials found a 230% to 306% increase in skill transfer for the surgeons who trained with their platform.

Military and firefighting training: The US military uses VR-simulated combat exercises. In such online learning, you can play with various

---

[14] https://www.virtamed.com/en/medical-training-simulators/overview/
[15] https://www.ossovr.com/

variables and change them to present different or harder scenarios to solve. Even firefighter training is being done virtually with more realistic games.

Several more examples are evolving and emerging daily as technology evolves with additional features. For instance, Microsoft HoloLens boasts of integrating analytics and haptic sensors in their next-generation gadgets, which will make hands-on skill acquisition far faster. Check out additional examples in subsequent chapters.

DESIGNING CONTEXTUALIZATION FOR ACCELERATION

There is a vast amount of research on contextualization dictating that learning for acceleration should be designed entirely with scenarios or around scenarios. However, most training designers and e-learning strategists give a blind eye to those proven strategies. Instead, they use a few examples, scenarios, or cases as an addendum to their slide-based, text-based, or video-based informational content. This could be mainly because scenario-based e-learning design requires them to start from scratch and is a highly effort-intensive endeavor.

Further, such an approach indeed increases the length of training. As a general rule, to compress overall TTP, one may have to increase overall training length by several folds. At the outset, it would look counterintuitive, but that's exactly how the overall proficiency path is shortened.

Often designers do not take this route. They resort to converting their conventional classroom material into an e-learning format, which, at best, can only reduce travel costs or training durations or make learning more accessible. However, such an approach fails to accelerate the learning.

SELF-GUIDED CONTEXTUALIZATION (PRE-ILT PHASE)

Here are some best practices for designing contextualized self-guided e-learning during the pre-ILT phase for accelerated employee development:

 Encapsulate any content you want learners to master into well-scoped realistic cases or scenarios relevant to produce the desired outcomes for a job.

 Put learners into deep thinking mode on day one instead of starting with basic things. Emphasize problem-solving skills as the foundation for a job instead of projecting information content.

 Avoid linear informational content, presentation-based material, or videos focused on the basics of jobs, operations, concepts, principles, facts, and figures. This can be searchable via PSSs and does not need self-learning upfront. Avoid putting learners into such passive reading or watching mode to learn the material.

 Create well-scoped scenarios from actual jobs to prepare learners for realistic job challenges that drive the need to understand concepts and principles.

 Focus on delivering relevant content to produce outcomes for a job. Link the task to be learned to the realist work environment and challenges one may face. Drive learning goals or outcomes closely or directly linked to on-the-job success or failure.

 Avoid giving all the content in one shot. Distribute the content over time and interleave consecutive scenarios with some active tasks in between, like performing a relevant task, noting observations, creating an outcome, interviewing an expert for a specific topic, etc.

 Avoid namesake quizzes and assessments on the material. Get learners into active processing mode whereby they need to submit something tangible like project deliverables, their analysis of the problem, making of a report, actual work output, or summaries of a coaching session, among others.

 Avoid assigning grades on quizzes or assessments. Improve the sense of achievement of learners by giving usable artifacts like credits, points, and awards.

VIRTUAL OR REMOTE CONTEXTUALIZATION (ILT PHASE)

Here are some best practices for designing instructor-led contextualized remote or virtual sessions for accelerated employee development:

☞ Avoid the traditional approach of lectures followed by hands-on activities and some case scenarios as supplementary material, cherry-sprinkled with quizzes or discussions.

☞ Flip the delivery around to make it realistic. Expose learners to representative case scenarios first, have them perform hands-on activities to solve the problems, assess them hard using on-the-job assessment criteria, and then cherry-sprinkle the lectures and presentations to facilitate the learning toward desired results.

☞ Avoid wasting time on icebreakers and usual training techniques. Drive learning with stakes and high emotional involvement rather than always design for a 'safe place to learn.' Give them an environment that conveys the same level of emotional loading, pressure, and expectations in which they are required to operate.

☞ Include stakes in the assessments similar to the ones they will encounter on the job, like consequences, failures, deliverables, and reviews, among other checkpoints. Build a sufficient amount of challenge, complexity, and difficulty level. Promote learners' emotional involvement, emotional reactions to stakes in learning, and sense of 'what is on the line.' Add a similar amount of pressure, deadlines, or time restrictions as it would be there in a real job.

☛ Use interactive case-study-based lectures, which involves having a case study as the main backbone embedded with lectures or instructor-led sessions. Identify a complex, larger-scope case scenario or fabricate one if something is not readily available. Such a scenario should run throughout the ILT as a backbone. Choose or simulate a case scenario that represents or involves all the critical skills and key aspects of a job that learners need to succeed. Design the scenario around the primary learning outcome that culminates in attaining the same outcomes or results as they would be required to produce in the job.

☛ Use the CBA-CDR model (see my upcoming book *"Stakes in Learning"*), which includes presenting the context (C) of the problem, briefing (B) about concepts involved, having them analyze the problem through activities (A), giving them content (C) to learn and apply the skills requires to solve that problem, conduct discussions and debrief (D) on what they just learned and end it with reflection (R) on the best practices.

☛ Design several sub-problems for secondary learning outcomes that can fit into the main backbone. Design a visual map of how the instructor will navigate and jump in and out of the case scenario.

☛ Map the learning outcomes on the case scenario backbone to ascertain where and how each learning outcome will be covered, either by the primary case scenario or sub-problems.

- Use variations of scenario-based e-learning, including problems, cases, games, VR, and simulation.

- Try several ways to incorporate context, such as analyzing a real-life scenario; solving the stated problem; describing the root cause; providing a recommendation on a solution; making decisions; To choose between available options; exploring or extending an option.

- Increase active participation by incorporating interactivity and encourage learning by executing. Build peer-to-peer communication and collaboration, which promote peer recognition.

- Ask learners to generate deliverables, compute something, process information actively, and transform content.

- Use thinking-based assessment, i.e., questions requiring research, active involvement, and deeper thinking. Trigger non-linear thinking process in learners by using higher-order scenarios, real-life cases, and job-relevant assessments.

- Do not offer long virtual or remote lectures, seminars, or sessions. Deliver a maximum of 1-2 hours of the virtual or remote session, consisting of not more than three micro-lessons.

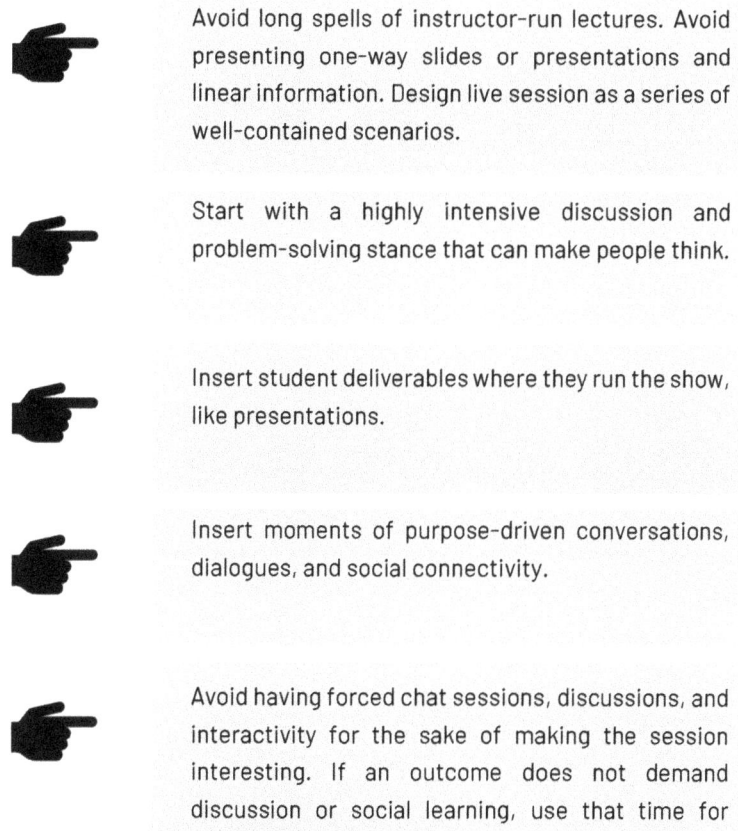

👉 Avoid long spells of instructor-run lectures. Avoid presenting one-way slides or presentations and linear information. Design live session as a series of well-contained scenarios.

👉 Start with a highly intensive discussion and problem-solving stance that can make people think.

👉 Insert student deliverables where they run the show, like presentations.

👉 Insert moments of purpose-driven conversations, dialogues, and social connectivity.

👉 Avoid having forced chat sessions, discussions, and interactivity for the sake of making the session interesting. If an outcome does not demand discussion or social learning, use that time for something more purposeful.

ON-THE-JOB CONTEXTUALIZATION (POST-ILT PHASE)

Here are some best practices for designing on-the-job contextualized e-learning for accelerated employee development:

☞ Avoid task-driven OJT check sheets. Don't use the S-OJT approach unless the job is highly task-focused and predictable. Instead, use result-driven OJT to prove they attained the results, not simply accomplished the tasks.

☞ Deliver PSS-enabled micro-lessons during the post-ILT phase designed around well-scoped case scenarios. The focus should be on unpredictable, non-routine events instead of routine, known ones. Use PSSs and searchable repositories for performance improvement on known/routine tasks.

☞ Assign field mentors who coach and test the employees through scenarios and actual on-the-job results instead of generic tips or sign-off for formality's sake.

☞ Use proficiency metrics to assess their performance. Measure on-the-job progress and performance with the exact metrics with which their annual or quarterly performance review is measured.

☞ Avoid assigning recurring streams of videos, bulletins, documents, or similar dry content to learners in the name of reinforcement or updates. Create scenario-driven communication and employ story-telling to provide context on what is happening and why and how they need to change methods.

CONTEXTUALIZATION TO MAINTAIN PROFICIENCY (SUSTENANCE PHASE)

Here are some best practices for contextualized e-learning to maintain proficiency and accelerate employee development:

 Avoid one-way communication for refresher and reinforcement. The pushed assignment should ask for the submission of clear job-related deliverables or artifacts. Extend it with purpose-driven conversations, dialogues, and social connectivity.

 Be selective about what employees need to stay informed about during the sustenance phase and what is absolutely a must to stay proficient. Events and activities occurring on the actual job may be different in nature than the ones perceived by the learning strategists.

 Turn documents, bulletins, videos, or other notifications, required by employees to maintain proficiency, into a story-telling format, such as a real scenario that happened in the field.

 Not everything required to provide refresher or reinforcement to maintain proficiency can be designed or delivered as scenarios, mainly if it has never happened before. For instance, precautionary or compliance notices are meant to reduce the chances of something dreadful.

CHIEF E-LEARNING OFFICER

 Deliver refresher and reinforcement learning on an ongoing basis via PSSs rather than LMSs. Try to embed this learning into the workflow employees use to perform their job, like AR/VR gadgets and work-related mobile apps.

 Design proficiency-testing scenarios and deeply problem-solving-oriented assessments of learners, but program them to conduct as shorter on-the-go assessments, not taking more than a few minutes at a time.

REFLECTION TIME

Things go wrong when we start building slides and other content pieces, including videos, to create e-learning packages. The organizations that indeed made a difference in speeding up TTP focused on designing and exposing employees to well-designed scenarios, cases, or problems. If you are not using the strategies, methods, and technologies with appropriate contextualization, you may not be able to leverage the power of this strategy to accelerate the learning of skills.

Use the space below to reflect upon and note down your major takeaways to this point. ***Are you leveraging this powerful online training design strategy? If not, look at all the tasks you target in online learning.***

> ***Question to Think ahead!***
>
> *Which task does require deeper thinking and solving a range of problems to achieve business outcomes?*

Reflections

YOUR LEARNING JOURNEY

In this chapter, you learned the first strategy to design powerful scenario-based e-learning courses and programs, which significantly accelerates employee performance. You learned four principles that you must consider while designing scenarios. You learned various advancements making it possible to design experiences that can ensure much-accelerated workforce proficiency easily.

In the next chapter, you will learn how to design these scenarios into smaller chunks using the second strategy of time-spaced microlearning.

Chapter 1
E-LEARNING AND DIGITAL REVOLUTION

Chapter 2
A ROLE OF CHIEF E-LEARNING OFFICER

Chapter 3
SPEED OF EMPLOYEE DEVELOPMENT AS E-LEARNING KPIs

Chapter 4
STRATEGIC E-LEARNING FOR SPEED

Chapter 5
SCENARIO-BASED E-LEARNING

Chapter 6
TIME-SPACED MICROLEARNING CONTENT

Chapter 7
OPTIMALLY SEQUENCED E-LEARNING PATH

Chapter 8
ON-DEMAND PERFORMANCE SUPPORT SYSTEMS

Chapter 9
EXPERIENCE-RICH MULTI-TECHNOLOGY MIX

Chapter 10
SPEED-ENABLING E-LEARNING SYSTEMS APPRAOCH

Chapter 11
SUMMARY OF E-LEARNING DESIGN GUIDELINES FOR SPEED

Chapter 12
EMERGING E-LEARNING REVOLUTIONS

6

TIME-SPACED MICROLEARNING CONTENT

Research from my studies and others shows that technology-driven virtual training sessions and self-directed learning become more effective when splitting into shorter sessions or modules. It becomes even more effective when each session is focused on a few learning outcomes at a time.

This strategy is called by several names like 'chunking,' 'bite-size learning' (Mayer & Moreno 2003), 'microlearning' (Hug, Lindner & Bruck 2006), or 'segmenting' (Clark & Mayer 2011). Microlearning is a more contemporary concept: "Microlearning is a way of teaching and delivering content to learners in small, very specific bursts. The learners are in control of what and when they're learning" (Eades 2014).

Some studies have indicated that when traditional sessions are broken into microlearning sessions, it improves retention and far transfer (Clark & Mayer 2011; Hug, Lindner & Bruck 2006; Hug 2015; van der Meer et al. 2015). It has been reported to improve learning transfer by 17% compared to traditional learning methods. In addition, it generates 50% more engagement while reducing development costs by 50% and increasing development speed by 30% (Gutierrez 2018).

In general, e-learning, online or virtual sessions should be smaller in length and broken into smaller modules. Two examples of apps that use microlearning are here:

Duolingo[16], a popular language learning app, uses time-spaced microlearning to help users learn new languages. This app breaks down language lessons into small, bite-sized chunks that can be completed in just a few minutes each day. The lessons are spaced out over time, so users are able to review previous lessons and reinforce what they've learned. According to Duolingo, users who complete just 5 minutes of

---

[16] https://www.duolingo.com/

Duolingo lessons each day can learn as much as those who take a traditional language course.

Headspace[17] is a popular meditation app that uses time-spaced microlearning to help users develop mindfulness skills. The app offers a variety of guided meditations designed to be completed regularly, with users encouraged to meditate for a few minutes each day to reinforce their mindfulness practice.

DEBUNKING ATTENTION SPAN MYTH

Most designers relate the need for microlearning with decreasing attention spans. It is true to some extent, as it has been seen through studies and experimentation that people's attention span is reduced from 12 seconds in 2000 to 8 seconds in 2013 (Grovo, n.d.). You might have heard such claims or remarks on social media. However, as a designer or learning specialist, you must take such observations rationally. Many designers tend to apply attention span context quite non-contextually.

Often the low or decreasing attention span is talked about in the context of things like Facebook or social media advertisement where it matters that a reader be hooked onto a message within the first few seconds to explore or click further. Mention of attention span refers to the effectiveness of the hooks required to make the audience stay on your content. The drivers that have worsened attention spans are things like the culture of swiping, scrolling, and TikToking. People want more within a given time and don't stick around at one piece for long.

---

[17] https://www.headspace.com/

CH 6 - TIME-SPACED MICROLEARNING CONTENT

However, the problem happens when you apply attention span in the context of designing e-learning. To some extent, it is applicable but not to an insane level. If you over-apply it, it drives ineffective designs in an attempt to over-compress content into bite-size modules, some of which do not do good justice to the complexity of the skill.

In the learning domain, if you know that a given skill will make you successful in your job, no matter the complexity and rigor of the skill, you will try to hold your attention as long as needed. The reason is that there are consequences if you don't keep it well enough. Such emotional loading has a significant impact on your job performance. So, as a learning designer, do justice with the skills for which you are designing programs, and don't get too hung up on non-contextual statements about declining attention spans.

However, we also know the quality of learning declines when we sit on content for too long. The ability to focus on a range of information is a highly individual trait and is not the same across the board. In general, less is more, given that people need time to do many other things.

Here I want to clarify one thing. If your goal is to shorten TTP of learners, and you think the first thing you could do is to shorten the time they spend on the content, that is probably the wrong start. Giving less time to the content or shorter content does not accelerate learning. The learning speed with microlearning is enhanced with something else you will learn in this chapter.

PRINCIPLES OF MICROLEARNING

A microlearning strategy to positively impact TTP requires three pieces, as shown in Figure 6.1.

1. Chunking the content
2. Time-spacing and distributing
3. Interleaving chunks with relevant activities

Figure 6.1: Principles of microlearning-based e-learning

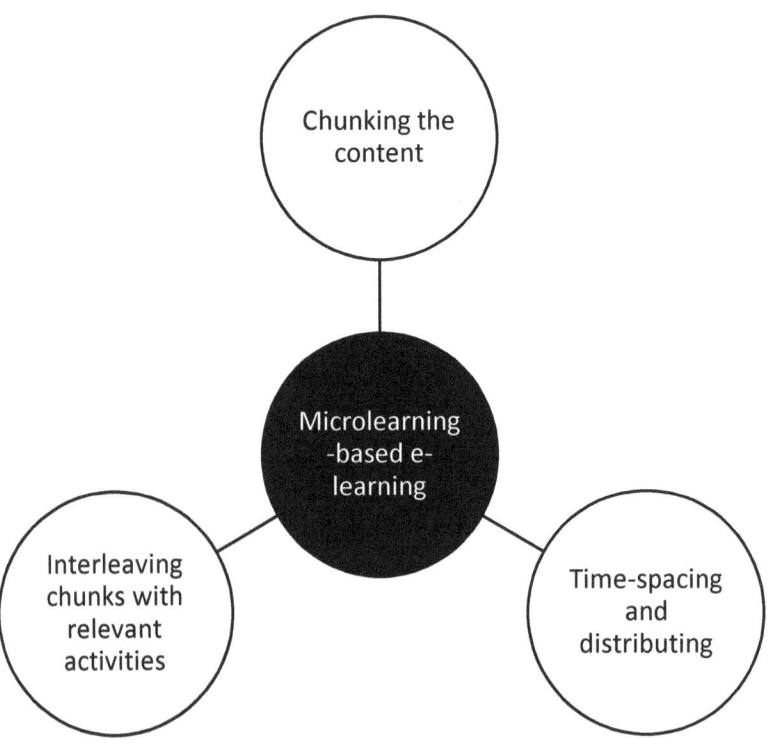

1. CHUNKING

The first piece of the microlearning strategy is to divide the learning in smaller chunks. The approach is called segmenting, chunking, or microlearning. This makes sense because people don't have enough

CH 6 - TIME-SPACED MICROLEARNING CONTENT

time. If you could design smaller chunks, each chunk focusing on one learning outcome at a time, you can make online learning painless.

Van der Meer et al. (2015) reported that when a traditional lecture was replaced with bite-sized videos, over 45% of the students found learning useful and preferred this method. Lingg (2014) recommends that "Rather than designing your next multi-hour course, consider creating several smaller 'learning snacks' instead" (p. 12).

The short, quick, on-the-job instructor-facilitated sessions or short videos targeting one learning outcome at a time could effectively drive retention and absorption, and hence speed-to-proficiency. As a design rule, each learning outcome can be designed as a microlearning session for drawing the best value and flexibility of time-spaced microlearning.

But how long a content can be a 'chunk,' that's debatable. Some pieces of research and certain evidence are there to specify its length. For example, TED talks are designed maximum to be 18 minutes. They consulted several scientific studies and found that the proximity of 20 minutes was a sweet spot for a learning-worthy talk. More than that becomes unbearable. They also recommended that a talk should not cover multiple learning outcomes.

The latest research by Microsoft suggests that a virtual instructor-led session should not be longer than two hours. That is when you get serious content that must be learned. But organizations sometimes are too interested in offering day-long virtual sessions to save their resource costs.

So, the chunks could vary depending upon the amount of information and level of skills to be learned.

It is seen that the short, quick, on-the-job instructor-facilitated sessions or short videos of not more than 4 minutes or so, targeting one learning outcome at a time, can effectively drive retention and absorption and hence, speed-to-proficiency. If each microlearning video or session is designed around one learning outcome, it is possible to leverage the e-learning path approach to sequence the sessions by learning outcomes toward the desired proficiency during pre-training, ILT, and on-the-job learning phases to support the learners.

2. SPACING AND DISTRIBUTING

In my research, I came across programs that were as long as 8 weeks in face-to-face settings. The traditional approach is to break them into smaller chunks but then assign an aggressive timeline to learners to finish all the chunks.

In a recent program design at a $50 billion corporation, one week's worth of face-to-face training was converted into video-based chunks, each spanning 30 minutes, but total learning amounted to 40 hours. Learners were reserved one week dedicated to watching such self-driven videos. This type of ineffective design only slows down learning.

The correct design practice is to break larger content into shorter sessions, modules, or chunks and space them out. The idea is to insert a reasonable space between two consecutive chunks or modules and then distribute those chunks over a fairly reasonable period of time.

Doing so provides reinforcement or boost to the learners at regular intervals. This leads to better retention of skills or knowledge being learned (Birnbaum et al. 2013). For learners, it reduces the cognitive load of a complex skill. It also gives a sense of achievement incrementally to the learners. Other benefits are less resource needs to deliver learning in short chunks. One could use technology and automation to make delivery and learning more efficient.

The shorter e-learning sessions spaced out in time are effective and accelerate speed-to-proficiency. This strategy also complements scenario-based contextualization. Each chunk can be a well-scoped case or scenario instead of one-dimensional, linear informational content.

3. INTERLEAVING WITH REINFORCEMENT

A usual mistake with microlearning design is that designers rely only on smaller chunks and spacing. However, research suggests that most online training, e-learning programs, or even virtual sessions fail because they lack moments of reflection. That's where the third piece of microlearning strategy, called 'interleaving,' comes into play.

The idea of interleaving is to use other tasks and activities between microlearning chunks, which could allow more practice and reflection. Such spaced, shorter sessions embedded with interleaved assignments allow appropriate reflection and practice required to learn a complex skill. A varied type of tasks or assignments could be used to internalize those smaller chunks.

DESIGNING MICROLEARNING FOR ACCELERATION

There is a vast amount of research on the effectiveness of microlearning. However, most designers and e-learning strategists give a blind eye to those proven strategies. This could be mainly due to time pressures from upper management. The focus is always on reducing costs, but executives fail to relate to TTP and continue to exert their uneducated stance on cost reduction in travel and training durations. As a general rule, to compress overall TTP, one may have to increase overall training length by several folds. At the outset, it would look counterintuitive, but that's exactly how the overall proficiency path is shortened. Ironically, while everybody loves learning, hardly anyone knows how to design learning to accelerate the path.

SELF-GUIDED MICROLEARNING (PRE-ILT PHASE)

Here are some best practices for designing self-guided microlearning during the pre-ILT phase for accelerated employee development.

Create shorter micro-lessons (10 to 20 minutes) addressing one specific learning outcome at a time.

Avoid offering self-guided micro-lessons as packaged web-based training modules through traditional LMSs for a fixed block of time each day. Avoid assigning more than 1-2 hours of daily cumulative learning via micro-lessons.

Don't design micro-lessons around video-based content only. Mix various pieces of content such as videos, text, slides, internet-based material, third-party content, assessments, case studies, games, and simulated runs in micro-lessons.

Avoid loading micro-lessons solely with preparatory or foundational content like information or facts/figures. Design each micro-lesson around a

CH 6 – TIME-SPACED MICROLEARNING CONTENT

well-scoped realistic case or scenario relevant to producing the outcomes for the job. Emphasize thinking skills and problem-solving skills as a solid foundation.

☞ Don't assign due dates for completion to a package of micro-lessons within a blocked time. Schedule and push each micro-lesson individually at regular intervals to user accounts or mobile phones based on a time-spaced learning path.

☞ Don't offer standard fixed content, fixed length learning paths. Conduct a micro-assessment before each micro-lesson. Change the learning path adaptively based on the experience and accomplishments of the users.

☞ Avoid terminating each micro-lesson with traditional quizzes. Ask learners to produce something. Design clear and evidence-based finishing or a micro-lesson that ends up submitting something active: quiz, deliverable, or starting a chat.

☞ Don't just settle for time-spacing alone to distribute the lessons. Interleave two consecutive micro-lessons with an 'active' task like performing a relevant task, noting observations, creating an outcome, interviewing an expert for a specific topic, etc.

VIRTUAL OR REMOTE MICROLEARNING (ILT PHASE)

Here are some best practices for designing instructor-led remote or virtual sessions using microlearning for accelerated employee development.

- 👉 Treat each virtual session as an independent micro-lesson designed around one specific learning outcome, limited to not more than 20-30 minutes each.

- 👉 Do not offer long virtual or remote lectures, seminars, or sessions. Deliver a maximum of 1-2 hours of the virtual or remote session, consisting of not more than three micro-lessons.

- 👉 Design each micro-lesson around a well-scoped scenario relevant to the job or results.

- 👉 Interleave two consecutive micro-lessons on the same day with a thinking-intensive break and assign them pre- or post-work, specific tasks, group discussions, etc., to put them into a profoundly reflective state.

- 👉 Avoid the mindset that a remote or virtual session must be a contiguous, day-long session to save resource costs.

CH 6 – TIME-SPACED MICROLEARNING CONTENT

☞ If you have more than one virtual or remote session, spread them over a reasonably long time instead of delivering on consecutive days.

☞ Assign tasks and activities between consecutive virtual sessions, allowing more practice, application, and reflection.

☞ Avoid long spells of instructor-run lectures. Avoid presenting one-way slides or presentations and linear information. Design live session as a series of well-contained scenarios.

☞ Start with a highly intensive discussion and problem-solving stance that can make people think.

Insert student deliverables where they run the show, like presentations.

☞ Insert moments of purpose-driven conversations, dialogues, and social connectivity.

☞ Avoid having forced chat sessions, discussions, and interactivity for the sake of making the session interesting. If an outcome does not demand discussion or social learning, use that time for something more purposeful.

Do not slice your session too short and over-compress content into bite-size modules, which could impair the depth and quality of learning. Take attention span claims in the correct context. Do justice to the complexity of skills.

 Be selective about which skill really qualifies for microlearning and which requires a larger contiguous block of time to master.

ON-THE-JOB MICROLEARNING (POST-ILT PHASE)

Here are some best practices for designing on-the-job training using microlearning for accelerated employee development.

 Deliver PSS-enabled micro-lessons during the post-ILT phase designed around well-scoped case scenarios. The focus should be on unpredictable, non-routine events instead of routine, known ones.

 Encourage using PSSs and searchable repositories for performance improvement on known/routine tasks.

 Assign field mentors who coach and test the employees through nano-coaching and nano-mentoring instead of generic tips or sign-off for formality's sake.

CH 6 - TIME-SPACED MICROLEARNING CONTENT

 Avoid assigning recurring streams of videos, bulletins, documents, or similar dry content to learners in the name of reinforcement or updates. Create scenario-driven micro-lessons and employ story-telling to provide context on what is happening and why and how they need to change to new methods.

MICROLEARNING TO MAINTAIN PROFICIENCY (SUSTENANCE PHASE)

Here are some best practices for designing microlearning to maintain proficiency and accelerate employee development.

 Be selective about the nature of microlearning content sent to learners during this phase. Not everything required to provide refresher or reinforcement to maintain proficiency can be designed or delivered as microlearning if it requires a larger contiguous block of time to master.

 Avoid sending the e-learning content in an email to learners. Avoid one-way, click-a-button types of non-value-add tasks not directly impacting the results of a job. Push meaningful content on-the-go as written content, messages, reminders, write-ups, summaries, videos, documents, or assessments on users' mobile devices.

☛ Do not send links or attachments of large documents to read or for reference. Convert any large documents into shorter segments of bulletins and push them as time-spaced micro-lessons.

☛ Design each micro-lesson, whether a document, bulletin, video, or other notification, into a storytelling format, such as a real scenario that happened in the field.

☛ Deliver refresher and reinforcement learning on an ongoing basis via PSS rather than LMSs. Try to embed this learning into the workflow employees use to perform their job, like AR/VR gadgets and work-related mobile apps.

☛ Avoid one-way communication for refresher and reinforcement. The pushed assignment should ask for the submission of clear job-related deliverables or artifacts. Extend it with purpose-driven conversations, dialogues, and social connectivity.

☛ Design proficiency-testing scenarios and deeply problem-solving-oriented assessments of learners, but program them to conduct as shorter on-the-go assessments, not taking more than a few minutes at a time.

Some of the above guidelines may either be unconventional or straight unorthodox challenging mainstream guidelines you otherwise might have been practicing. If you want to go deeper into this subject with examples and an exact implementation framework, stay tuned for my upcoming book, *Stakes in Learning*.

REFLECTION TIME

Breaking down e-learning content into smaller, focused sessions or modules can improve retention and learning transfer. However, you should not over-apply the concept of attention span decline to e-learning design, as learners will remain engaged if the skill is perceived as valuable. Microlearning should be designed around one learning outcome at a time, in smaller sessions, spaced out and interleaved with reinforcement activities. This approach not only improves retention and absorption but also accelerates speed-to-proficiency and reduces resource needs. Remember that not every skill or content qualifies for microlearning or time-spacing.

Use the space below to reflect upon and note down your major takeaways to this point. *Are you chunking, spacing, and interleaving the microlearning segments in your settings to build solid online training?*

> **Question to think ahead!**
>
> *Which skill can be packed in shorter e-learning that learners can apply immediately at the job?*

Reflections

YOUR LEARNING JOURNEY

In this chapter, you learned the second strategy to split larger mass of content into smaller chunks using time-spaced microlearning. You learned three key principles governing a good microlearning e-learning design meant to shorter TTP faster than other means. You understood key considerations and techniques to apply microlearning at various stages of proficiency journey.

In the next chapter, you will learn the third strategy in which you will be able to arrange these microlearning chunks, spaced or distributed in time through a sequence or order which is optimally sequenced for speed.

Chapter 1
E-LEARNING AND DIGITAL REVOLUTION

Chapter 2
A ROLE OF CHIEF E-LEARNING OFFICER

Chapter 3
SPEED OF EMPLOYEE DEVELOPMENT AS E-LEARNING KPIs

Chapter 4
STRATEGIC E-LEARNING FOR SPEED

Chapter 5
SCENARIO-BASED E-LEARNING

Chapter 6
TIME-SPACED MICROLEARNING CONTENT

Chapter 7
OPTIMALLY SEQUENCED E-LEARNING PATH

Chapter 8
ON-DEMAND PERFORMANCE SUPPORT SYSTEMS

Chapter 9
EXPERIENCE-RICH MULTI-TECHNOLOGY MIX

Chapter 10
SPEED-ENABLING E-LEARNING SYSTEMS APPRAOCH

Chapter 11
SUMMARY OF E-LEARNING DESIGN GUIDELINES FOR SPEED

Chapter 12
EMERGING E-LEARNING REVOLUTIONS

7
OPTIMALLY SEQUENCED E-LEARNING PATH

At the workplace, people don't learn just by sitting in front of the computer. They need to do a certain task, practice on something, deliver something for the job, and participate in or conduct some assignments. All of these, including the learning activities, online learning modules, and other training activities, need to be sequenced optimally to enable them to reach desired proficiency in a shorter time.

My research revealed that TTP is significantly impacted by carefully sequencing the learning activities, tasks, or assignments in a very efficient path, called a 'learning path' or 'learning pathway.'

CONCEPT OF E-LEARNING PATH

The concept of a learning path is to eliminate redundant, irrelevant, or wasteful activities in the learning path by selecting the most essential and relevant learning activities (e-learning or otherwise) required for a stated proficiency goal and then sequencing those through readily available resources (e-learning modules or otherwise) to achieve that goal in shortest possible time.

The essence of the strategy is that if you sequence those activities over time, you can deliberately create certain events and not wait for the universe to provide them to the learners. In a nutshell, it accelerates learning by being deliberate about how soon and in what order learners are exposed to events required to master their skills.

In the context of e-learning, activities including online courses, use of electronic resources, practice on PSS, other knowledge tools, and a range of other e-learning activities, when sequenced optimally, are termed as 'e-learning path.'

Note that the learning sequence I suggest here is not the same as what most academic literature portrays, i.e., individualized or personalized learning paths created in typical LMS systems for a learner. That learning path is created in reference to learning the material rather than gaining proficiency. Here we are talking about a total journey until someone really reaches desired proficiency. If your LMS allows building a start-to-end learning path to create a total journey until on-the-job proficiency is attained, then we are discussing the same thing.

Figure 7.1: Concept of an optimal path[18]

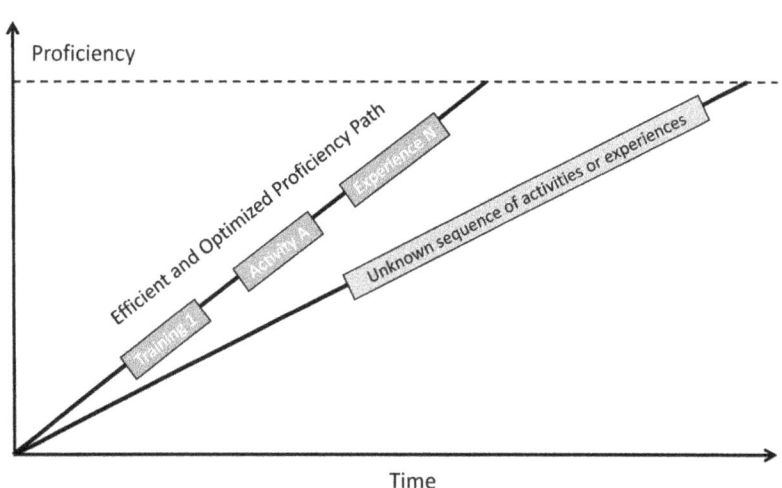

Previously, in the context of complex jobs, Darrah (1996) showed the use of a sequence of organized activities in a computer manufacturing company, while Hutchins & Palen (1997) explained it for a flight engineer's role. This was seen as an influential strategy for

---

[18] Image inspired by Steve Rosenbaum, Learning Paths International 2010, learningatlightspeed.wordpress.com

accelerated proficiency. Rosenbaum and Williams (2004) demonstrated the use of the learning path concept in many commercial settings.

By approaching the sequence from a learner's proficiency angle, a designer could map available e-learning modules in a path in optimal order of activities that shorten the TTP as suggested in Figure 7.1.

The bottom line is that if you can set up a very systematic set of cases and experiences and organize them in a sequence, you could speed up the process of proficiency acquisition.

PRINCIPLES OF OPTIMALLY SEQUENCED E-LEARNING PATH

Building an optimal e-learning path is the key to designing a learning experience that can ensure the acceleration of learning and proficiency. This includes selecting only the most essential and relevant learning activities and focused assignments required for a stated proficiency goal, then sequencing how learners should go through it. This follows an optimization to make the length of that path the shortest possible. There are five principles determining this path, as shown in Figure 7.2.

1. *Remove unnecessary activities*
2. *Criteria-driven optimization*
3. *Assign time targets*
4. *Include resources in place of training*
5. *Create adaptive sequence*

Figure 7.2: Principles of optimally sequenced e-learning path

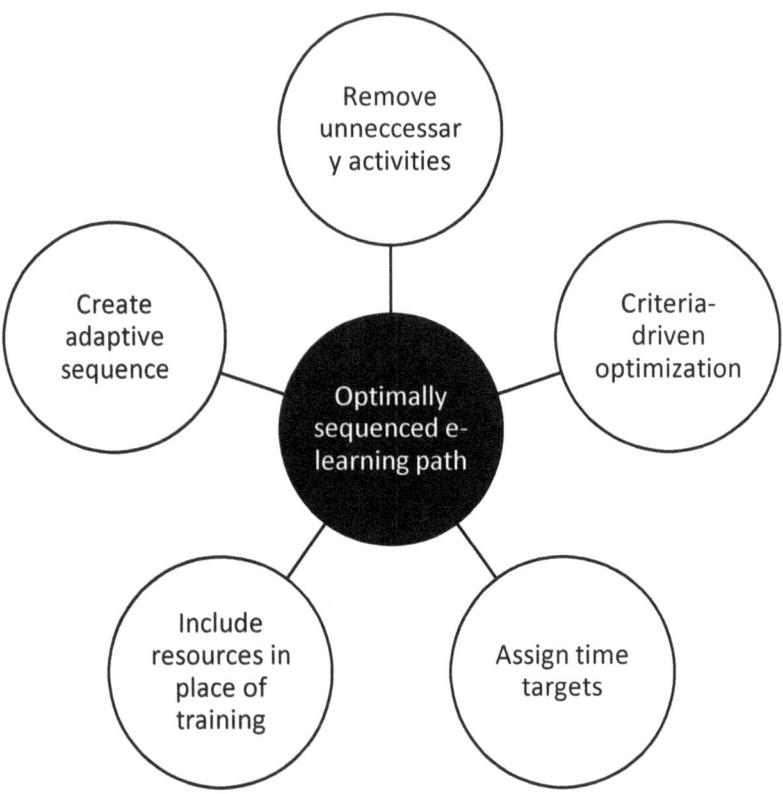

1. REMOVE UNNECESSARY ACTIVITIES

The idea here is to select only the most essential and relevant learning activities and focused assignments required for a stated proficiency goal, then sequence them according to how learners should go through them. The goal is to optimize the learning path and make its length as short as possible by eliminating redundant, irrelevant, or wasteful activities.

2. CRITERIA-DRIVEN OPTIMIZATION

The other thing you can do is assess what activities you are putting into the sequence. For instance, if you are creating a training course for a facility analyst, they might need to create a specific government audit report once every five years. Is there any point in teaching them a skill that won't be used for five years? So, you must look at what is immediately relevant and optimize the path accordingly.

The sequencing is made optimal by using some criteria like:

- Frequency of occurrence of the task (very frequent to rare)
- Usage of the knowledge or skill (very often to hardly)
- The complexity of the task (simple to complex)
- The difficulty level of the problem (very simple to very hard)

When such business criteria are used to sequence the e-learning modules, resources, activities, and microlearning sessions, the result is an efficient and lean learning path. This efficient learning path then contributes significantly toward attaining proficiency faster.

3. ASSIGN TIME TARGETS

Now, when you start putting time targets on each item in that sequence, the learning is automatically accelerated, or at least you'll know how long it would take to finish the sequence.

By assigning time targets to each activity, including online and e-learning activities, the total TTP can be estimated and tracked, and then focused efforts can be made to shorten the time.

4. INCLUDE RESOURCES IN PLACE OF TRAINING

Another thing that you can do is to use PSS, tools, reference repositories, or readily available resources, which may eliminate the need for any online training. Probably simple instructions to use the tools may be enough.

5. CREATE ADAPTIVE SEQUENCE

When learners are provided with a headstart based on their prior learning, current skill assessment, and other experience, it could accelerate TTP. Systematic profiling of learners needs to be done using smart technologies. Such profiling (or assessment) can be used to build an adaptive learning path to shorten the journey to proficiency collectively.

In a study, a case-based contextualized approach was used in which cases could be profiled based on complexity and skill levels and then can be sequenced in such a way as to allow learners to reach desired proficiency goals (Arnold et al. 2013). Thus, the adaptive e-learning path approach could be applied to accelerate the speed-to-proficiency further.

Here are three examples of adaptive sequence:

Pearson MyITLab[19]: A classic example of this strategy is Pearson Education's MyITLab online e-learning system which performs an initial assessment of the learner and allows different 'adaptive' entry and exit points depending on current skills, knowledge, or experience. Further, it conducts continuous assessments tied to learning outcomes. Based on

---

[19] https://mlm.pearson.com/northamerica/myitlab/

the results, it dynamically selects activities or modules in the learning path.

Smart Sparrow[20]*:* It is an adaptive learning platform that uses an optimally sequenced learning path to personalize the learning experience for each student. The platform uses AI and data analytics to assess the learner's knowledge and adjust the learning path accordingly. A study conducted by Arizona State University found that students who used Smart Sparrow for physics instruction had higher exam scores compared to those who used traditional instruction methods.

Carnegie Learning: Carnegie Learning uses AI to create personalized learning paths for cognitive teaching, such as math curricula. It adapts to each student's individual strengths and weaknesses (RAND 2013).

Cornerstone[21]: This is an AI-powered system to accomplish this adaptive function to optimize the content presented to learners based on their goals and current state of knowledge. This personalized learning experience can help learners better retain new information.

OPTIMIZING E-LEARNING PATH FOR ACCELERATION

There is a vast amount of research on the personalized learning path. However, the e-learning path you need to design is larger than the path a typical LMS system supports. You have to look at the entire learning journey of an employee from day one till they become proficient. In some

---

[20] https://www.smartsparrow.com/what-is-adaptive-learning/
[21] https://www.cornerstoneondemand.com/sg/solutions/learning-and-development-lms

cases, you also have to look at their path during proficiency maintenance phases to help them maintain it.

However, most training designers and e-learning strategists give a blind eye to designing a holistic, start-to-end learning path. A tiny percentage of them do design certification paths, but certification in most jobs denotes basic readiness. It does not convey proficiency. Moreover, once employees are out of the learning program, the e-learning strategist has no say or control over their remaining e-learning path. That's why they resort to a 'limited-view' e-learning path that typically starts from onboarding and goes until required training requirements have been completed. Even the best of the best training programs does not impart proficiency. Thus, the learners walk out non-proficient from any training setting.

Further, such an approach of 'limited-view' presents a rosy picture of training-related metrics, including the number of trainees qualified or certified, their impression or feedback scores, the number of programs offered, the number of video hours watched, and other non-value-added metrics. None of their metrics are related to TTP or proficiency measurements, simply because that would require a complete e-learning path design. A primary pushback is that the moment they design a full e-learning path, they do not have a definite number on the length of that path in days, weeks, or months to look good in front of executives.

However, unless you design a total, holistic e-learning path for a job role, your goal to shorten TTP and accelerate employee development will not become a practical reality.

CH 7 - OPTIMALLY SEQUENCED E-LEARNING PATH

SELF-GUIDED E-LEARNING PATH (PRE-ILT PHASE)

Here are some best practices for designing an optimal, efficient, and lean e-learning path for self-guided learning during the pre-ILT phase for accelerated employee development.

 Conduct skill profiling based on complexity and difficulty and then determine the placement of a task appropriately on the employee proficiency development path.

 Approach from business goals or the job outcomes instead of developing individualized or personalized learning path. Sequence all elements of pre-work, ILT sessions, homework, etc., as an e-learning path.

 Eliminate redundant, irrelevant, or wasteful activities in the learning path. Select the most essential and relevant learning activities for a stated proficiency goal.

 Start from the outcome and determine all the essential activities or tasks required to achieve the outcomes. Design an efficient and optimal path.

 Design all the self-guided learning activities as micro-lessons. And then sequence them on a lean path. Sequence that path through readily available resources and avenues in natural settings to achieve that goal in the shortest possible time.

CHIEF E-LEARNING OFFICER

☛ Time-space all the self-guided micro-lesson and then distribute them over a period of time. Interleave two consecutive micro-lessons with an 'active' task like performing a relevant task, noting observations, creating an outcome, interviewing an expert for a specific topic, etc.

☛ Don't offer standard fixed content, fixed length learning paths. Conduct a micro-assessment before each micro-lesson. Change the learning path adaptively based on the experience and accomplishments of the users.

☛ Design a learning path that allows different 'adaptive' entry and exit points based on the learner's profile, providing a headstart to learners.

☛ Conduct a continuous assessment of learning outcomes and dynamically select activities or modules in the learning path to collectively shorten the journey to proficiency.

☛ Map the learning activities vs. available opportunities and focus on the optimal order.

☛ Use smart technologies to systematically profile learners' current knowledge, skill, and experience during the journey.

CH 7 - OPTIMALLY SEQUENCED E-LEARNING PATH

 Don't design an e-learning path solely around video-based content or other passive reading/watching activities. Leverage various pieces of content such as videos, text, slides, internet-based material, third-party content, assessments, case studies, games, and simulated runs, which can demonstrate the active involvement of learners throughout the path.

VIRTUAL OR REMOTE E-LEARNING PATH (ILT PHASE)

Here are some best practices for designing an optimal, efficient, and lean e-learning path for instructor-led remote or virtual sessions for accelerated employee development.

 Do not offer long virtual or remote lectures, seminars, or sessions. Deliver a maximum of 1-2 hours of the virtual or remote session, consisting of not more than three micro-lessons.

 Design an e-learning path showing a series of virtual or remote sessions required to obtain desired outcomes. If you have more than one virtual or remote session, spread them over a reasonably long time over the entire e-learning path pertaining to ILT.

 Include interleaving activities between virtual sessions with pre- or post-work, specific tasks, group discussions, etc., to put them into a profoundly

reflective state. Insert tasks and activities between allowing more practice and application of what they learned. Insert moments of purpose-driven conversations, dialogues, and social connectivity as properly defined assignments or activities rather than leaving them to flow independently.

☞ Design each virtual or remote session around a series of well-scoped scenarios relevant to the job or results.

☞ Design self-guided homework assignments that include highly complex skills requiring deeper thinking. Allow space, time, and opportunity for reflection before the next day's ILT session.

☞ Include only the most essential tasks and activities directly related to producing a given outcome at the job or obtaining results. Remove anything which is 'nice to have' information.

☞ Avoid information, one-way presentation, or other linear virtual/remote session content. Instead, put tasks entirely dependent on information access using PSS or knowledge repository as activities on the path.

☞ Assign time targets to each activity on the e-learning path, starting from the end goal and working backward to assign reasonable and achievable time targets.

CH 7 - OPTIMALLY SEQUENCED E-LEARNING PATH

 Do not compress the sessions in length or quantity. Do justice to the complexity of the skills and compute the required length of the overall e-learning path based on that.

 Insert student deliverables like creating reports, presentations, material, and other artifacts as assessments embedded in the e-learning path and suitably allocated in time and defined with a specific sequence.

ON-THE-JOB E-LEARNING PATH (POST-ILT PHASE)

Here are some best practices for designing an optimal, efficient, and lean e-learning path for on-the-job training for accelerated employee development.

 Use adaptive LMSs to change and optimize the e-learning path for each employee based on their performance, learning speed, accomplishments, and results. Expose employees to only necessary activities. Not all employees need to have the same fixed e-learning path.

 Design a careful e-learning path for the post-ILT phase because this is where learners are likely to be assigned by their managers on ad-hoc assignments, interrupting their proficiency.

- Integrate online learning sources, documentation, PSSs, and on-the-job activities properly sequenced on the on-the-job e-learning path.

- Identify coaching or mentoring opportunities as events or activities. Include those field mentoring and coaching activities suitably on the e-learning path focused on specific outcomes.

- Use PSSs and searchable repositories for performance improvement on known/routine tasks.

- Measure a learner's progress through an on-the-job e-learning path at regular intervals in terms of proficiency metrics defined for that job.

- Deliberately manufacture the activities or leverage ongoing events to create an experience on the learning path for unpredictable, non-routine events instead of routine, known ones.

- Put high-frequency events first on the e-learning path, followed by mid and low-frequency events. This prepares employees for essential tasks. However, try to put the highly complex ahead of others. Learners can gain mastery in their overall job faster when they are exposed to highly complex tasks first.

CH 7 - OPTIMALLY SEQUENCED E-LEARNING PATH

 Conduct a continuous assessment of learning outcomes and dynamically select activities or modules in the learning path to collectively shorten the journey to proficiency. Design a learning path that allows different 'adaptive' entry and exit points based on the learner's profile, providing a headstart to learners.

 Continuously optimize the post-ILT e-learning path to ensure that unnecessary or wasteful activities are constantly removed. Perform criteria-driven optimization to scrutinize each activity on the path. Optimize the e-learning path by assigning realistic goals.

 Track time spent by employees on each activity on the path and track how soon each employee achieves desired proficiency. Marry this data with the proficiency level of employees. Determine the baseline length of the e-learning path based on a given composition.

E-LEARNING PATH TO MAINTAIN PROFICIENCY (SUSTENANCE PHASE)

Here are some best practices for designing an optimal, efficient, and lean e-learning path to maintain proficiency and accelerate employee development.

 Use proficiency metrics, learning, and HR analytics to gather data on the frequency, complexity, importance, and urgency of various activities done by employees and associate how those are related to the speed of proficiency attainment.

 Use analytics to analyze the e-learning path of seasoned employees who have attained proficiency. Use this data to optimize the path for new employees and make it shorter based on new targets.

 Use intelligent technologies and analytics to systematically profile past, present, and future learners' knowledge, skill, experience, accomplishments, and proficiency at every point during the journey. Draw an organization-level picture out of this analysis.

Some of the above guidelines may either be unconventional or straight unorthodox, challenging mainstream guidelines you otherwise might have been practicing. If you want to go deeper into this subject with examples and an exact implementation framework, stay tuned for my upcoming book *"Proficiency Made Visible: Accelerated On-the-job Learning with ProPath and ProMap Tools."*

CH 7 - OPTIMALLY SEQUENCED E-LEARNING PATH

REFLECTION TIME

Several organizations create comprehensive certifications in the LMS, which dictates a well-scoped sequence for the learners. The advantage of such implementation is that anyone can get a report to track learners' journey toward desired proficiency. For such a business-relevant learning path, you must involve the direct manager in establishing a sequence particular to a job role.

Use the space below to reflect upon and note down your major takeaways to this point. *Are you leveraging this powerful thought process in your settings? If not, you need to review the learning paths applied to the most critical job roles.*

Question to think ahead!

Which e-learning activities make someone reach proficiency quickly, and which do not?

CHIEF E-LEARNING OFFICER

Reflections

CH 7 - OPTIMALLY SEQUENCED E-LEARNING PATH

YOUR LEARNING JOURNEY

In this chapter, you learned the third strategy to design an optimally sequenced and lean e-learning path by removing unwanted or time-wasting activities and focusing on the essential activities required to attain the outcomes for the job. You learned how you could arrange scenario-based microlearning content to hasten the proficiency of your learners.

In the next chapter, you will learn the fourth strategy to replace training with suitable performance support systems to allow just-in-time learning during the workflow of a job instead of spending unproductive time on unnecessary training intervention.

Chapter 1
E-LEARNING AND DIGITAL REVOLUTION

Chapter 2
A ROLE OF CHIEF E-LEARNING OFFICER

Chapter 3
SPEED OF EMPLOYEE DEVELOPMENT AS E-LEARNING KPIs

Chapter 4
STRATEGIC E-LEARNING FOR SPEED

Chapter 5
SCENARIO-BASED E-LEARNING

Chapter 6
TIME-SPACED MICROLEARNING CONTENT

Chapter 7
OPTIMALLY SEQUENCED E-LEARNING PATH

Chapter 8
ON-DEMAND PERFORMANCE SUPPORT SYSTEMS

Chapter 9
EXPERIENCE-RICH MULTI-TECHNOLOGY MIX

Chapter 10
SPEED-ENABLING E-LEARNING SYSTEMS APPRAOCH

Chapter 11
SUMMARY OF E-LEARNING DESIGN GUIDELINES FOR SPEED

Chapter 12
EMERGING E-LEARNING REVOLUTIONS

8
ON-DEMAND PERFORMANCE SUPPORT SYSTEMS

CH 8 - ON-DEMAND PERFORMANCE SUPPORT SYSTEMS

Managers tend to rely heavily on training and more often underestimate the value of PSS.

When you make information, knowledge, and learning available to employees just-in-time at the point of need or the teachable moment during the job, they can apply it in the context of the job. If people's questions could get answers at the point of need, it would speed up their on-the-job proficiency way faster. Simple things like job aids, checklists, task sheets, flow charts, procedures, a model, algorithms, decision tables, etc., can do wonders in speeding up performance.

PSSs are meant to achieve that goal. They may include a range of electronic resources like online learning content, reference material, knowledge-based procedures, mobile applications, decision-making software, etc., which, according to the project leaders, can provide just-in-time training or support.

The recent pandemic has increased the importance of this technology to the point that it has become the core of most organizational learning endeavors. As we have seen, organizational learning moves from being a training event to which employees need to be invited to something that happens automatically as employees seek assistance on-the-job from PSSs. PSSs are powerful tools that are now used in place of or in the augmentation of training. These are not some tools that are used sitting on the sideline but rather used during the task as part of the workflow.

Incidentally, this is also the space where technologies are evolving at a rapid pace. With the availability of new technologies, the shape and extent of PSSs are also changing beyond their original role of just-in-time resources for training, support, or information. This is the single most element of the ecosystem you, as an e-learning strategist, can rely on if your workforce is geographically dispersed. When in-person training is not feasible or when training itself does not give your results in terms of faster readiness of your teams, then you need to implement PSSs strategically to provide employees with JIT coaching and mentoring.

My research suggests eight types of PSSs, as shown in Figure 8.1, that are shaping workforce learning and proficiency.

A PSS can be simply a learning delivery resource like LMS to get self-paced content and on-demand videos. It may be a document repository of the organization or simply a repository of YouTube-type videos. The primary goal is to get learning on-demand and just-in-time when someone needs it. As simple as checklists or job aids to more sophisticated ones like AR-based job instructions, Contextual on-screen help, Decision-support software, and AI-based search engine. Others may include more straightforward but easy-to-implement, like on-the-go push notifications, mobile apps, chatbots, skill self-assessments and procedures, and manuals.

CH 8 – ON-DEMAND PERFORMANCE SUPPORT SYSTEMS

Figure 8.1: Eight types of PSS

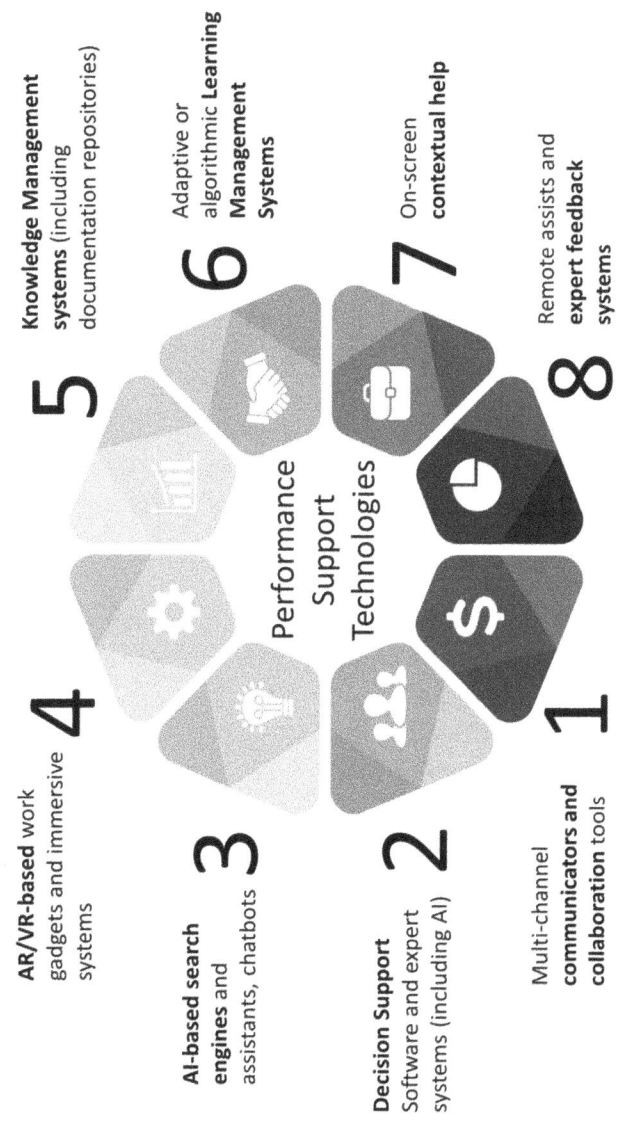

1. MULTI-CHANNEL COMMUNICATORS AND COLLABORATION TOOLS

Most basic forms of PSS technologies include multi-channel communicators to instantly connect with anyone to ask questions or help. Real-time collaboration technologies allow individuals and teams to work together seamlessly in real time, regardless of their physical location. Some technologies can be project-driven, team-driven, or function-driven. In the end, the goal of any implementation is to enable real-time work with each other, start conversations, and keep it going.

Most collaboration tools have inbuilt communicators. For instance, Slack and Microsoft Teams enable real-time text communication, allowing teams to stay connected and collaborate more efficiently. Collaboration tools include desktop-sharing features to enable remote teams to view and control each other's screens, facilitating remote troubleshooting and training.

Modern platforms allow businesses to build messaging, voice, and video into their apps using APIs. For instance, Twilio[22], a cloud communication platform, offers a range of channels, including SMS, voice, video, chat, and WhatsApp. CRM systems like HubSpot[23] and Salesforce[24] not only include a range of tools for sales, marketing, and customer service but also support multi-channel communication tools, including email marketing, SMS, live chat, and social media management. Slack[25] is another messaging platform designed for team communication through various channels, including direct messaging, group messaging, and channels.

---

[22] https://www.twilio.com/
[23] https://www.hubspot.com/
[24] https://www.salesforce.com/
[25] https://slack.com/

CH 8 - ON-DEMAND PERFORMANCE SUPPORT SYSTEMS

Platforms like Zoom, Skype, and Google Meet enable remote teams to have real-time face-to-face meetings, reducing travel costs and improving communication. On top of that, most collaborators support features similar to Microsoft Whiteboard or Zoom Whiteboard to enable teams to collaborate on visual projects in real time, allowing for remote brainstorming and ideation. The collaborations are enhanced with cloud-based document editing and sharing tools like Google Drive, Dropbox Paper, and Microsoft SharePoint, allowing teams to collaborate on documents in real time.

Other enterprise systems like Microsoft Teams, Zoom, WhatsApp Business, and Facebook support powerful communicators, including messaging, video calls, voice calls, and file sharing. Overall, real-time collaboration technologies have become essential tools for modern workplaces, especially those with distributed or remote teams. These technologies help improve efficiency, productivity, and team collaboration by enabling seamless communication and collaboration.

2. DECISION-SUPPORT AND EXPERT SYSTEMS

Decision-support systems are software or expert systems to support executives, leaders, and managers in making quick and accurate decisions based on data or qualitative inferences.

These systems range from dashboard-based analytics to data visualization tools to AI-driven data insights.

Here are some leading examples:

IBM Watson Analytics[26]: It is a cloud-based data analysis and visualization platform which is used to help executives make quicker and

---

[26] https://www.ibm.com/cloud/watson-studio

more effective decisions based on several parameters. Such a system can help organizations identify patterns and insights in their data. It can be used to help employees make better decisions by providing them with real-time insights and predictions based on the data they are working with.

TIBCO Spotfire[27]: It is a business intelligence and analytics software that can help organizations make better decisions by providing them with real-time data visualizations and insights. It can be used to analyze data from multiple sources, including spreadsheets, databases, and cloud-based applications, and can help employees identify patterns and trends in their data.

Microsoft Power BI[28]: It is a business analytics service that provides interactive visualizations and business intelligence capabilities with an interface simple enough for end users to create their own reports and dashboards. Power BI is cloud-based and can be used to analyze data from a wide range of sources, including Excel spreadsheets, on-premises and cloud-based data sources, and other cloud-based applications.

SAP Lumira[29]: It is a data visualization and analysis tool that can help organizations make better decisions by providing them real-time insights and predictions based on the data they are working with. It can be used to analyze data from multiple sources, including spreadsheets, databases, and cloud-based applications, and can help employees identify patterns and trends in data.

QlikView[30]: QlikView is a business intelligence and data visualization tool that can help organizations make better decisions by providing them with real-time insights and predictions based on their data. It can be used to analyze data from multiple sources, including spreadsheets,

---

[27] https://www.tibco.com/products/tibco-spotfire
[28] https://powerbi.microsoft.com/en-us/
[29] https://www.sap.com/products/technology-platform/lumira.html
[30] https://www.qlik.com/us/

CH 8 - ON-DEMAND PERFORMANCE SUPPORT SYSTEMS

databases, and cloud-based applications, and can help employees identify patterns and trends in their data.

Decision-support software can be an incredibly powerful tool for enhancing employee performance. By providing employees with real-time data insights and predictions, they can make informed decisions that can help them achieve their goals and improve their overall performance.

3. ADVANCED AI-BASED SEARCH ENGINES AND ASSISTANTS

AI-based search engines allow your employees to quickly and precisely find what they need depending upon the context of the case or problem, or customer issues. These search engines now allow you to precisely and rapidly find what you want, whether it is documentation, specification, product details, how-to video, or anything from corporate repositories.

There are several excellent examples of AI-based search engines available today. They are becoming increasingly popular due to their ability to provide personalized and relevant search results. Some are simply powerful search engineers. Others are context-based chatbots that can help your employees get precise answers to business information.

Here are some of the most notable ones:

ChatGPT[31]*:* An AI chatbot from OpenAI, this revolutionary tool can answer a wide range of questions and provide information on various topics. Lately, it has been integrated into Microsoft's Bing search engine to provide personalized search results, suggestions, and visual search

---

[31] https://chat.openai.com/

features. As an e-learning strategist, you can draw upon its power by connecting API to your organization's knowledge repository and teaching AI about your know-how.

IBM Watson AI assistant[32]: It is a natural language chatbot that can help your employees to deliver exceptional customer experiences that are faster and more accurate. This chatbot understands your customers' queries in context so your employees can deliver fast, consistent, and accurate solutions when and where your customers need them.

Hundreds of new AI chatbots and search engineers are evolving daily. Tall claims, as well as some compelling results, are being demonstrated by the players. For instance, NeevaAI is a subscription-based search engine that uses AI to provide relevant and personalized search results. YouChat is an AI-powered chatbot integrated into the You.com search engine. Like NeevaAI, it provides summarized paragraphs and cited sources for search results. Algolia AI uses AI to understand user intent and deliver personalized search experiences.

Remember that these search engines' power is leveraged when integrated into your organization's technological infrastructure over documentation repositories, knowledge bases, video libraries, and other intellectual properties that need to be processed to draw quick insights.

Also, check out Chapter 11 for a detailed section on AI-based e-learning developments.

4. AR AND VR-BASED GADGETS

In the previous section, I explained the application of AR and VR gadgets as learning technologies. However, the application of AR and VR is far

---

[32] https://www.ibm.com/products/watson-assistant

more impactful as performance support technology. These are setting standards for rethinking learning, social, and performance technologies.

The underlying philosophy of AR/VR technology is simple. If you get precise, contextual instructions on what to do at a given point, it shortens the time to training and allows you to be productive independently faster. Using an augmented headset, an employee can access instructions, videos, or other help while working on a task with his hands. They don't have to look for manuals or papers. It does not restrict the vision; it superimposes work instructions onto employees' normal vision while keeping hands free for doing complex tasks.

AR headsets can support tons of different media to make work highly successful, like even pointing out errors to the employees in real time. Those instructions are JIT during the workflow. It has seen much success in shortening TTP in complex tasks like building products or repairing equipment.

Here are some great examples of AR-based PSSs:

Employee onboarding: Companies can use AR technology to create interactive department signs that guide new employees to learn more about the office and the people who work there.

Industrial uses: AR smart glasses can be used in manufacturing, warehousing, and field service environments to provide workers with real-time information and support while they perform their tasks.

Technical support: AR can be used as a performance support tool during the workflow to do a task. For example, in complex field services domains like the repair of machines, maintenance, troubleshooting, equipment, and power stations, AR/VR hand-free headsets are changing the way we bring field service engineers up to speed. It can provide technicians with step-by-step instructions on repairing a machine or troubleshooting an issue. The headsets allow them to step-by-step instructors and resources to solve a problem. With such technologies, you can pretty much put field service staff into the field with minimal training and let the rest happen onsite.

Customer service: Companies like CSS Corp offer AR solutions that can transform customer experience and cut operating costs by providing intelligent visual support.

Smart Glasses

A simpler version is augmented smart glasses in which the screen is made available in the headset as a teaching aid. For instance, RealWear[33] and Google SmartGlasses (now stopped) offer displays on the glasses whereby employees can play step-by-step instructions or videos on these augmented screens while learning to do the task with their hands.

AR Headsets

AR technology overlays digital information onto the real world via an augmented or heads-up display, enhancing the user's experience. AR can be used for gaming, education, and marketing. Among the latest technologies, Microsoft HoloLens[34] and Oculus Quest[35] have an augmented screen in front of eyes on which employees can run immersive models, videos, instructions, procedures, or other learning material while doing a task with their hands. For example, repairing a machine needs both hands. Many of you have experienced or seen it in some videos. They can control with voice commands or gestures and learn a step and perform that step or check back instructions to do it again.

---

[33] https://www.realwear.com/field-services/
[34] https://www.microsoft.com/en-us/hololens/hardware
[35] https://www.meta.com/quest/products/quest-2/

CH 8 - ON-DEMAND PERFORMANCE SUPPORT SYSTEMS

AR Handheld Devices and Apps

Handheld AR is using handheld devices such as smartphones or tablets on which AR apps are installed to access and apply AR. These are easy to use and cheap. An example of a smartphone-based app is ScopeAR[36] which runs an AR model to repair and maintain the equipment with the help of remote experts. Another example is Medical Realities[37] App which uses AR and VR for medical training using gamified learning. Trainees can view medical procedures and lessons, full medical procedure simulations, instructions, and videos using Oculus and other VR devices. It is used in hospitals and medical colleges for assessment and delivery of training in medical courses.

VR Gadgets

The next extension is VR which puts you close to the real world. A fully digital environment that surrounds the user and makes them feel like they are in a real place. VR can be used for various purposes, such as gaming, education, and training.

Some tasks may not be practical or may be risky to do in the actual environment. For example, practicing putting out a fire, handling medical emergencies, or even combat situations in war. Those can be effectively taught using VR.

Some other examples are where a more immersive experience is needed. For instance, Mondly VR[38], a language learning platform, enables students to have real conversations with real people in virtual reality, enhancing their language skills and making learning more engaging and effective.

---

[36] https://www.scopear.com/
[37] https://www.medicalrealities.com/technology
[38] https://www.mondly.com/vr

VR can break the boundaries of experiences. For instance, Nearpod VR[39] offers virtual field trips to places that are otherwise inaccessible or harmful, such as ancient Egypt or the bottom of the ocean. This technology appeals to visual learners and provides engaging, real-life experiences.

The above examples demonstrate the vast potential of AR and VR technologies in enhancing and speeding up the learning experience. In the long run, it is seen that several corporations are able to shorten TTP when they use AR and VR as part of their training delivery.

5. KNOWLEDGE MANAGEMENT SYSTEMS AND DOCUMENTATION REPOSITORIES

Knowledge capture and management are other kinds of systems that are widely used as e-learning resources. Document management tools help organizations improve efficiency and productivity by making access and sharing of information easier. If strategically deployed, knowledge management systems could either augment or completely replace the training interventions. For instance, it can be your document repository. When field staff can access that knowledge precisely at the point of need, it significantly impacts how fast they can come up to speed. Some service operations have decision-support software on the field staff's tablets or smartphones that guides them through the customer cases.

Arnold & Collier (2013) demonstrated that an e-learning system, designed using knowledge management around an expert system and case-based e-learning, accelerated the expertise of new financial analysts, providing highly complex decision-making to business corporations without actually requiring any training.

---

[39] https://nearpod.com/nearpod-vr

CH 8 - ON-DEMAND PERFORMANCE SUPPORT SYSTEMS

The knowledge management systems become a robust online learning platform by integrating the learning material (such as scenario-based questions) into the business procedures. Additionally, if integrated with an LMS, you can track employee progress through the procedure-based exercises they must complete to achieve and prove competence. Such a technology strategy provides a comprehensive map of organizational learning and competence.

6. ON-DEMAND AND JUST-IN-TIME LEARNING

Taking informational content and making it available to employees as self-guided online searchable content can ensure just-in-time access. Such just-in-time knowledge access at the point of need makes a huge difference in learning what you need, when you need it, and as much as you need. It saves a lot of time.

It is suggested to take the content out from instructor-led sessions and make it accessible through electronics PSS as self-paced learning activities to prepare the learners. By doing so, employees can access the resources at their own pace rather than at the instructor's pace, significantly reducing the time from the proficiency cycle. This makes good use of the learner's time while waiting for the instructor-led session and allows the formal training intervention to focus more on critical and complex hands-on skills.

An attempt to remove unnecessary informational content from the training modules can lead to a shorter training time.

There is a trend to use EPSSs to provide individualized online access instead of the information content-heavy training upfront. Learners can use or access content based on the need of the task at hand rather than learning it beforehand. By using PSS to deliver informational content, the formal training intervention can focus more on critical human skills required for proficiency. One reason PSS could accelerate proficiency is its ability to reinforce learning and knowledge at specified intervals.

The new LMS systems are becoming powerful now with the unmatchable capability to provide on-demand informational content, procedures, documents, videos, and web-based training at the time of need. Component Content Management systems (CCMS) now integrate content and training into one platform, making on-demand learning much more efficient. Mobile-enabled CCMS and content delivery systems have broken the boundaries of jobs and can provide on-demand learning on-the-go or directly at the job.

Mobile Learning

Mobile learning technologies offer a range of options to speed up learning, from gamification and microlearning apps to VR and personalized learning paths. Employing a combination of these technologies can help learners engage with and retain information more effectively.

However, remember that mobile learning must be integrated into on-demand, just-in-time PSS to make a dent in learning speed. Such PSS deliver learning as short modules or microlearning chunks over a period of time.

Mobile apps accessible on users' smartphones provide a convenient and accessible way to learn on-the-go. These can offer a range of content, including videos and interactive videos, to enhance learning outcomes. Microlearning apps like Your Primer offer short courses in various disciplines. These apps allow learners to learn on-the-go and in short bursts, increasing retention and application of knowledge.

Quizzes and Simulations

Mobile learning also includes quizzes and simulations to encourage continuous practice and hone previously learned skills. These mobile learning examples can include a range of formats, including multiple-choice, true or false, and drag-and-drop, among others.

7. CONTEXTUAL ON-SCREEN HELP

A large financial service call center in the US used to provide 11 weeks of ILT to its agents. They found that agents would take an additional three months to become fully proficient. Then they implemented a technology that identified where an employee was on the screen or step and then provided contextual help to employees, like what to check and what questions to ask from the customer. The software provided decision-making, like how and when to escalate the call to others. By providing the basic orientation to the software and remaining moved as PSS on their screen, the company was able to reduce TTP by almost 70%. The software basically eliminated the training completely for the most part.

Such software appears directly within the application interface to help users complete their tasks or overcome issues they may encounter. They also provide users with real-time support while using the app. Here are some great examples of on-screen contextual help software:

KnowledgeOwl[40]*:* KnowledgeOwl's contextual help solution is designed to appear within the application interface when users need it the most. This solution is meant to reduce the need for users to consult manuals or support documents when they encounter an issue while using an application.

ScreenSteps[41]*:* The ScreenSteps context-sensitive help browser extension is a tool that puts training and reference documents directly in the web application where employees need them. With this tool, users

---

[40] https://www.knowledgeowl.com/features/
[41] https://www.screensteps.com/

no longer have to search endless tabs or documents to find the necessary information.

Userlane[42]*:* Userlane is software that allows companies to measure how employees use applications, identify areas for improvement and create on-screen interactive guides and tours for software users. This solution aims to enable users to immediately use any software without needing instructions or training.

Microsoft Power Automate[43]*:* Microsoft Power Automate provides in-product contextual help that displays content relevant to the currently selected action, trigger, or connector. When users display the in-product help, they can select any link from the list of help topics, and the corresponding documentation will open.

OnScreen[44]*:* OnScreen Professional Services is software that digitizes existing documentation and converts content into in-app walkthroughs. This solution is designed to help users onboard and refresh their knowledge with the needed context provided by world-class trainers.

These are just a few examples of on-screen contextual help software that can help users navigate software applications more quickly and efficiently. Keep in mind that such applications, though they improve efficiency, their end goal should remain as shortening TTP.

---

[42] https://www.userlane.com/platform/context-sensitive-help/
[43] https://powerautomate.microsoft.com/en-us/
[44] https://onscreen.us/onscreen-for-web-apps/

8. REMOTE ASSISTS AND EXPERT FEEDBACK

Remote Assistance Technologies

Some of the latest technologies allow employees to seek remote assistance from experts in real time when stuck at work. For instance, plant and equipment repair technicians use AR headsets with inbuilt capabilities to remotely pull relevant experts into the scene when needed. The experts on the other side of the globe can see what these technicians see in real-time. There are real-time conversations, discussions, and collaborative troubleshooting. Research tells us that with such instant feedback, JIT coaching hugely accelerates TTP.

Also such technologies also allow for building a network of coaches from different corners with different sets of expertise. Research shows that having multiple coaches with diverse experience if we tap it correctly, could help employees master new behaviors quickly.

The advantage is that you don't have to wait for an employee to be 100% ready during a training event on everything before you can use them to support field issues. These augmented expert systems and remote assist technologies provide performance support when they really need it.

Expert Directories or Expert locators

An internal expert directory is a tool used by organizations to identify and leverage the expertise of their employees. Behind those technologies are the well-managed, cloud-based database of experts and employees in terms of who has done what, who has worked with a specific large customer, and who has won large deals. Imagine how powerful is that kind of know-how. Your employees can go to that person immediately to seek tips to shorten their journeys. Otherwise, they would have to start from scratch.

More detail on this emerging trend is explained in Chapter 11. For now, expert directories allow project teams, work groups, departments, communities, and employees across the enterprise to find the expertise resident in their organizations. Often, they include experts from external sources. Organizations use such internal expert directories to leverage the knowledge and skills of their employees. Companies deploying such tools include IBM, Deloitte, Cisco, Microsoft, and Siemens.

Nano-coaching and Nano-mentoring

Nano-coaching and nano-mentoring are emerging trends in the coaching and mentoring space where individuals are provided with bite-sized, quick, and personalized guidance to enhance their skills and improve their performance. Nano-coaching happens when technologies such as mobile enable experts or managers to provide short, targeted, asynchronous coaching or timely feedback to enhance employee performance.

Continuous mentoring and coaching are warranted during any problem-solving process to help learners cross the hurdle with proper guidance. Nano-coaching can happen in a matter of minutes. These are usually quick, short, and targeted. For instance, a manager coaches a new customer service representative via a chat messenger to create a process for resolving and escalating customer issues rather than simply telling them to 'get through the backlog.'

Timely nano-coaching has the potential to accelerate skill acquisition by providing learners with coaching in a timely fashion from a 'network of coaches' at the 'moment of need' without having to browse through the piles of information. This allows the learner to reach out to experts or peers in no time. Further, It can leverage social interactivity strategies that prompt learning by doing and interacting with others. Nano-coaching opens up an additional channel for meaningful and purposeful interconnectivity.

The key to nano-coaching success is how apps and platforms allow reaching out to experts and quickly seeking help. Instant messengers, expert networks, and coaching forums are some of the mechanisms for making it possible. Some research has shown the good potential of mobile devices in providing just-in-time learning and nano-coaching (Bolton 1999, Quinn 2011).

When employees get timely and quick resolutions to overcome their hurdles, they typically gain mastery faster.

LEVERAGING PSS FOR ACCELERATION

Now, organizational learning has moved from a training event to something that happens as employees seek assistance on-the-job from electronics PSS. With the availability of new technologies, the shape and extent of PSSs are also changing beyond their original role of just-in-time resources for training, support, or information. More and more PSSs are being integrated into the workflow. There is vast evidence that PSSs can significantly impact shortening TTP when you can replace formal training with PSSs.

However, e-learning designers continue to believe that their job is to teach their learners 'how to operate' a given PSS. Thus, several designers build massive, multi-day training programs for every use case or step involved in operating any new PSS technology they implement.

However, they need to understand that learning to use a PSS vs. using the PSS to learn are two different philosophies. But most e-learning strategists do not get it right.

Thus, the focus needs to be shifted to teaching employees how to obtain the desired results for their role using PSSs in the context of their job or workflow instead of learning to use some sample examples.

That means two things: first, how to learn and master PSSs just-in-time during the workflow, and second, how to seek just-in-time support from PSSs just enough in the moment of need to accomplish the goal at hand.

As a Chief E-learning Officer, you must be clear that PSSs are not some optional sideline resources. Instead, these are now mainstream resources that can eliminate the need for training if used strategically. Unless you enable your employees to use PSSs during their scenario-solving, the need for in-context PSS will not arise. Unless PSSs are used as an avenue to accomplish some tasks on the e-learning path, it will not lead to any impact on shortening TTP.

In the following sections, I provide some best practices for various phases of the proficiency journey. Remember that PSS is the only strategy with consistently the same guidance across all phases. Thus, the guideline presented is applicable across various phases, even though its relevance is under the phase where it is described.

PSS FOR SELF-GUIDED E-LEARNING TOOLS (PRE-ILT PHASE)

Here are some best practices for leveraging PSSs as e-learning avenues during the pre-ILT phase for accelerated employee development.

CH 8 - ON-DEMAND PERFORMANCE SUPPORT SYSTEMS

☞ Replace or slim down the training curriculum with just-in-time, on-demand PSSs, which one can access at the point of need during the workflow.

☞ Remove unnecessary informational content from self-guided training modules and disposition them to a searchable PSS or searchable repository instead.

☞ Use LMSs that enable on-demand self-guided informational content, procedures, documents, videos, and web-based training at the time of need.

☞ Integrate PSSs with mobile learning to deliver learning material as short modules or microlearning chunks over a period of time.

☞ Make advanced AI-based search engines available to your employees to precisely and rapidly find what they need when they need it, including documentation, specification, product details, how-to video, or anything from corporate repositories.

☞ Use decision-support software or systems to provide real-time data insights and predictions to make informed decisions.

☞ Use the latest technologies like AR/VR headsets to enable employees to access precise, contextual instructions, documents, or videos on what to do at a given point while working on a task by hand.

☛ Integrate your knowledge management systems which allows searching for scenario-based learning material.

☛ Make mobile apps accessible on users' smartphones that could provide a convenient and accessible way to learn on-the-go. These can offer a range of content, including videos and interactive videos, to enhance learning outcomes.

Implement or leverage PSSs during the task workflow instead of sideline resources.

☛ Make an inventory or map of all the available PSSs before you begin designing training. Then suitably replace training sessions with PSSs.

☛ Instead of creating training to operate PSS with generic examples, teach employees how to obtain the desired results for their job role using PSSs in their job or workflow context.

☛ Deliver micro-lessons of self-guided material using PSSs which can push the lessons to learners, which is time-spaced and distributed over a fair amount of time.

PSS FOR VIRTUAL OR REMOTE E-LEARNING TOOLS (ILT PHASE)

Here are some best practices for leveraging PSSs as e-learning avenues for instructor-led remote or virtual sessions for accelerated employee development.

 Assess the best combination of multiple channels of technologies, modes, media, and formats to deliver experience-rich learning to master each identified skill.

 Leverage PSSs that allow moments of purpose-driven conversations, dialogues, and social connectivity via multiple channels and technologies as properly defined assignments or activities rather than leaving them to flow on their own.

 Use various channels, including PSSs, and facilitate virtually via video, text, and email, among other methods.

PSS FOR ON-THE-JOB E-LEARNING TOOLS (POST-ILT PHASE)

Here are some best practices for leveraging PSSs as e-learning avenues for on-the-job training for accelerated employee development.

👉 Make PSSs accessible to learners and coaches to allow short, targeted, asynchronous coaching or timely feedback to enhance employee performance.

👉 Enable PSSs, which allow accessing expert directories and build a network of coaches with diverse experiences. Provide coaching in a timely fashion from a 'network of coaches' at the 'moment of need,' eliminating the need for learners to browse through the piles of information.

👉 Allows learners to connect and interact with anyone and everyone instantly at the 'moment of need.' Implement multi-channel collaborators for meaningful social interactivity and purposeful interconnectivity.

👉 Deliver PSS-enabled micro-lessons during the post-ILT phase designed around well-scoped case scenarios. The focus should be on unpredictable, non-routine events instead of routine, known ones.

👉 Encourage using PSSs and searchable repositories for performance improvement on known/routine tasks.

👉 Use adaptive LMSs to change and optimize the e-learning path for each employee based on their performance, learning speed, accomplishments, and results.

CH 8 - ON-DEMAND PERFORMANCE SUPPORT SYSTEMS

 Integrate online learning sources, documentation, PSSs, and on-the-job activities properly sequenced on the on-the-job e-learning path.

 Implement a range of PSSs and technologies that makes post-ILT learning boundaryless rather than forcing learners to choose a specific media to maintain proficiency.

PSS TO MAINTAIN PROFICIENCY (SUSTENANCE PHASE)

Here are some best for leveraging PSSs as e-learning avenues to maintain proficiency and accelerate employee development.

 Deliver refresher and reinforcement learning on an ongoing basis via PSS rather than LMSs.

 Embed this learning into the workflow employees use to perform their job, like AR/VR gadgets and work-related mobile apps.

 Use analytics to analyze the field events to identify PSSs, repeatable algorithms, rule-based automation, and AI-based workflow that can support employee proficiency.

👉 Implement a range of PSSs and technologies that makes learning boundaryless during the post-ILT and sustenance phase by leveraging multiple channels, modes, and formats.

👉 Design proficiency-testing scenarios and deeply problem-solving-oriented assessments of learners, but program them to conduct as shorter on-the-go assessments, not taking more than a few minutes at a time.

👉 Make learners submit clear job-related deliverables or artifacts via PSSs or LMSs, instead of emails against the assignments or assessments as evidence of their proficiency development.

👉 Design proficiency-testing scenarios and deeply problem-solving-oriented assessments of learners, but program them to conduct as shorter on-the-go assessments, not taking more than a few minutes at a time.

REFLECTION TIME

When proficiency goals are viewed holistically, several non-training resources, such as PSS, can be used in conjunction with training-focused events. You are not pushing or forcing employees to learn. Instead, you are looking for what is available to employees when they are doing a job or what new tools can be made available that either reduce or eliminate the training requirement. The result could be highly targeted and much shorter training while relying heavily on PSSs as the first line of defense. Such complementation allows a learner to attain proficiency in several complex skills within a shorter time. As an e-learning strategist, keep in mind that the real impact of PSSs is seen when integrated into the workflow.

Use the space below to reflect upon and note down your major takeaways to this point. *Are you leveraging PSS as the core of your e-learning strategy? If not, then you need to flip your e-learning philosophy upside down.*

> **Question to think ahead!**
>
> Which skills can be addressed or taught more effectively using organizational systems, resources, and PSS as just-in-time learning or support instead of relying on training events?

Reflections

YOUR LEARNING JOURNEY

In this chapter, you learned the fourth strategy to leverage the power of performance support systems. You learned how you could replace irrelevant or unproductive training with suitable just-in-time performance support systems to allow learners to attain proficiency in achieving desired outcomes during the workflow of the task.

In the following chapter, you will learn the last strategy to enrich learners' experience via a mix of multiple technologies to support multiple channels of learning. You will learn how you can multiply the speed of skill acquisition by employing experience-rich channels.

Chapter 1
E-LEARNING AND DIGITAL REVOLUTION

Chapter 2
A ROLE OF CHIEF E-LEARNING OFFICER

Chapter 3
SPEED OF EMPLOYEE DEVELOPMENT AS E-LEARNING KPIs

Chapter 4
STRATEGIC E-LEARNING FOR SPEED

Chapter 5
SCENARIO-BASED E-LEARNING

Chapter 6
TIME-SPACED MICROLEARNING CONTENT

Chapter 7
OPTIMALLY SEQUENCED E-LEARNING PATH

Chapter 8
ON-DEMAND PERFORMANCE SUPPORT SYSTEMS

Chapter 9
EXPERIENCE-RICH MULTI-TECHNOLOGY MIX

Chapter 10
SPEED-ENABLING E-LEARNING SYSTEMS APPRAOCH

Chapter 11
SUMMARY OF E-LEARNING DESIGN GUIDELINES FOR SPEED

Chapter 12
EMERGING E-LEARNING REVOLUTIONS

9
EXPERIENCE-RICH MULTI-TECHNOLOGY MIX

In the year 2015, Bower et al. (2015, p. 15) predicted: "Ideally in the years to come, rich-media collaborative technologies will become so invisible that students and teachers interacting from different locations will feel as though they are in the same room." We have witnessed that happening in the last decade, particularly during the COVID-19 pandemic. The question remains, does traditional blended learning, the way we know it, accelerate TTP? If not, then what do we need to do about it?

RISE OF BLENDED LEARNING

In an earlier study, Sims et al. (2008, p. 26) suggested that such a 'blended' learning approach may be more effective than a training session that relies completely on one mode or strategy.

With recent tremendous technological advances in smart and mobile technologies, traditional in-person training has been enriched with several new channels supported by technologies.

As we see today, blended learning combines the power of online learning, e-learning, and instructor-driven training (in-person or virtual). For instance, you may use a live Zoom session and then post a video on a platform to view later. In other cases, it could be all online recorded videos before attending an ILT. Such combinations, as a blanket term, are called blended learning.

This is further enhanced with self-paced learning.

In blended learning, the instructor-led portion can be in-person, or it can be virtual. Virtual and remote classrooms are now the standard norm for large-scale learning. For virtual mode, it is supported by conference technologies (like Zoom, telepresence, and streaming) which offer powerful virtual interactions, rich experience, and multiple learning channels. Bower et al. (2015) demonstrated that various technologies like web conferencing, video conferencing, and the virtual world make learning highly active with positive student feedback. Similarly, Yilmaz (2015) showed that students who attended live virtual lectures achieved significantly higher scores than those who only watched recorded sessions.

During the pandemic, the blended learning concept has expanded far beyond its original definition. Now, most e-learning designers use multiple delivery channels blended together. For instance, learners may be required to attend a virtual lecture for a certain part. Some segments require them to use social media. Others may require peer-to-peer coaching, discussion forums, project work, fieldwork, etc. There are unlimited variations of how one can design an e-learning journey by blending these in-person, remote, virtual, self-learning, and field learning modes best suit the job at hand.

Multiple enriched channels extend interactions beyond the instructor to peers and others. Some even have argued that virtual classrooms are more effective than traditional classrooms because they allow good face time and extended interactions beyond instructor to peers and others across geographies. Lending newer e-learning technologies can enhance virtual training sessions that allow multi-sensory interaction with the content and caters to the different preferences and requirements of the learners.

Now technologies exist for managing each blended channel seamlessly. Most modern LMSs and several dedicated learning platforms now support the blended curriculum by default. Such systems allow scheduling, assessment, and tracking across all elements of a blended learning journey. Universities and corporate learning have long moved to such enriched blended learning programs.

The blended technology is highly efficient and scalable, where hundreds of learners can be reached in a shorter time, allowing breaking the capacity barriers. This key advantage certainly allows you to train many people in a shorter time. Another advantage is the availability of multiple assets, learning materials, collaterals, and resources you can give to your employees in any order, thus shortening their wait time and also shortening training duration.

But does it help you shorten TTP? Not truly. A reduction in training length does not mean a reduction in TTP. A reduction in training rather elongates the TTP. If your goal is to shorten TTP, you need to rethink blended learning.

PRINCIPLES OF MULTI-CHANNEL LEARNING

Blended learning can be made more effective by using an e-learning path to put all the available modules in the right sequence. Well-designed blended learning modules, set up as pre-work in the pre-training phase, are instrumental in raising the entry-level proficiency of learners as they enter the formal ILT sessions. One of the approaches can be to design low-complexity skills, including informational content, as a pre-training course to provide a headstart to learners.

Highly complex skills are covered during ILT sessions which are spread over time. Self-guided homework assignments are designed to cover highly complex skills which require deeper thinking and reflection. Such reflective practices are considered to accelerate skill transfer. Then multiple e-learning modules are designed to cover medium complexity skills as a bridge between consecutive ILT sessions. Leveraging blended e-learning-based pre-work and homework strategically to supplement ILT sessions during pre-training and the ILT phase can make blended learning more effective.

While blended learning is a great approach, its flaws do not let learners learn at a faster rate. If a job requires complex thinking skills, social skills, and hands-on technical skills, a blended approach does not always lead to acceleration. Over-reliance on self-learning and virtual learning actually leads to reduced social interactions. The lack of in-person dynamics makes blended learning ineffective. Ultimately, it shows up as the slow speed of learners' skill acquisition.

Blended learning has one key issue; one kind of content is available in one specific format and is offered only through one specific channel. For instance, if the content is provided as a video, that's your best choice as a learner. You will be offered this content either as packaged web-based training (WBT) via an LMS or pushed to your devices. However, that content is not offered in any other format or media.

As a learner, when you attend a live virtual session, the content you are exposed to is limited to slides or other collateral used to orchestrate the live virtual session.

One of the key findings in research is that you need to engage all the senses in a body to encode the information, knowledge, and skills in the brain to learn faster. In today's complex jobs, your mind, body, feelings, emotions, and thinking are triggered at the same time. A video can evoke certain thoughts, but in the absence of social pressure, it may not drive the required emotional loading. That's the foundational reason why most e-learning programs do not 'stick' long enough.

How can you ensure the multi-sensory involvement of learners in the learning process?

You need a big-picture strategy. You need to be clear about the nature of the skills you teach and what media, mode, or channel can deepen that learning.

There are three pieces to such a strategy, as shown in Figure 9.1:

1. **Segmentation:** Analyze the skills involved in doing a job and segment the skills based on their nature (knowledge-based, hands-on-based, thinking-based, behavior-based, problem-solving based, etc.).
2. **Learner-content interactions:** Establish the nature of learner-content interactions required to master each identified skill
3. **Experience-rich multiple channel access:** Assess the best combination of multiple channels of technologies, multiple modes of learning, and multiple media to deliver experience-rich learning to master each identified skill

Figure 9.1: Principles of experience-rich multi-channel learning

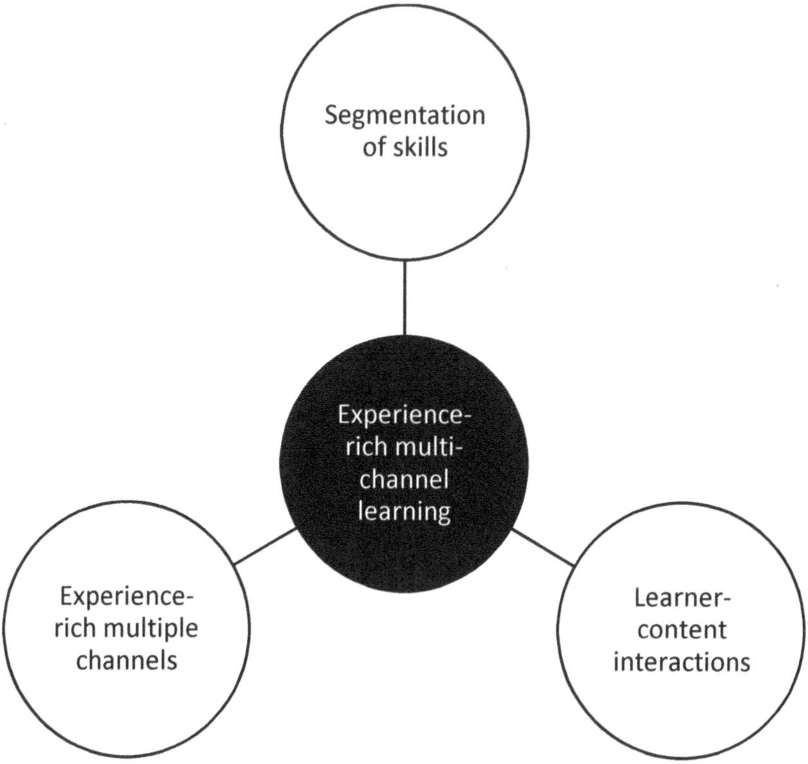

1. SEGMENTATION OF SKILLS

Before any design is put in place, it is necessary to understand the nature of tasks/skills involved in a given job. Segmentation is to classify the nature of learning outcomes. Not all tasks in a given job require information mastery. Some need knowledge mastery. Some need hands-on mastery. Some need thinking mastery, while other needs changes in behaviors. Different tasks require a different mix of skills. Thus, it is absolutely a must to have such segmentation by category.

The usual approach is to build a matrix of skills and use a taxonomy to classify them. The most common taxonomy is Blooms' taxonomy of learning objectives. However, it has its own flaws as the nature of skills is no longer based on root elements like remembering, understanding, applying, evaluating, etc. Neither is the perceived hierarchy of skills applicable in today's world. If someone can access the information via a search engine, there is no point in remembering facts and figures.

A more accurate approach is to use extensive data analytics to identify underlying success behaviors with the outcomes to determine how successful employees have attained the results. For instance, in one petroleum refinery plant, they identified the star employees among their process control technicians who were more efficient and faster than others. Then they analyzed their on-the-job behaviors and found that the star players were actually controlling one specific valve upstream instead of the ones mentioned in the manuals. This skill to figure out upstream vs. downstream flow was highly analytical in nature, which was not a required skill from process technicians. Their job was to simply follow provided standard operating procedures without questioning. Once they identified it, they knew they had to build their e-learning programs to teach exactly that skill. This example illustrates that once you have segmented the results to the underlying success behaviors, you will be able to build an extensive matrix by the nature of skills.

CH 9 - EXPERIENCE-RICH MULTI-TECHNOLOGY MIX

Regardless of the nature of the job, this principle advocates using data to segment the nature of the tasks based on their characteristics.

2. LEARNER-CONTENT INTERACTIONS

The nature of skills then dictates the type of content most appropriate to master that skill. The nature of skills also dictates how learners should interact with the content to learn it faster. For instance, in the last example, they figured they needed thinking-oriented examples to develop computational and analytical thinking among technicians. They designed the learner-content interactions in two parts. First, they developed a scenario-based app that could run on technicians' cell phones. Every two hours, a short message popped up on their screen, presenting them with a scenario in which they were to choose the correct valve for the adjustment. In others, they were to choose the correct amount of adjustment. This took less than 1-2 minutes of their time. Such 4-5 scenarios were presented to them daily over 30 days. Each submitted response received feedback with the correct options and reasoning. Now, all this is happening on the job using microlearning and time-spaced assessment. At the end of 30 days, they were called for the second phase, where they were to work with one assessor for 30 minutes (in-person or remotely) and physically adjust the valves based on the measurements shown on their dashboards. This is where they applied all that they learned during the last 30 days of microlearning.

While this example is simple, the point is to build a detailed matrix of content types for each identified skill and plan for how learners will interact with the content to master it. Often, one skill may need a range of varied content and a range of interactions.

The segmentation in the previous step also tells what can be learned in a self-paced mode, what can be learned on the job, what can be provided through PSSs, and what must require formal in-person or remote live training. In turn, segmentation also tells us what goes in at different phases like pre-ILT, ILT, and post-ILT phases.

3. EXPERIENCE-RICH MULTIPLE CHANNELS

During learning, you should be able to employ your ability to read, listen, watch, write, feel, and touch seamlessly in any situation. You should not be contained by the content design to use only one specific mode. When you expose learners to one specific channel of information, for instance, by watching videos and responding to questions, you are not engaging all senses. The experience is not rich enough to accelerate learning.

When all senses are involved in learning, skill acquisition is accelerated heavily. My research showed that organizations that did great in shortening TTP offered the same content through multiple formats (text, video, procedure, AR, audio, transcription, slides, animation, assessments), multiple modes (live in-person, self-paced, virtual, remote, peer coaching, managed mentoring, structured OJT, nano-coaching), and used multiple channels (AR/VR gadgets, Zoom, computers, web, mobiles, guided walkthroughs, animation, simulators, actual equipment, on-the-job). They specified the primary or recommended format, mode, and channel based on their segmentation of skills and learner-content interaction matrix. But they did not mandate one specific format, mode, or channel for a given skill. Rather, they provided a range of additional or secondary avenues. One thing they

Then "truly" blended multiple formats, multiple modes, and multiple channels seamlessly in such a way that they provide learners with a range of choices from primary channels as well as secondary channels to learn the same content or skill. Learners could choose anything they prefer and could switch to a different format, mode, or channel if one does not work for them for a given content or skill.

Such an approach truly blends the power of multiple technologies to create experience-rich learning. The level of experience learners draw from such an approach is unparalleled.

Catering to the Diverse Nature of Tasks

Different tasks may require different types of content. For instance, just plain informational content is good enough for some tasks. For more complex tasks, one may need enrichment via video or animation. For highly complex tasks, one may need information, video, animation content, and flowcharts to master the skill deeply. This is where the segmentation and learner-content interaction matrix come into the picture behind the scenes to orchestrate access for the learners.

Catering to Multiple Options or Modalities to Learn the Same Thing

The same employee may need various resources to learn one thing. Let's take another example. If your employee needs to master a skill to repair a machine, they may be comfortable with the procedures themselves in native form. If the native procedure is hard to understand, they could use AI to summarize and use it. They could take it to the next level and run an animation of the procedure. If the task has workflow-based automation tools, they may ask for access to a PSS that can give them step-by-step instructions during the workflow. If that is still not enriched enough, they could access the video of the same. They may even watch previously recorded lessons on the same. Assuming they still need to understand a few additional things on the same task, they could even access instructor-led remote sessions from the ongoing offerings and join the same. If that's not enough to build confidence, they could access AR or VR models for the same procedure. They might request peer coaching if the task requires social interaction or feedback. If they still don't grasp well, they could ask for an expert 1:1.

Catering to the Diversity of Learning Styles

A diverse global workforce comes from various parts of the world where they learn and get groomed with different learning styles, preferences, and work ethics. Among them, no two people learn things in the same way. Learning is a highly individualized phenomenon. You can't manage the process of learning. All you can manage is the ecosystem around learning. When the learning ecosystem you design or establish allows learners to pick and choose the most effective format, mode, and channel for their challenge, they learn much faster. But the point here is that 'effectiveness' is determined by them, not by you.

The point is that you don't give them a recipe for 'how they learn' but only specify 'what to learn.' And you make every single thing available in multiple formats, multiple modes, and multiple channels.

Now virtual, hybrid, blended, and then VR modes give you many options to develop multiple routes for learning. You can mix several learning modalities into an overall program. Leverage and mix these all. Don't stick to one specific way of designing and delivering online learning. By providing multiple experience-rich channels of information and content delivery to match the learning styles of the diverse workforce, organizations can cut the time to readiness. Collectively, multiple channels provide several learning routes to employees, cutting overall TTP significantly.

MIXING CHANNELS FOR ACCELERATION

The value of multi-format, multi-mode, and multi-channel is clear. However, most e-learning strategists are pressed hard on timelines and don't invest in more than one type of content for a given challenge. Saving resources, investment, and time does not have great ROI because this does not shorten TTP. While mixing multiple channels, modes, and formats sounds expensive, ROI from a shorter TTP is enormous in the long run.

SELF-GUIDED E-LEARNING WITH MULTI-CHANNEL TECHNOLOGIES (PRE-ILT PHASE)

Here are some best practices for implementing multiple channels of learning and support during the pre-ILT phase for accelerated employee development.

 Focus on managing the ecosystem around learning, not the process of learning. Design a learning ecosystem that allows learners to pick and choose the most effective format, mode, and channel for their challenge.

 Use multiple formats, modes, and channels to deliver the same information for learners to learn anything using any modality suitable to their learning

style. Effectiveness is determined by learners, not you, regarding what works best for them.

☞ Don't give learners a recipe for 'how they learn' but only specify 'what to learn.' Allow learners to choose anything they prefer and switch to a different format, mode, or channel if one doesn't work for them for a given content or skill.

☞ Don't offer standard fixed content, fixed length learning paths using a preset media, channel, or format. Blend multiple formats, modes, and channels seamlessly so that they provide learners with a range of choices from primary and secondary channels to learn the same content or skill.

☞ Design a learning path that allows not only different 'adaptive' entry and exit points based on the learner's progress but also adaptive across, letting learners choose any available channels, media, and formats to learn the same skill.

☞ Map the learning activities vs. all feasible channels, modes, and formats. Focus on sequencing the learning outcomes on the e-learning path, not the learning modes.

☞ Keep the standards of assessments consistent regardless of the mix of channels, modes, and formats. You don't have to create assessments only in the form of quizzes tied to one specific learning mode. Focus on evaluation or completion of assigned learning content in reference to the job outcomes and results, i.e., 'what an employee should be capable of doing' instead of 'how much or how well an employee learned a piece of content.'

 Design low-complexity skills, including informational content, as a pre-training course to provide a headstart to learners.

VIRTUAL OR REMOTE E-LEARNING WITH MULTI-CHANNEL TECHNOLOGIES (ILT PHASE)

Here are some best practices for implementing multiple channels of learning and support for accelerated employee development.

 Use extensive data analytics to identify underlying success behaviors and skills with the outcomes to determine how successful employees have attained the results.

 Analyze the skills involved in a job and segment them based on their nature (knowledge-based, hands-on-based, thinking-based, behavior-based, problem-solving based, etc.)

☞ One skill may need a range of varied content and interactions. Build a detailed matrix of content types for each identified skill and plan how learners will interact with the content to master it.

☞ Engage all the senses in a body and trigger maximum elements of learners' mind, body, feelings, emotions, and thinking at the same time. Use media-rich channels which allow hands-on experience and multi-sensory processing of information.

☞ Schedule ILT sessions over time through technology-enabled channels. An instructor-led session does not need to have an instructor available on the screen. It can be a combination of teaching, facilitation, and coaching through the intelligent use of multiple technologies.

☞ Assess the best combination of multiple channels of technologies, modes, media, and formats to deliver experience-rich learning to master each identified skill. Use various channels, including PSSs, and facilitate virtually via video, text, and email, among other methods.

☞ Leverage blended pre-work and homework strategically to supplement ILT sessions. Cover highly complex skills during ILT sessions. Embed self-guided homework and bridge assignments between consecutive ILT sessions requiring deeper thinking and reflection.

☞ Incorporate the latest technologies like mobile learning, VR, AR, video conference, remote sharing, and others, allowing more interactions.

☞ Insert student-generated deliverables as one of the assessment approaches. Do not stick to one specific assessment mode restricted by media. Provide freedom to learners to demonstrate capability in any qualified manner, like creating a report, giving presentations, verbal explanation, doing something with hands, producing a written essay, or other artifacts that convey mastery in the assignment. Restrict a specific type of assessment if warranted by the nature of skills or proficiency measures.

☞ Insert moments of purpose-driven conversations, dialogues, and social connectivity via multiple channels and technologies as properly defined assignments or activities rather than leaving them to flow on their own.

ON-THE-JOB E-LEARNING WITH MULTI-CHANNEL TECHNOLOGIES (POST-ILT PHASE)

Here are some best practices for implementing multiple learning channels and support for accelerated employee development.

 Identify coaching or mentoring opportunities and use a range of channels and media to connect learners with the experts. Create flexibility of technology-driven connectivity for learners.

 Implement a range of PSSs listed in Chapter 8, including search engines, documentation repositories, AR/VR, on-demand self-guided material, decision-support systems, multi-channel communicators and collaborating platforms, on-screen help, and remote assistance, among other new-generation technologies.

MAINTAIN PROFICIENCY WITH MULTI-CHANNEL TECHNOLOGIES (SUSTENANCE PHASE)

Here are some best for implementing multiple channels of learning and support to maintain proficiency and accelerate employee development.

 Provide refresher and reinforcement training content in multi-channel, multi-mode, and multi-format well after attaining desired proficiency.

- Provide coaching in a timely fashion from a 'network of coaches' at the 'moment of need,' eliminating the need for learners to browse through the piles of information.

- Allow learners to connect and interact with anyone and everyone instantly (preferred) at the 'moment of need.'

- Implement a range of PSSs and technologies that makes post-ILT learning boundaryless rather than forcing learners to choose a specific media to maintain proficiency.

REFLECTION TIME

Several e-learning strategists and CLOs boast of providing a multi-channel learning experience to their learners. When people have to access ten different places to access various formats, modes, or channels, things go wrong. Thus, at the technology level, you must remove boundaries to access and create a one-entry portal for them to choose what works best based on their competence, comfort, and confidence. When you integrate multiple formats, modes, and channels, you can use e-learning platforms to access even the traditional resources which otherwise are not called e-learning (like peer coaching).

Use the space below to reflect upon and note down your major takeaways to this point. ***Are you integrating multiple formats, modes, and technologies for seamless, boundaryless, experience-rich learning of your employees? If not, then you need to think about being an organizational change-maker.***

> **Question to think ahead!**
>
> *Which e-learning format, channels, and technologies can deliver the intended skills to provide learners with an enriched experience and deeper learning?*

CH 10 – SPEED-ENABLING E-LEARNING SYSTEMS APPROACH

Reflections

YOUR LEARNING JOURNEY

In this chapter, you learned the fifth and the last strategy to use multiple channels, multiple formats, and mixing experience-rich technologies to ensure that learners acquire the skills in the fastest possible time. You learned how to enrich learners' experiences via a mix of multiple technologies and multiple channels of learning.

Until this point, you have learned five powerful e-learning design strategies geared toward speeding up employee development. However, one strategy all alone may not give you the desired speed. In the next chapter, you will learn how to implement these strategies holistically on a learner's journey. You will learn the core guiding forces to ensure that any implementation is driven toward deeper learning and accelerated TTP of employees.

Chapter 1
E-LEARNING AND DIGITAL REVOLUTION

Chapter 2
A ROLE OF CHIEF E-LEARNING OFFICER

Chapter 3
SPEED OF EMPLOYEE DEVELOPMENT AS E-LEARNING KPIs

Chapter 4
STRATEGIC E-LEARNING FOR SPEED

Chapter 5
SCENARIO-BASED E-LEARNING

Chapter 6
TIME-SPACED MICROLEARNING CONTENT

Chapter 7
OPTIMALLY SEQUENCED E-LEARNING PATH

Chapter 8
ON-DEMAND PERFORMANCE SUPPORT SYSTEMS

Chapter 9
EXPERIENCE-RICH MULTI-TECHNOLOGY MIX

**Chapter 10
SPEED-ENABLING E-LEARNING SYSTEMS APPRAOCH**

Chapter 11
SUMMARY OF E-LEARNING DESIGN GUIDELINES FOR SPEED

Chapter 12
EMERGING E-LEARNING REVOLUTIONS

10
SPEED-ENABLING E-LEARNING SYSTEMS APPROACH

THINKING E-LEARNING OUT-OF-THE-BOX

Sometimes, advantages or push for e-learning are more 'trend-driven' than 'need-driven.' Because your competitor is doing it, you might feel as if you are missing out or lagging behind. Designing e-learning to look cool would not bring accelerated proficiency to your learners. If effectiveness is your goal, your e-learning design will not bring your learners an accelerated pace of proficiency. If efficiency is your goal, your e-learning design will not bring faster speed to learning. Unless your goal is explicitly shortening TTP, your e-learning design will not cater to hasten employee development.

At this point, I also want to share two important premises.

E-learning Is Not Self-Guided Learning

A large portion of e-learning is misunderstood or deliberately designed as self-guided learning. The reasons are obvious: it frees up resources and can be scaled big time with a small investment.

However, what most designers and e-learning leaders miss out on is that learners may not be in the state of readiness to take their learning on a self-directed rocket. There is a foundational state of readiness, after which they can learn anything of their own.

In that regard, the mistake is building the foundation itself with e-learning. How many companies are out there that expose their new hires through e-learning-based orientation for hours and hours? In reality, instead of working, this approach would disengage them just at the door of entry. The problem with building foundations with self-directed e-learning is that the moment these learners go to new, more complex scenarios, their foundation is so weak that it will not hold for too long.

Our mind is not an optimal machine to learn everything in self-learn mode. From a learner's side, there are certain areas in which we can learn ourselves. We will always need help, coaching, and teaching in certain areas.

Relying on One Modality Is a Recipe for Failure

There are certain things that you can self-learn. While there must be other things where you'll need teaching, mentoring, or training, all these aspects are not really well thought out while designing e-learning. For instance, for certain things, you need some external facilitation to put you into the situation to help you learn to solve the problem. For another set of things, you need some level of coaching whereby you would need someone to ask you a series of questions to reflect deeply. You may need someone to teach you what to do for an entirely different kind of thing, and you follow afterward. Sometimes, you need mentoring, whereby you learn from other experiences. Designers generally do not think of all types of learning modalities appropriate to solve different situations.

An effective e-learning design geared to speed up skill acquisition toward on-the-job proficiency has to employ a combination of all these strategies. Relying on one single strategy of making everything self-directed and asking you to go home and learn yourself - is a disaster.

OUTCOME-DRIVEN DESIGN

I advocate an outcome-driven e-learning design that can help you put all five strategies into play. The result could be powerful e-learning that can ensure accelerated learning of your learners.

Start with an overall comprehensive analysis of the learning outcomes. A detailed matrix of learning outcomes (what to learn), delivery methods (how to deliver), and delivery modes (when to deliver) should be prepared for design decisions. Such a matrix or blueprint of learning outcomes allows designers to assess which learning outcomes should be delivered using e-learning and which can be attained only in the classroom settings. This blueprint will also enable you to decide what learners can learn before formal classroom training and what makes the best sense to learn alongside the task in the actual job.

Each learning outcome can then be designed as small chunks of content or as a microlearning session. These sessions should be distributed in time with appropriate spacing. The sessions can then be sequenced in the form of an e-learning path to help learners progress in their proficiency in quick short steps. You may be able to insert various self-paced and instructor-led sessions at the most appropriate points in the path based on the complexity and difficulty levels of the learning outcomes. For example, if the topic demands attention, reflection, and deeper thinking to prepare for the next ILT session, then corresponding pre-work can be inserted as self-paced homework activities between the consecutive ILT sessions.

An attempt should be made to design each microlearning session around scenarios and problems. The scenario-based short sessions can be delivered through EPSSs, including a range of tools like LMS, learning on-the-go, mobile learning, and decision-support systems.

To demonstrate the above process, in one case study, an expert system was used as an e-learning system to accelerate financial analyst learning. An extensive database of pre-design financial analysis cases was loaded. The cases were profiled based on complexity, skill levels, and other subject matter. These cases were then sequenced based on the blueprints of learning outcomes targeted for the job of financial analysts. The cases were presented to learners on their devices in a suitable progression of complexity, which guided them to reach the desired proficiency goal in a shorter time.

5 GUIDE QUESTIONS TO DESIGN E-LEARNING

In the following figure, the same model with a different perspective allows you to ask design questions systematically. These questions are listed below.

Question #1–Which task requires deeper thinking and solving a range of problems to achieve business outcomes? Such tasks are your candidates for designing scenarios.

Question #2–Which skill can be packed in shorter learning units that can be applied immediately at the job?

Question #3 - Which e-learning activities make someone reach proficiency quickly and which do not?

Question #4–Which channel or technology can deliver the intended skill to provide enriched experience and deeper learning?

Question #5–Which skills can be delivered through EPSS to provide JIT support at the moment of need? It will undoubtedly accelerate learning if you can deliver skills, content, and scenarios through PSS at the point of need.

After this, for each strategy, you ask four questions pointing at that particular strategy at hand. Everything is linked up in a very cyclic fashion, and none of the strategies works in isolation, as suggested by Figure 10.1. When you apply an isolated strategy without integrating the other four strategies, you end up having ineffective e-learning or online training that does not serve your goals. Thus, use these five strategies as a system.

CH 10 – SPEED –ENABLING E-LEARNING SYSTEMS APPROACH

Figure 10.1: Meta questions for five e-learning strategies to accelerate proficiency

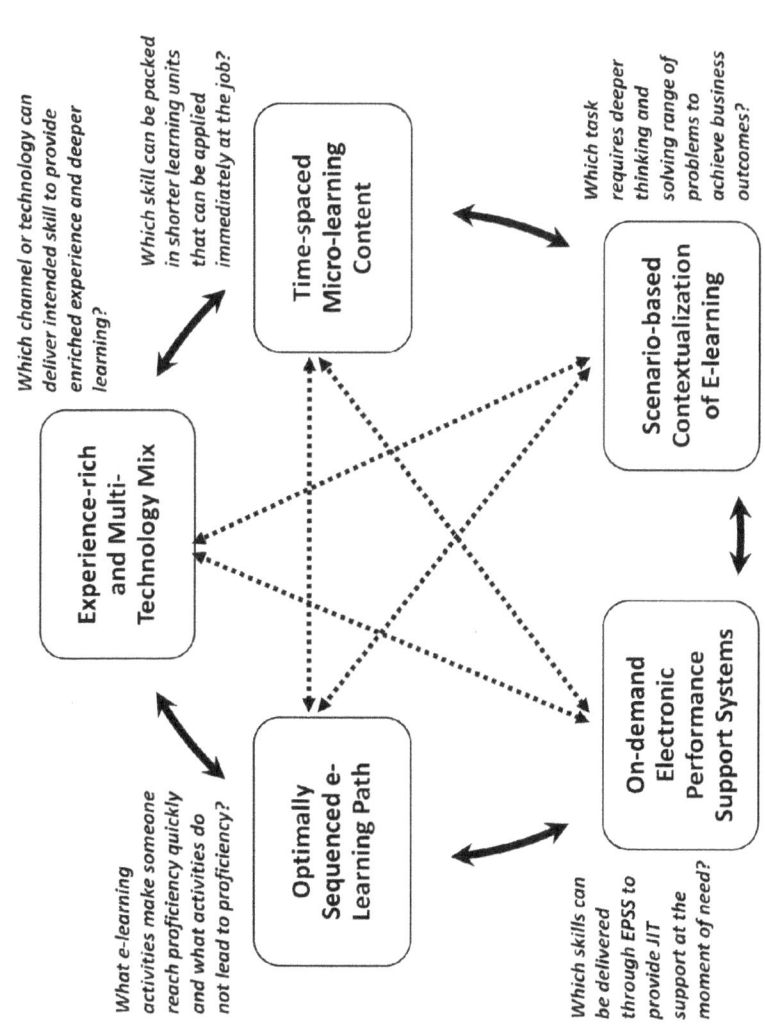

5 CORE GUIDING FORCES

I bought a revolutionary Microsoft HoloLens 2.0 headset, a great AR technology taking the market by storm as a flagship e-learning strategy.

I was playing it with my usual adult learning techniques, like going through the vast amount of learning modules available everywhere, reading the manuals, and learning how to do it step-by-step.

In the meantime, my kid interrupted me and eagerly wanted to try as well. He played with all the buttons for a few minutes, and here it goes. He ended up playing virtually with a 3D inbuilt AR game 'in the air' for an hour. He mastered the skills of next-generation technology in a few minutes while I struggled with it despite being an engineer.

What's the difference?

He used a natural human learning mechanism called 'learning by doing' and 'experiential learning.' On the other hand, I was using a taught mechanism of how the world has groomed us to learn from somebody's lengthy online learning modules.

That had me thinking that when we design online learning, we forget that we are designing it for humans. And we put all the technology, tools, resources, and frills we come across and over-glamourize it to the point that we simply make it inhuman learning.

This is now the time to think differently about online learning. Perhaps we need to design it for kids to make it the best.

The model is driven by a set of core philosophies that anchor 1-to-many relationships and dependencies among various strategies. Five common threads or core guiding forces allow you to center your e-learning design around humans.

1. BUILD CRITICAL THINKING

At the core of all these strategies is a guiding philosophy that employees don't perform tasks now. They are actively engaged in thinking and making complex decisions. If your goal is to design e-learning specifically for accelerating learning and skill acquisition, then make sure that you deliberately design or build moments of critical thinking, more profound reflections, and problem-solving encounters. Unless you build 'critical' critical thinking moments, realizing the advantage of speed is hard. Your aim should be to design e-learning that can drive people to think critically.

2. IMPART PROBLEM-SOLVING SKILLS

On the same lines, online learning needs to be problem-solving-focused. After all, employees are required to solve workplace problems or challenges daily. Now the nature of problems employees encounter is far more complex, far more multi-factored, and far more multidisciplinary than it was a decade ago. If you don't build realistic enough problem-solving in your e-learning, you will not see any benefits in the speed of skill acquisition.

3. LEVERAGE EMOTIONAL LOADING

We all produce remarkable outcomes at work, and usually, those get produced or done far more quickly. The reason is that you are surrounded by an ecosystem driven by peer pressure, harsh deadlines, and performance goals. Besides that, you fear the repercussions of missing the deliverables, pressures imposed by your manager, and the impact of your ability to do a good job on your 'earning ability.' All these factors create an emotional loading on you.

This emotional loading is what accelerates your skills, learning, and performance and gets things done faster. Here we are not talking about the stress caused by those pressures but the emotional triggers that make you a high performer. Along similar lines, unless your e-learning programs drive your employees to be emotionally involved in the task or content, you don't get an acceleration of the skills. Unless they are emotionally aware of the impacts of mastering or not mastering tasks, there are far fewer chances that their learning will get accelerated. You must put pressure, challenges, deadlines, commitments, and performance goals into your e-learning programs.

4. DELIVER IN THE CONTEXT OF THE JOB

You need to ensure that online learning is in the context of the job. Thus, everything you design in e-learning needs to be in the context of producing outcomes or results for the job rather than in the context of learning a piece of content or information. Learning skills in isolation has no impact on shortening TTP unless one learns in the context of how to integrate various skills and knowledge pieces to produce an outcome for the job.

Thus, e-learning's value is if it is delivered, absorbed, and used during the job while doing the tasks rather than some kind of forced 'information download' upfront. When your goal becomes delivering learning, you become a content-focused e-learning strategist. However, when you shift your focus on results, you become a proficiency-focused e-e-learning officer.

5. BEYOND CONTENT OR INFORMATION SHARING

A mistake most e-learning strategists make is that they design e-learning that is information-heavy or content-heavy but context-light. Such a design only delivers content loaded with information, facts, figures, and knowledge but lacks enough coverage of skills. The key idea here is your online training should focus on teaching and delivering skills. For information content, you can use PSSs or search-based systems. You don't need to invest in designing a training course for those information-seeking tasks.

HOLISTIC IMPLEMENTATION OF E-LEARNING

Most instructional designers for e-learning work in isolation, irrespective of instructor-led virtual or face-to-face training modalities or on-the-job learning resources. The result is that such isolated e-learning programs never accelerate learning.

Five e-learning strategies are presented in previous chapters in their silos based on the nature of learning. However, pure e-learning does not work in its silos. There is quite an overlap and interconnection among strategies for e-learning, ILT, and on-the-job workplace learning.

Thus, if your goal is to speed up learners' learning and proficiency, then you have to include strategies for ILT as well as on-the-job learning. A detailed treatment of instructor-led and on-the-job workplace learning strategies can be found in my book *"Designing Training to Shorten Time to Proficiency."*

A holistic implementation considering all elements of the learner's experience throughout the proficiency journey leads to a total of nine strategies that must be implemented. It must be noted that no single training and learning strategy might be powerful enough to impact the overall TTP of the learners. However, when these strategies work in tandem with each other, the overall impact might be amplified.

While training might be a smaller portion of overall efforts to reduce TTP, a bad training design may basically hamper acceleration. As discussed in Chapter 4, inefficient training design may lead to a longer TTP instead. Thus, it is important to orchestrate these strategies in such a way that training acts as an enabler toward accelerating proficiency.

You can view this holistic system as shown in Figure 10.2 in terms of how you will deploy e-learning solutions during four phases of proficiency growth: Pre-ILT, ILT, Post-ILT, and sustain/maintain phase. Conventional use of e-learning happens mostly during instructor-driven sessions. Another conventional mechanism is to rely heavily on self-paced learning to bring learners up to speed. Both mechanisms lead to a slower rate of proficiency acquisition.

Strategic thinking is to leverage the correct amount of self-paced learning before providing learners with intense instructor-driven virtual learning. It has been seen that strategically deployed self-paced learning lifts the initial proficiency level of learners. Such learning is controlled, managed, and measured. Typically, organizations throw a basket full of self-paced videos and material for learners to master. However, you learned in this book that you have to design an efficient lean path for them to master in a sequence determined by your design or determined by an adaptive algorithm.

Providing an initial headstart prior to instructor-driven e-learning (like virtual sessions, remote training, etc.) leads to accelerated learning during the ILT phase. In turn, it means the shorter time required to master things on-the-job. There is an increased likelihood of attaining a shorter TTP with such an arrangement.

CH 10 - SPEED-ENABLING E-LEARNING SYSTEMS APPROACH

Figure 10.2: e-learning used strategically to shorten TTP

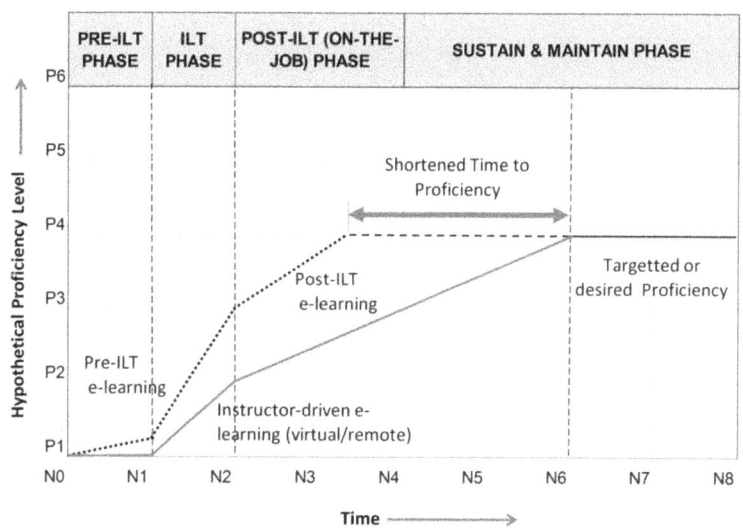

Keep one thing in mind. While a solid line shows instructor-led learning as happening between N1 to N2, it is not meant to be a single event. If you apply the principle of time-spaced microlearning and optimize the e-learning path, you will design several time-distributed virtual sessions spaced with appropriate on-the-job assignments. The dots in the upper lines show that spacing. In that view, pre-learning is also not a continuous block of time. Rather, those are distributed e-learning activities designed using the above two principles. If you keep it strategic and do not load the learners with mammoth content and information, you can shorten the TTP of your workforce in any job role.

In any organization, e-learning as a standalone solution is bound to fail. Several organizations have taken that route only to revert back to their conventional old-school approach. Organizations are in a hurry, driven by massive cost savings, to replace every opportunity for face-to-face or classroom-based training with e-learning packages. Heavy reliance only on e-learning or depending on old-style instructor-driven in-person training are both recipes for a much longer TTP.

Instead, you have to implement e-learning in the context of the job. Any e-learning must be implemented in conjunction with standard instructor-led or classroom-based training. The best bet is to use four phases of the learner's journey toward proficiency development. In my research, I observed that most organizations used nine methods overlayed on four phases of proficiency growth strategically, some implemented together, and some staggered in time. The representation is shown in Figure 10.3 in the form of horizontal bars that runs for specific phases. The underlying goal is to lift the entry-level proficiency during the pre-ILT phase and then exit the learners at a higher level of proficiency from training sessions before they go into the on-the-job phase. When they go to the on-the-job phase with that groundwork, they acquire proficiency at a much higher rate, resulting in a shorter TTP.

The nine methods seen in the holistic e-learning model are listed and described in the following sections:

1. *Segmentation of critical tasks*
2. *Optimally sequenced learning path*
3. *Self-guided pre-work*
4. *Contextualized learning with scenarios*
5. *Emotional loading and involvement*
6. *Multi-channel experience-rich delivery modes*
7. *Manufactured and structured on-the-job experiences*
8. *Time-spaced distributed microlearning*
9. *On-demand PSS*

CH 10 - SPEED -ENABLING E-LEARNING SYSTEMS APPROACH

Figure 10.3: A holistic e-learning design and implementation

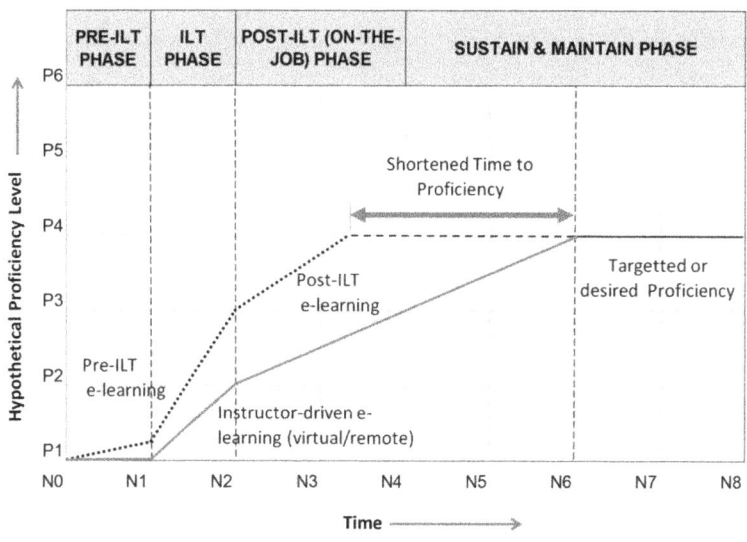

[1]	Segmentation of critcal tasks
[2]	Optimally sequenced learning path
[3]	Self-guided pre-work
[4]	Contextualized learning with scenarios
[5]	Emotional loading and involvement
[6]	Multi-channel experience-rich delivery modes
[7]	Structured on-the-job experiences
[8]	Time-spaced distributed microlearning
[9]	On-demand performance support systems

1. SEGMENTATION OF CRITICAL TASKS

Before any design is put in place, it is necessary to understand the nature of tasks/skills involved in a given job. Segmentation is to classify the nature of learning outcomes and determine what needs to be learned first, what can be learned in a self-paced mode and on the job, what can be provided through PSSs, and what must require formal training. Segmentation also tells us what goes in at different phases like pre-ILT, ILT, and post-ILT phases. The strategy advocates using data to segment the nature of the tasks based on their characteristics.

2. OPTIMALLY SEQUENCED LEARNING PATH

Once you have correctly segmented tasks/skills, the next step early on is to design an optimal sequence of the activities through which those tasks/skills are learned, leading to the development of an efficient learning path. The well-sequenced learning path holds the most potential in cutting out the significant time from the learning journey of the learners. It has an application for both optimizing e-learning as well as on-the-job learning. Therefore, this strategy is all prevailing throughout proficiency growth.

3. SELF-GUIDED PRE-WORK

Once you are clear on how the learning interventions are spread across pre-ILT, ILT, and post-ILT phases, you can design self-guided pre-work for the pre-ILT phase. A well-designed pre-work focusing on thinking skills instead of informational content can uplift learners' proficiency levels before introducing them to classroom-based formal training interventions. This method can be leveraged for designing self-guided homework for multi-day formal training that allows learners to ingrain a deeper level of learning.

4. CONTEXTUALIZED LEARNING WITH SCENARIOS

Before you design any e-learning content, you must create cases, scenarios, and problems from real job challenges and pressing problems one may encounter. Your goal should be to deliver all the learning outcomes using scenario-based learning. This strategy is crucial for training design in the pre-ILT and ILT phases. This allows active involvement of learners online and in formal training while solving realistic problems they may encounter on the job. Such preemptive involvement contributes toward preparing learners to become proficient faster when deployed on the job.

5. EMOTIONAL LOADING AND INVOLVEMENT

Actively involving the learners, regardless of the phase, emotional loading, and emotional involvement, goes a long way toward accelerating TTP. The contextualization strategy ensures necessary emotional loading and involvement in pre-ILT and ILT phases. It would be best to build pressure and consequences into the learning for it to work. Emotional loading may have one of the most significant impacts on how fast learners come up to speed. It must be designed into all the interventions throughout the proficiency acquisition journey. During the post-ILT and sustenance phases, the job will introduce constant emotional loading, which helps them to attain desired proficiency faster.

6. DELIBERATE ON-THE-JOB EXPERIENCES

During the post-ILT phase, employees must be made to leverage on-the-job assignments. Once you can segment the tasks appropriate for on-the-job learning, you identify events and opportunities for realistic assignments at work. Their proficiency speed is enhanced when you time-space or distribute these identified activities over some time. However, in all that, you do not encourage any ad-hoc involvement. Rather, you include these identified activities and sequence them deliberately on your learning path. You do not wait for events to happen. If certain events necessary to gain proficiency are not happening, you need to manufacture those experiences on-the-job or off the job. You can use the workplace ecosystem or simulators to structure those experiences. The moment you do so, it becomes an e-learning task. The level of emotional loading experienced by the learners also depends on how sound the on-the-job experiences are designed, manufactured, and structured.

7. MULTI-CHANNEL EXPERIENCE-RICH DELIVERY MODES

Learners learn faster when you provide them with experiences through experience-rich and multi-channel modes that allow efficient transfer of information. This strategy aims to offer the same content via multiple modes. You can use various channels to deliver the same content. The newer technologies allow several modes like audio, text, videos, AR, VR, immersive gaming, and simulated challenges. Learners are made to use any appropriate learning mechanism and are not restricted by specific content types. You can use a mix of technologies to achieve this goal. Technologies also ensure time-spaced, distributed learning in smaller chunks. Additionally, you can integrate on-demand PSSs and LMSs to make the delivery experience-rich.

8. TIME-SPACED DISTRIBUTED MICROLEARNING

The contextualized scenarios are designed in smaller chunks so you can sequence them efficiently on the learning path. While doing so, you can time-space and distribute these sessions over a more extended period. The method can be used during the pre-ILT, ILT phase, and post-ILT phases. Care must be taken to interleave consecutive microlearning sessions with relevant on-the-job activities or assignments. This strategy is essential in both e-learning and classroom training design.

9. ON-DEMAND PSS

In usual instructional design, PSSs are hardly considered as learning interventions. But in reality, deploying PSSs is promising e-learning as well as a workplace learning strategy that shows the most potential to replace or reduce the amount of formal training. If you analyze it in the context of the learning path, you can determine which tasks you should train employees in and for which tasks you should let them seek support from PSSs. Once you do that, deploy PSSs throughout the proficiency acquisition journey. It should become your primary mechanism to maintain proficiency during the post-ILT and sustenance phase to handle tasks that do not occur frequently.

THINKING AHEAD

If your goal is to design e-learning specifically for accelerating learning and skill acquisition, make sure that you ground the e-learning or online learning design to build moments of critical thinking, deeper reflections, and problem-solving moments. While you do so, focus on skills rather than information or content download. You need to give the learners realistic challenges and as much emotional loading as feasible. To encode that learning deeply and accelerate it, use multiple experience-rich channels. You can leverage a range of resources available to deliver learning in such a way that it is nearer to the point of need or application in the context of job. Once you make it contextual, you speed up learning at an unimaginable rate.

Reflections

Chapter 1
E-LEARNING AND DIGITAL REVOLUTION

Chapter 2
A ROLE OF CHIEF E-LEARNING OFFICER

Chapter 3
SPEED OF EMPLOYEE DEVELOPMENT AS E-LEARNING KPIs

Chapter 4
STRATEGIC E-LEARNING FOR SPEED

Chapter 5
SCENARIO-BASED E-LEARNING

Chapter 6
TIME-SPACED MICROLEARNING CONTENT

Chapter 7
OPTIMALLY SEQUENCED E-LEARNING PATH

Chapter 8
ON-DEMAND PERFORMANCE SUPPORT SYSTEMS

Chapter 9
EXPERIENCE-RICH MULTI-TECHNOLOGY MIX

Chapter 10
SPEED-ENABLING E-LEARNING SYSTEMS APPRAOCH

Chapter 11
SUMMARY OF E-LEARNING DESIGN GUIDELINES FOR SPEED

Chapter 12
EMERGING E-LEARNING REVOLUTIONS

11
SUMMARY OF E-LEARNING DESIGN GUIDELINES FOR SPEED

CH 11 – SUMMARY OF E-LEARNING GUIDELINES FOR SPEED

In the previous chapters, detailed guidelines are presented, which are segmented into four phases of the employee proficiency journey. This chapter provides a highly condensed summary of those guidelines for each phase of the proficiency journey, grouped by five e-learning strategies.

SELF-GUIDED E-LEARNING GUIDELINES (PRE-ILT PHASE)

Scenario-based E-learning Contextualization

- Encapsulate content into realistic cases or scenarios relevant to job outcomes.
- Use actual job scenarios to prepare learners for realistic job challenges.
- Focus on problem-solving skills and link learning goals to on-the-job success or failure.
- Avoid passive learning modes and linear content; instead, use active processing tasks such as project deliverables or analyses.
- Replace traditional quizzes and assessments with usable artifacts like credits, points, and awards.

Time-spaced Microlearning

- Create shorter micro-lessons (10-20 minutes) addressing one learning outcome at a time.
- Avoid assigning more than 1-2 hours of daily cumulative learning via micro-lessons.
- Design micro-lessons around realistic cases and scenarios, emphasizing thinking and problem-solving skills.
- Distribute micro-lessons individually at regular intervals.

- Schedule and push micro-lessons individually at regular intervals based on a time-spaced learning path.
- Interleave micro-lessons with active tasks, such as performing relevant tasks or interviewing experts.

Optimally Sequenced E-learning Path

- Design learning paths with adaptive entry and exit points based on learners' profiles and experiences.
- Distribute content over time and interleave with active tasks.
- Sequence pre-work, ILT sessions, and homework on an e-learning path, focusing on essential and relevant learning activities.
- Conduct micro-assessments before each micro-lesson to adapt learning paths.
- Implement continuous assessment and dynamically select activities to shorten the proficiency journey.
- Include various content types, such as videos, text, slides, case studies, and simulations, to ensure active learner involvement.

On-demand Performance Support Systems

- Deliver micro-lessons using PSSs for time-spaced and distributed learning.
- Replace or reduce training curriculum with just-in-time, on-demand PSS accessible at the point of need during workflows.
- Integrate PSS with mobile learning to deliver short modules or microlearning chunks over time.
- Use advanced AI-based search engines and decision-support systems to help employees make informed decisions.
- Teach employees how to obtain desired results using PSSs in their job or workflow context.

CH 11 – SUMMARY OF E-LEARNING GUIDELINES FOR SPEED

Experience-rich Multi-channel Technology Mix

- Focus on managing the learning ecosystem rather than the learning process.
- Design a learning ecosystem that allows learners to choose the most effective format, mode, and channel for their needs.
- Blend multiple formats, modes, and channels seamlessly to provide learners with a range of choices.
- Utilize a mix of content types, such as videos, text, slides, and games.
- Maintain consistent assessment standards regardless of the mix of channels, modes, and formats, focusing on job outcomes and results.
- Design low-complexity skills and informational content as pre-training courses to give learners a headstart.

VIRTUAL OR REMOTE E-LEARNING GUIDELINES (ILT PHASE)

Scenario-based E-learning Contextualization

- Expose learners to job-relevant scenarios and hands-on problem-solving instead of traditional lectures and presentations.
- Use interactive case-study-based lectures with a complex, larger-scope case scenario as a backbone.
- Incorporate variations of scenario-based e-learning, such as problems, cases, games, VR, and simulations.
- Emphasize emotional involvement by incorporating stakes, consequences, and deadlines similar to real job situations.

- Design assessments that require research, active involvement, and higher-order thinking.
- Increase active participation through interactivity and peer-to-peer communication.

Time-spaced Microlearning

- Treat each virtual session as an independent micro-lesson limited to 20-30 minutes.
- Limit virtual sessions to 1-2 hours, with no more than three micro-lessons (20-30 minutes each).
- Design each micro-lesson around a well-scoped scenario relevant to the job or desired results.
- Space out virtual sessions over time and include pre- or post-work assignments for reflection and practice.
- Be selective about which skill qualifies for microlearning and which requires a larger contiguous block of time to master.

Optimally Sequenced E-learning Path

- Design an e-learning path with a series of virtual or remote sessions spread over time.
- Interleave activities between virtual sessions and include moments of purpose-driven conversations, dialogues, and social connectivity.
- Assign time targets for each activity and avoid compressing sessions in length or quantity.

On-demand Performance Support Systems

- Use PSS to facilitate purpose-driven conversations, dialogues, and social connectivity.
- Remove non-essential information from virtual sessions and instead provide access to PSS or knowledge repositories.

- Leverage blended pre-work and homework strategically to supplement ILT sessions.

Experience-rich Multi-channel Technology Mix

- Assess the best combination of technologies, modes, media, and formats to deliver experience-rich learning.
- Engage all senses and leverage technologies like mobile learning, VR, AR, video conference, and remote sharing.
- Insert student-generated deliverables as assessments and provide freedom to learners to demonstrate capability in any qualified manner.

ON-THE-JOB E-LEARNING GUIDELINES (POST-ILT PHASE)

Scenario-based E-learning Contextualization

- Employ story-telling and scenario-driven communication to provide context.
- Avoid task-driven OJT check sheets. Focus on result-driven OJT.
- Assign field mentors to coach and test employees through nano-coaching and nano-mentoring.
- Utilize PSS-enabled micro-lessons designed around well-scoped case scenarios focusing on unpredictable, non-routine events.

Time-spaced Microlearning

- Deliver PSS-enabled micro-lessons during the post-ILT phase focusing on unpredictable, non-routine events.
- Create scenario-driven micro-lessons employing story-telling to provide context.

- Encourage usage of PSSs and searchable repositories for performance improvement on known/routine tasks.
- Use nano-coaching and nano-mentoring techniques for personalized support.

Optimally Sequenced E-learning Path

- Use adaptive LMSs to optimize the e-learning path for each employee based on performance, learning speed, accomplishments, and results.
- Integrate online learning sources, documentation, PSSs, and on-the-job activities in a properly sequenced e-learning path.
- Identify coaching or mentoring opportunities and include field mentoring activities focused on specific outcomes.
- Continuously optimize the post-ILT e-learning path by removing unnecessary activities and assigning realistic goals.
- Measure learner progress through proficiency metrics and align them with annual or quarterly performance reviews.

On-demand Performance Support Systems

- Use PSSs for performance improvement on known/routine tasks.
- Make PSSs accessible to learners and coaches for short, targeted, asynchronous coaching or timely feedback.
- Enable PSSs that allow access to expert directories and build a network of coaches with diverse experiences.
- Implement a range of PSSs, including search engines, documentation repositories, AR/VR, on-demand self-guided material, decision-support systems, multi-channel communicators, and collaborating platforms, among other new-generation technologies.

Experience-rich Multi-channel Technology Mix:

- Create flexibility in technology-driven connectivity for learners by implementing a range of PSSs and technologies that make post-ILT learning boundaryless.
- Implement multi-channel collaborators for meaningful social interactivity and purposeful interconnectivity, allowing learners to connect and interact with experts instantly at the 'moment of need.'

E-LEARNING GUIDELINES FOR PROFICIENCY MAINTENANCE (SUSTENANCE PHASE)

Scenario-based E-learning Contextualization

- Transform documents, bulletins, videos, and notifications into real-world scenarios that engage learners.
- Design problem-solving-oriented assessments and proficiency-testing scenarios while keeping assessments short to accommodate on-the-go learning.
- Request submission of clear job-related deliverables or artifacts as evidence of proficiency development.
- Encourage purpose-driven conversations, dialogues, and social connectivity to enhance the learning experience.

Time-spaced Microlearning

- Create targeted, time-spaced micro-lessons by converting large documents into shorter segments.
- Be selective about microlearning content, ensuring it is appropriate for maintaining proficiency without demanding excessive time commitment from learners.

CHIEF E-LEARNING OFFICER

Optimally Sequenced E-learning Path

- Utilize proficiency metrics, learning, and HR analytics to optimize the e-learning path for new employees.
- Study seasoned employees' learning paths to identify successful patterns and implement intelligent technologies for profiling learners' knowledge, skills, and experiences at every point in their journey.
- Provide coaching through a network of coaches at the moment of need and facilitate instant connections between learners.

On-demand Performance Support Systems

- Deliver ongoing refresher and reinforcement learning via PSS instead of traditional LMSs.
- Embed learning into employees' workflows using technologies such as AR/VR gadgets and work-related mobile apps.
- Use analytics to identify PSSs, repeatable algorithms, rule-based automation, and AI-based workflows that support employee proficiency.

Experience-rich Multi-channel Technology Mix

- Focus on delivering refresher and reinforcement training content across multi-channel, multi-mode, and multi-format platforms.
- Avoid sending content through emails and aim for meaningful delivery on mobile devices through written content, messages, reminders, videos, or assessments.
- Implement a range of PSSs and technologies to make learning boundaryless, leveraging multiple channels, modes, and formats.

TAKING IT FORWARD

In the last five chapters, you learned five powerful e-learning design and development strategies that can give your organization a competitive edge in the market. By leveraging these strategies and strategies discussed in previous chapters, you can positively speed up the development of workforce skills, performance, and proficiency. That's when you, as a CeLO, can demonstrate your commitment to caring for employees. In the long run, you establish your unwavering leadership and ensure an executive seat in the CXO suite.

Use the space below to reflect upon and develop an action plan for each of the five e-learning design strategies in your context. Review the action plan with your executives. Start incorporating one element at a time in your annual strategic plans. Institute a culture of "speed" in your organization and be a change agent to educate management staff to speak the language of *time-to-proficiency*. Once you accomplish that, it will be far easier for you to win any ROI battle and stay as a leader who is ahead of the technology.

Action Plan

Strategy #1: Scenario-based contextualization of e-learning

Action plan:

Strategy #2: Time-spaced microlearning content

Action plan:

Strategy #3: Optimally sequenced e-learning path

Action plan:

Strategy #4: On-demand performance support systems

Action plan:

CH 11 - SUMMARY OF E-LEARNING GUIDELINES FOR SPEED

Strategy #5: Experience-rich and multi-technology mix
Action plan:
Overall system implementation, including ecosystem:
Key things to focus on this year:
Key things to focus on next year:
Your plan to secure the role of CeLO:

Reflections

Chapter 1
E-LEARNING AND DIGITAL REVOLUTION

Chapter 2
A ROLE OF CHIEF E-LEARNING OFFICER

Chapter 3
SPEED OF EMPLOYEE DEVELOPMENT AS E-LEARNING KPIs

Chapter 4
STRATEGIC E-LEARNING FOR SPEED

Chapter 5
SCENARIO-BASED E-LEARNING

Chapter 6
TIME-SPACED MICROLEARNING CONTENT

Chapter 7
OPTIMALLY SEQUENCED E-LEARNING PATH

Chapter 8
ON-DEMAND PERFORMANCE SUPPORT SYSTEMS

Chapter 9
EXPERIENCE-RICH MULTI-TECHNOLOGY MIX

Chapter 10
SPEED-ENABLING E-LEARNING SYSTEMS APPRAOCH

Chapter 11
SUMMARY OF E-LEARNING DESIGN GUIDELINES FOR SPEED

Chapter 12
EMERGING E-LEARNING REVOLUTIONS

12

EMERGING E-LEARNING REVOLUTIONS

In addition to the larger scope of strategies I presented earlier, the e-learning space keeps evolving daily in terms of new technologies, tools, apps, software, methods, and techniques. If you focus on a more tactical level, then your focus on leveraging or using e-learning to impact shortening TTP may become blurry.

However, e-learning designers tend to ride upon trendy buzzwords and make it a point to rely on that one world alone. For instance, a couple of years back, when the 'flipped classroom' term was coined, thousands of e-learning courses were flooded into the market designed fully around those concepts alone. That's the real reason why we don't see the impact of e-learning on TTP. The point is not to rely on one strategy wholly but synchronize multiple proven strategies to work in unison, supplementing or complementing each other.

In this chapter, I aim to share some of the 'most talked about' methods that have the potential to enrich the previous five strategies.

EMERGING LEARNING TECHNOLOGIES

Next set of technologies that impact speed is related to training and learning. Perhaps the term 'learning techs' is not that intuitive anymore because now the boundary between learning and work is diffused. Most of the learning technologies can make learning accessible, flexible, low cost, and more scalable, among other benefits. But only a few of them really have the potential to impact the speed-to-proficiency. In order to influence TTP, learning technologies must cut the time out of the employee development journey.

I observed five kinds of learning technologies in my research that showed good potential and success stories for shortening TTP.

1. *Adaptive LMSs*
2. *Training delivery technologies*
3. *On-demand and mobile learning technologies*
4. *AR/VR learning technologies*
5. *Immersive and gamification technologies*

1. ADAPTIVE LMS

The first group of technologies is those related to LMSs. LMSs typically are comparable across the board and do not directly impact the speed of employee development. Two kinds of LMSs that hold the potential to impact TTP are those LMSs that either support on-demand online learning or support adaptive learning paths. The adaptive paths are explained in detail in Chapter 6. In a nutshell, adaptive paths can enable differently skilled people to complete learning requirements via different routes if the system determines them qualified. That shortens times for certain employees.

Several LMSs provide adaptive learning paths, including Absorb LMS, Cornerstone, iSpring Learn, TalentLMS, Moodle, Litmos, Canvas LMS, Blackboard Learn, and Google Classroom. These systems use algorithms to optimize each learner's experience, resulting in better retention of new information and a more personalized learning experience. Some of these systems use machine learning-based adaptive systems, while others use advanced algorithm, rules-based, or decision-tree adaptive systems.

2. TRAINING DELIVERY TECHNOLOGIES

The second technology group is related to training or delivering learning, content, skills, or classroom experiences.

CH 12 – EMERGING E-LEARNING REVOLUTIONS

Virtual Training Delivery Technologies

During the pandemic, you have seen vast applications of virtual or remote training technologies. Now the world is moving to virtual learning platforms, which allow adding much capacity quickly to run many people through programs. If people wait for ILT to start their jobs, adding capacity via virtual mode can help shorten the curve.

Keep in mind that while training delivery technologies make learning more accessible, they may also hinder the speed of employee development. For instance, in a social interaction-intensive job role, try putting them through an endless stream of online learning, and you would see speed gets hampered negatively.

The reason is that most of the technologies in the learning space still tend to be largely content-focused. Thus, when choosing learning technology, focus on skills, not content.

Teaching technologies also include those used to conduct skill assessments, tools, and resources for coaching and mentoring.

Assessment Technologies

Among them, the technologies that allow conducting multi-level assessments of employees can significantly increase employee speed. However, remember that the assessment only adds to speed if integrated into LMS or workforce analytics.

Mentoring and Coaching Technologies

Experiencing the job under someone qualified allows much faster proficiency than learning the same task in the classroom. However, organizations are often too focused on implementing formal training technologies that they don't invest enough in technologies that could enable efficient coaching and mentoring processes.

The technologies which support distributed coaching and mentoring access to anyone, anywhere, at any time, hold the most potential to accelerate proficiency. If employees are geographically dispersed or mostly work in the field, your organizations must invest in 'on-the-go' coaching platforms that provide learners coaching when needed. Such platforms also equip experts with tools, templates, tracking, and other mechanisms to coach employees efficiently.

3. ON-DEMAND AND MOBILE LEARNING TECHNOLOGIES

On-demand, just-in-time learning resources have been described in Chapter 8. As a recap, when employees get just enough information, at the time of need, during the workflow, it is seen to improve their speed of learning. The third group is mobile learning and self-paced learning technologies, which allow just-in-time learning. These are used to enable employees to learn on-the-go. It can speed up the process of acquiring and accessing the learning content faster when and where they need it.

4. AR/VR LEARNING TECHNOLOGIES

AR/VR technologies as learning tools and PSSs have been described in Chapter 8. As a recap, AR and VR technologies are revolutionizing the education industry by providing students with immersive experiences that enhance learning outcomes. In cases where it is necessary to explore specific equipment and learn how to use it, an AR application can present the required 3D model and helpful explanations. This adds practical value to traditional learning materials and increases student engagement.

5. IMMERSIVE, GAMIFICATION, AND MIXED-REALITY LEARNING TECHNOLOGIES

Leveraging immersive gaming and gamification methods has been described in Chapter 5. However, any successful gamification has immersive technology behind it. Immersive technology refers to a class of tools that create immersive experiences with digital elements that feel real to the user, while gamification is a technique used to engage users and increase their participation by adding game-like features to non-game contexts.

EMERGING SOCIAL TECHNOLOGIES

What do you do when you get into a problem or forget something? You ask your buddy in the next cubicle or someone on the phone. And you get things solved fast by talking to others. Imagine how much wait time is cut out in your journey to produce outcomes and become proficient.

That's where technologies like instant communicators, collaboration platforms, expert directories, or even community of practices platforms are highly useful. Its relevance has become even more important post-pandemic because people don't sit next to each other. These techs can be integrated into Outlook, teams, mobile, and any other device.

In my observation, implementing social technologies is probably the most overlooked in organizations. As a leader, you have to make sure you have a strategy behind how these social technologies are deployed. In fact, too many of these may even be a distraction to productivity if proper strategy is not considered.

Several training experts cited that the acquisition of complex skills and knowledge gets accelerated by learning with a group, by doing with each other, having discussions, conversations with peers, and asking questions from experts (and even from peers).

Social connectivity can have a significant impact on the acquisition of skills. When we interact with others, we have the opportunity to observe their behavior, learn from their experiences, and gain new insights into our own abilities. Through social connections, individuals can access resources, such as mentors, coaches, and other professionals who can provide guidance and support. Moreover, social connectivity can provide a motivating and supportive environment that can help individuals to persevere in their learning efforts. When we feel connected to others, we are more likely to feel accountable and responsible for our own learning. This, in turn, can lead to greater self-efficacy, which is the belief in one's ability to achieve goals and succeed.

Research has shown that social connectivity can accelerate skill acquisition by providing a rich learning environment that includes diverse perspectives and experiences. Social connections can help individuals to identify new opportunities for learning, practice new skills in a supportive setting, and receive feedback that can help them to refine their abilities. In addition, social connectivity can provide access to new ideas, innovations, and best practices that can help individuals to stay current in their field.

In order to leverage this finding, design an e-learning system that allows learners to connect and interact with anyone and everyone. A typical e-learning system may have some static offline interactions like discussion boards, blogging, commenting, etc., but real-time and instant interactions at the moment of need are critical elements. An e-learning platform may leverage 'social networking' platforms, but the focus is on 'learning by socializing' and 'learning by connecting.' Such a system drives interactions and connectivity through learning outcomes.

Figure 12.1: Four types of social technologies

Four major categories of social technologies have been making waves, as shown in Figure 12.1. As more technologies converge, we see movement toward integrating all four technology categories into one platform. The closest example of such convergence is IBM Connections Engagement Suite[45]. If applied strategically, you can shorten TTP of your employees.

---

[45] IBM Connections Engagement Suite offers an integrated set of solutions for increasing employee engagement, collaboration, and productivity.

CHIEF E-LEARNING OFFICER

1. *Real-time collaboration tools*
2. *Expert directories*
3. *Community of practice platforms*
4. *Multi-channel communicators*

1. REAL-TIME COLLABORATION TOOLS

For a moment, think about how the work is typically done in teams in any organization. It involves group work, collaboration, exchange, and feedback. There is a multi-pronged evaluation by various stakeholders during the workflow till a perfect outcome is achieved. Incorporating all those work dynamics and social interactions into a suitable technology could hasten employees' learning curve, apart from being efficient. All that can be achieved in the new world using real-time collaboration technologies. The advantages of such innovation are explained in Chapter 8 as one of the PSSs.

2. EXPERT DIRECTORIES OR LOCATORS

This is explained in Chapter 8 as one of the PSSs. However, not many companies do a good job of building fully validated, up-to-date, accomplishment-based expert directories with social connectivity and collaboration function. More often, companies maintain directories highlighting the experiences and skills of experts rather than building a portfolio of their accomplishments, projects, and results. A massive effort is required to identify the expertise taxonomy and then apply granular taxonomy to each job role in the company.

---

https://www.ibm.com/common/ssi/ShowDoc.wss?docURL=/common/ssi/rep_ca/5/897/ENUS217-535/index.html&lang=en&request_locale=en

There is no approach to expertise locators from a technology procurement and implementation standpoint. Stan Garfield[46], a noted knowledge management author and speaker, revealed some great recommendations for various approaches in his article. Expertise databases can be self-filled by employees where they fill their skills and accomplishments and be more discoverable. Alternatively, HR can fill it based on what they know, or the system may be able to pull available data from repositories like LinkedIn. Good expertise locators will incorporate rich metadata schemas of job titles, organization structures, company-specific terminology, business processes, content taxonomies, etc., to provide highly accurate results. People can quickly find the experts they need to solve problems and stop wasting time looking for information.

Stan Garfield suggested the next level approach is to use a social profile method which includes self-tagging, peer tagging, or rating. This could allow employees to search for colleagues by name, job title, location, and expertise. Another possible way is to implement crawlers into work-related content, contributed content, or community discussions. Such an expertise locator can provide information about the employee's experience, publications, and other relevant information. Above all, a searchable option is required to search for expertise and locate experts in context. With that, the expertise locator tool enables employees to search for colleagues with specific skills or knowledge. This can allow project teams and work groups to access and utilize this expertise.

---

[46] Garfield, S. 2021. Expertise Locators and Ask the Expert. https://lucidea.com/blog/km-component-35-expertise-locators-and-ask-the-expert/

3. COMMUNITY OF PRACTICES PLATFORMS

One large IT company practiced a Friday afternoon pizza hour for several weeks. They would gather their high performers and new performers together, eat, and share on a specific topic facilitated by someone who sets the agenda. This simple act does something wonderful. It would allow new performers to access the high performers who may have solved a similar problem and could quickly guide these new team members. They connect and learn from the master performer rather than waiting for formal training classes or relying on unmanaged informal learning. This is an example of purpose-driven social connectivity. Now, if you can implement the platforms and technologies to enable similar kinds of connectivity and networks, you may be able to speed up TTP.

The reality is that employees work with each other to produce results as a group. They don't work in isolation. There are usual team interactions. They learn socially and informally from those interactions. They do so by doing work with each other, talking to each other, sharing with others, and supporting each other. These interactions act as a powerful multiplier of skill or competency.

That's why the social techs, called the Communities of Practice (CoPs) platforms, significantly impact speed. These platforms allow people at work to create groups and purpose-driven networks on specific topics, issues, or functions.

CoPs platforms are a great way for organizations to increase employee social interactions and promote knowledge sharing and collaboration. For instance, Yammer[47] and Jive[48] are examples of private social networks for businesses that allow employees to collaborate and communicate in a secure online environment. It provides a platform for

---

[47] https://www.microsoft.com/en-us/microsoft-365/yammer/yammer-overview
[48] https://www.jivesoftware.com/

CoPs where employees can share knowledge, discuss ideas, and ask questions. COPs platforms like Slack[49], Confluence[50], and Microsoft Teams[51] are team communication and collaboration platforms that allow employees to connect and work together in real time.

As an executive or leader of the organization, you need to figure out what is the right technology or platform for setting up learning networks for specific purposes. It may be based on projects or functions or the tenure of the employees. In fact, for every new hire, there should be a defined network to start with. Tools like Microsoft Teams and Slack allow you some features where you can create groups and networks. And if done right, you achieve this without sacrificing productivity. Rather, you will add speed to performance. The technologies that allow embedding purpose-driven discussions, conversations, and interactions among the performers in these networks would actually help toward speeding up proficiency.

But care must be taken that such technologies do not become another file-dump system or email alternative. If you need to make a difference with these technologies, there must be a targeted knowledge creation that can be fed back to new people to accelerate their proficiency. For instance, if you have a network of the best practices on risk assessment, make sure refined knowledge is created, shared, and made as a corporate culture, like how things should happen moving forward.

4. MULTI-CHANNEL COMMUNICATORS

This is described in Chapter 8. As a recap, multi-channel communicators are tools and platforms that allow for communication across multiple

---

[49] https://slack.com/
[50] https://www.atlassian.com/software/confluence
[51] https://www.microsoft.com/en-ww/microsoft-teams/teams-for-work

channels, such as email, SMS, social media, and chat. Several years ago, there used to be separate technologies or standalone applications that were required to be integrated into a company's infrastructure. However, with the convergence of technologies, such communicators are built into LMS, PSS, and CoPs platforms. Choosing the right multi-channel communicator for your organization depends on your specific needs and the channels your customers prefer to communicate through.

EMERGING AI-BASED E-LEARNING

AI-based e-learning, also known as intelligent e-learning, refers to the use of AI technologies to enhance the effectiveness and efficiency of e-learning. AI has been evolving in the learning design space for several decades. Initially, it was used for routine tasks such as grading and assessment. However, with the advent of ML and deep learning, AI has been used for more complex tasks such as personalized learning and content creation. The development of Natural Language Processing (NLP) has also enabled AI to understand and interpret human languages, leading to the creation of conversational AI chatbots (Tuomi 2018).

However, in 2023, AI-driven e-learning is, beyond doubt, a rapidly evolving field transforming how we learn. ChatGPT, a language model developed by OpenAI[52] and other AI tools, has recently emerged as a next-generation e-learning tool. This technology can potentially revolutionize education by providing learners with personalized, adaptive, and efficient learning experiences. For instance, AI can improve learners' engagement, satisfaction, and outcomes by personalizing learning paths, providing real-time feedback, and offering adaptive learning opportunities.

---

[52] https://openai.com/

CH 12 - EMERGING E-LEARNING REVOLUTIONS

It can also be used to create e-learning content, and ChatGPT is an excellent example. Certainly, these can cut off a large percentage of your time as a content developer, but how would it ensure the shortening TTP of your learners? Unless you apply it in such a way that makes learners' proficiency faster, it has no significant impact.

At this moment, four major trends in the use of AI in the context of e-learning are emerging:

1. **E-learning content creation**
2. **Personalized e-learning**
3. **E-learning tutor**
4. **Content practice**

1. AI E-LEARNING CONTENT CREATION

AI-powered content creation tools can analyze the learner's performance data and create personalized learning content based on their strengths and weaknesses (Michelle 2023). Not only that, AI can also be used to create e-learning content. For example, ChatGPT, can generate high-quality text content for e-learning.

One example of AI in creating e-learning content is Educative[53] platform where OpenAI ChatGPT models are integrated into the courses to help learners build the applications. Another is Quillionz[54], an AI-powered platform that helps educators and trainers generate questions and assessments based on their existing content. By analyzing text and identifying key concepts, Quillionz can create quizzes, flashcards, and learning activities, significantly reducing content creation time.

---

[53] https://www.educative.io/
[54] https://app.quillionz.com/

AI can also be used to enhance content development by generating insights from the data gathered from e-learning platforms. With AI, e-learning platforms can analyze large amounts of data to identify patterns and trends that can be used to improve the curriculum and teaching methods (Michelle 2023). This can lead to the creation of more engaging and relevant learning materials that are better suited to the learner's needs.

Some latest examples of AI-driven content generation include Descript (Video generation), Colossyan (AI-generated onboarding videos), Picttory (Ai-generated video from text script, procedure, or written material), Slide.io (AI-generated automated presentation slides), MindGrasp (AI-generated summaries), AutoDraw (rough sketches to proper drawing), among hundreds of others.

2. AI PERSONALIZED E-LEARNING

Organizations increasingly use AI as an e-learning tool to improve learner engagement, retention, and outcomes. AI-powered e-learning tools can personalize the learning experience by adapting to the learner's needs and preferences. For example, an AI-powered chatbot can provide instant feedback to learners, answer their questions, and offer personalized learning recommendations based on their learning history (Wang et al. 2020).

AI-enabled e-learning platforms are becoming more intelligent and personalized, providing students with a unique learning experience that is tailored to their needs and preferences. AI algorithms can analyze student data and identify their strengths and weaknesses, enabling them to provide a customized learning experience.

IBM's Watson[55] is a prime example of how AI can be used to create personalized learning experiences. Watson's Talent Frameworks leverage AI to analyze employees' skills, identify knowledge gaps, and recommend targeted learning content, helping employees stay relevant and engaged.

Personalized learning paths ensure that students are presented with relevant content at the right time, increasing the effectiveness of the learning process. This approach has been used by companies like Coursera, which leverages AI to provide learners with personalized recommendations on what courses to take next based on their previous learning activities. One example of AI as an e-learning tool is Knewton[56], an adaptive learning platform that uses AI to personalize learning for individual learners.

AI can also personalize learning paths by determining appropriate content for each learner based on their level of comprehension and preferred modes of learning (Murtaza et al. 2022).

AI can also make e-learning more accessible to everyone. AI-driven solutions can recommend personalized resources, grade papers, and answer learners' questions. This has been implemented in e-learning platforms like Khan Academy[57], which uses AI to provide personalized recommendations for learners.

3. AI E-LEARNING TUTOR

AI-based e-learning platforms can also act as a tutor by providing real-time answers to student questions. Learners often face difficulties getting clarification on specific subject matters while learning is going

---

[55] https://www.ibm.com/watson
[56] https://www.knewton.com/
[57] https://khanacademy.org/

on. For example, ALEKS[58], an AI-based e-learning platform, uses adaptive questioning to determine what an employee knows and doesn't know. It then provides targeted instruction and guidance, ensuring that employees receive the support they need to succeed. Carnegie Learning[59] offers an AI-driven math learning platform that acts as a personal tutor, providing real-time feedback and guidance to students as they work through problems, ensuring they receive the support they need to succeed.

AI-based platforms can offer solutions by providing real-time answers to student questions. AI-driven solutions can answer learners' questions, recommend personalized resources, and grade papers. AI-powered Sherlock system has been used for several decades to teach Air Force technicians to diagnose electrical system problems in aircraft.

It can further assist students who need additional help. For instance, Microsoft Presentation Translator[60] translates real-time subtitles when a teacher speaks.

4. AI CONTENT PRACTICE

Another way AI can be used in e-learning is to create chatbot experiences for learners to practice real-time conversations. Language learning platforms like Duolingo[61] use NLP to create chatbot experiences, allowing language learners to practice their skills and gain confidence before interacting with a real person[62]. The chatbot also provides

---

[58] https://www.aleks.com/
[59] https://www.carnegielearning.com/solutions/math/mathia/
[60] https://www.microsoft.com/en-us/translator/education/
[61] https://www.duolingo.com/
[62] Learndash. 2020. 4 examples of Ai being Used In E-learning. https://www.learndash.com/4-examples-of-ai-being-used-in-e-learning/

immediate feedback, allowing learners to identify their mistakes and improve their skills.

As another example, Sana Labs[63], an AI-powered adaptive learning platform, adjusts the learning path for each employee based on their performance. The platform fetches the right information and knowledge from company repositories and uses it to create content, questions, or even entire courses with a few clicks. It generates explanations and images to let employee practices the concepts.

EMERGING WORKFORCE ANALYTICS

Analytics are the life and blood of e-learning and most corporate decisions. They can inform learning design as well as the implementation of e-learning platforms. As a CeLO, you need powerful analytics to design and strategize your e-learning programs. Analytics reveal powerful insights and gaps and guide the organization to take the right step to develop e-learning that can address specific business goals.

The real reason you as a CeLO need analytics is to measure, baseline, and then improve TTP of employees. On the surface, you might think you need only learning-related analytics. But in reality, if your goal is to shorten TTP, learning analytics can help you only so much. You need access to multiple analytics beyond your learning analytics.

Several analytics are now available to business leaders. Some examples are people analytics, Talent analytics, Human capital analytics, HR analytics, workforce analytics, and learning analytics. Many of these terms may have overlapping meanings. The names are often adopted by the supplier or vendor, even if the intent of the analytics is similar to

---

[63] https://www.sanalabs.com/

other analytics. Despite the differences among these terms, it sometimes becomes hard to draw boundaries. One common thing is that all of these involve the use of data analytics to better understand and manage human resources in organizations. The good news is that technologies are converging. We call the collection of these analytics 'workplace analytics,' as shown in Figure 12.2, which conveys the characteristics of the people as well as the characteristics of the work they do.

Figure 12.2: Various terms for workplace analytics

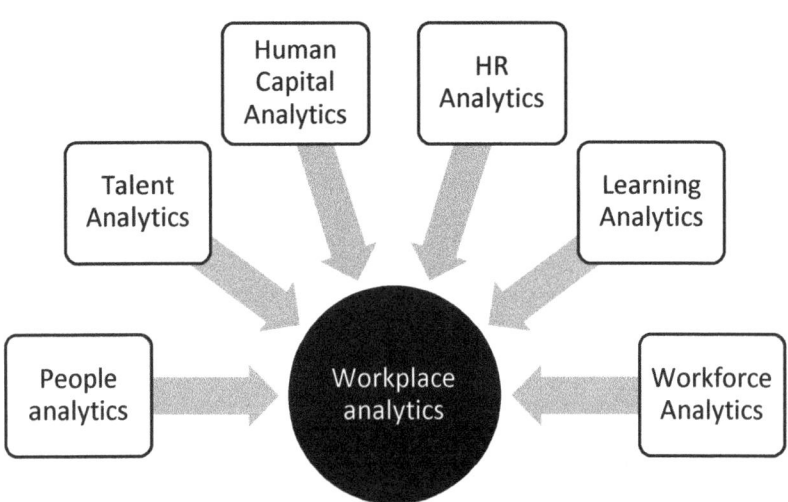

Out of such a vast spectrum of analytics, you need several of them to institute e-learning efforts to speed up employee development strategically. Not all analytics may fall under your purview or control. Thus, integrating information from diverse, incompatible analytics might be a big problem. To solve it, I recommend first looking at analytics in the context of the employee proficiency journey shown in Figure 3.2. Such a view helps you identify which data from those analytics is important to focus on TTP.

At each phase of the employee development journey, the analytics mentioned have some specific purpose. However, not all analytics are owned by the learning department. Most workplace analytics are procured and implemented by associated functional departments for a specific purpose or goal. Business units own some, some by HR department, some by finance, and some by IT.

As summarized in Table 12.1, you see that most of the data collected by traditional analytics, specifically by learning analytics, do not add much value to measuring or tracking TTP.

Table 12.1: Analytics at various phases of the employee development

Hiring stage	Onboarding and orientation stage	Training or coaching stage	On-the-job support stage	Proficiency stage
Education profiles	Dropout rate	Training records	OJT records	Customer sat scores
Diversity distribution	Time to orientation	Time in training	Mentor ratings	Customer calls
Age distribution	Manager's ratings	Performance in training	Time to certification	Revenue generated
Talent profiles	First 90-days performance	Trainer's scores	Field performance	Sales closures
Retention metrics	Compliance training records	Assessment scores	Skill assessment scores	Case resolutions
Time to hire trends	90-days skill assessments	Manager's ratings	Manager's ratings	Time to resolution
Compensation comparisons		Compliance scores	Performance ratings	Financials & expenses
Skill/experience analytics		Mentor ratings	Engagement metrics	
Service time		Training costs		
Average experience				

Education			
Service time			
Project experience			
Past achievements			
Past role history			
Diversity eligibility			
Potential ratings			
Past performance ratings			
Talent profiles			
Skill assessments			

Analytics at the Hiring Stage

Whether internal or external, some organizations have analytics that deals with talent distribution, experience profiles, recruitment sources, time to hire, and things like that. Some examples are listed in Table 12.1. The most relevant data to TTP is skill assessment, but it is not always complete enough to make conclusions.

Analytics at the Onboarding & Orientation Stage

We have some analytics on completing mandatory WBT or other compliance training data via LMSs Some examples are listed in Table 12.1. There is hardly any useful data captured at this stage to enable the acceleration of TTP.

Analytics at the Training or Coaching Stage

We have some learning analytics showing us training modules taken, skill profiles, skill gaps, and coach assessments. Some examples are listed in Table 12.1. Metrics like time in training, performance, assessment, and manager's ratings can be used to ascertain the speed of employee development.

Analytics at the On-the-job Support Stage

Some analytics analyze field folks' case activities, events, and performance. Some examples are listed in Table 12.1. Metrics like field performance, skill assessment, performance ratings, and time to certification can help you build the definition of proficiency and measure them across the job roles.

Analytics at the Proficiency Stage

We have some analytics that measure business KPIs across departments, regions, or even at the employee level. Some examples are listed in Table 12.1. This is the ultimate data you must have to establish key KPIs that denote proficiency, and then you need to track them to baseline TTP.

While these analytics play an important role in each functional unit, there is no clear-cut anchor on how these analytics enable the speed of employee development. For instance, learning analytics may include metrics on time to certification, and workforce analytics may have analytics on measuring time to productivity in the field.

Due to those silos, no analytics can measure speed as a universal metric across an organization. These functional boundaries also don't give us a common anchor to measure and increase employee development speed. If you can't tie off different analytics, you will have difficulty building a collective picture to understand whether you are going slow or fast. Hence, the decision on strategies to speed up employee development becomes more qualitative in nature than based on data.

We can't accelerate employee performance unless we measure that acceleration and quantifiably cut the time out of the equation. The strategic questions you need to focus on are: How do we integrate different workplace analytics to help in bringing employees up to speed quickly? How do we rope them together so that it tells us a single high-level picture?

One way is to look at three categories of work analytics, irrespective of which functional department owns it:

1. *Analytics for performer profiling*
2. *Analytics for proficiency metrics*
3. *Analytics for work skills*

The detailed discussion of these metrics is out of the scope of this book. I recommend you get a copy of my book *"Chief Learning Technologist"* to understand more about these analytics and learn how analytics are used strategically to develop the workforce faster.

CH 12 – EMERGING E-LEARNING REVOLUTIONS

THINKING AHEAD

Most e-learning strategists get swayed and bogged down by waves of evolutionary technologies and tools. They feel they are doing next-generational, revolutionary, and breakthrough work by introducing miraculous technologies in their organization. However, that chase doesn't let them shine beyond their job role.

Technology obsolesces is at an all-time high. The technology that is the town's talk today will either fade away tomorrow or become an inseparable part of an organizational workflow. Thus, as a Chief E-learning Officer, your race is with technologies and tools to stay ahead of it. Ensure you keep looking at applications and possibilities as and when new technologies or e-learning breakthroughs come to the market. Take your time to absorb the innovation. Give time for technologies to impact and establish themselves as direction-changing technology significantly. Otherwise, you will be in a race to keep replacing your ecosystem. Besides, incorporating new e-learning modes just to look cool or to look competitive in the market is not a good idea. You will end up burning corporate dollars.

The master plan to manage such volatility is to stay strategic. To build your career as a revolutionary Chief E-learning Officer, you must learn to become strategic. This book delivered five e-learning strategies that are likely to remain stable and relevant over a reasonably long period and are independent of the nature, lifespan, and evolution of various tools and technologies available at different times.

To take your career further, I recommend looking for my other books on closely related subjects: *Chief Learning Technologist in the Era of Speed* and *Chief Learning Officer in the Era of Speed*.

Reflections

CAREER ACCELERATION RESOURCES

LEARN FROM POWER-PACKED BOOKS

Accelerate your learning, training, and technology leadership with the following books. Check out **amazon.com/authors/raman.k.attri** to purchase these books.

CHIEF E-LEARNING OFFICER

Chief Learning Technology Officer in the Era of Speed

Written for senior learning technology leaders who want to shine as a CXO executive. The book describes five strategies to leverage current technologies to shorten time-to-proficiency and provides leaders with a framework to evaluate future technologies to impact employee development speed. You will walk out with an integrated system thinking about measuring, tracking, and reducing time-to-proficiency while integrating time-to-proficiency metrics as technology KPIs

Releasing June 2023.

Training Impact Measurement

Written for training leaders, this book provides a practical and intuitive model for measuring the effectiveness of technical training programs, addressing the challenges faced by technical training managers and other technical managers in justifying the return on investment for large-scale and investment-intensive training programs. The 4-tier Return on Expectations (ROE) framework presented in this book, developed through years of research, observation, and experience, aims to reduce technical business managers' pains while presenting and return on investment (ROI) of their training programs.

Releasing July 2023.

Iconic Chief Learning Officer

Written for visionary training and learning leaders to guide them through a breakthrough framework to become a globally recognized iconic chief learning officer. The book teaches the art and science of impactful corporate learning leadership above ad beyond your job and your organization. Learn the secrets of accelerating your career to unimaginable heights.

Releasing Dec 2023

Designing Training to Shorten Time to Proficiency

Written for training designers, this book delivers over 21 training and learning strategies across online learning, classroom instructions, and on-the-job learning that can enable designing workplace training programs to shorten the time to proficiency of employees. The book provides practical guidance for implementation to equip corporate learning

REFERENCES

specialists, HR professionals, training leaders, performance consultants, and direct managers. (Released)

ENROLL IN ONLINE TRAINING COURSES

Accelerate your learning, training, and technology leadership with the following powerful online courses. For more such courses, head out to **get-there-faster.com/courses**.

L&D Leader and Strategist: Your Learning Leadership Accelerated

The learning, training, and development space is overcrowded and highly competitive now. Establishing yourself as a distinguished L&D leader is not easy anymore. You need to adopt a specific thought process and proven strategies to speed up your path to becoming a top L&D leader with unique specialization, positioning, and credibility. In this online course, learn the science of accelerating the path to becoming a top-notch learning and training leader. Master strategies, methods, and frameworks to put yourself onto the world map at an accelerated rate.

Enroll at **get-there-faster.com/learning-leadership-course**

Speed Learner: Accelerated Learning Skill in the Era of Speed

Have you ever wished to learn anything faster in your profession or business? You get overwhelmed by a humongous amount of content, tasks, activities, and projects to master. You don't know where to start. The end result is that it takes you a long time, sometimes years, to master everything you have to do in your job. You tried all possible methods, but you did not see a difference in your learning speed. More often, professionals and leaders are at a loss to set the appropriate goals for their speedier learning and then achieve them at a faster rate. In this course, you will learn breakthrough insights on how to position your approaches to learn faster for professional goals and set yourself apart from your peers. In this course, you will learn how someone is viewed as a fast learner by most organizations. In this course, you will learn a breakthrough technique from Dr. Raman to accelerate your learning for professional success in your profession or job.

Enroll at **get-there-faster.com/speed-learning-course**

Training Designer: Learn Powerful e-learning Design Practices to Speed Up Learning

Do you need to design online/e-learning courses to speed up the skill acquisition of your learners? But you don't know where to start? The life-changing skills are delivered when you design online or e-learning courses systematically using instructional design practices using the latest and greatest strategies. In this training course, you will learn a new framework to think about your e-learning training design. You will walk out with proven, practical e-learning training design strategies from research used by some of the most advanced training organizations across the world. You will learn 3 key elements of e-learning design that you just pay attention to. You will learn 5 strategies to make your e-learning courses powerful. You will adopt a new viewpoint of implementing 5 guiding principles in your e-learning or online courses.

Enroll at **get-there-faster.com/elearning-design-course**

Strategize Technologies to Speed Up Employee Development

The speed with which teams are developed is far more critical now to meet the challenges of complex next-generation projects amidst a fast-paced business environment. Technologies are now the first line of defense to impact how employees learn, develop, and perform at the workplace. In this revolutionary course, you will receive first-hand research-based wisdom on an integrated system thinking on measuring, tracking, and reducing time to proficiency using analytics strategically. You will acquire a renewed business acumen of marrying two things - 'workforce analytics' and 'time-to-proficiency metrics'- to build a people analytics strategy that can ensure improving employee performance faster. You will learn how futuristic thinking organizations have leveraged state-of-the-art technologies, analytics, tools, and systems to shorten time to proficiency of the workforce and teams at the speed of business.

REFERENCES

Enroll at **get-there-faster.com/strategic-technologies-course**

Artificial Intelligence for Enterprise Learning

Are you an executive or enterprise leader looking to implement AI and ChatGPT in your organization? Look no further! In this FREE course, structured around real demos of 25 different elements of Ai and ChatGPT for corporate applications, you will be taken through the evolution of this breakthrough technology. You'll learn how AI and ChatGPT can revolutionize how your organization can design, develop and manage large-scale training programs, e-learning solutions, and knowledge management processes. You will also see how ChatGPT can assist in writing procedures and managing your entire corporate e-learning and knowledge management space chain. You will shake up your traditional thinking and open your mind about how you can take such a powerful tool to your upper management and shine as a visionary leader.

Enroll at **get-there-faster.com/enterprise-ai**

GET CERTIFIED IN THE SCIENCE OF SPEED

Supercharge your learning leadership career to new heights by getting certified through a master certification program. For more such certifications, head out to **get-there-faster.com/pathways**.

Xcelerated Learning Strategist Certification: Speed-Savvy Chief Learning Officer
---

Designed for learning and training specialists, training managers, L&D professionals, human resources executives, and coaches to help them shine as world-class, speed-savvy learning thought leaders. The certification is awarded through rigorous training and qualification to develop the participants as the world's top-notch experts on accelerated learning in organizational space. Based on two decades of research, experience, experimentation, and authoring, this certification is structured around 5 power-packed tracks to qualify ambitious learning specialists who want to become master the science of speed in learning, training, performance, and employee development.

To apply for acceptance to this certification, check out **get-there-faster.com/xcelerated-learning-guru-pathway.**

Xcelerated Training Design Guru Certification: **Speed Savvy Training Officer**

Designed for learning and training specialists, training professionals, trainers, instructional designers, speakers, coaches, and teachers, to help them shine as highly sought-after training design strategists. The certification is awarded through rigorous training and qualification to develop the participants as the world's top-notch experts in designing complex training and mentoring programs. If you need to equip your learners and audience with complex skills and improve their performance faster, then this advanced certification is for you. Based on two decades of research, experience, experimentations, and authoring, this certification is structured around 5 power-packed tracks to teach you the breakthrough, advanced, integrated methodologies for start-to-end analysis, design, development, and delivery of your training programs. Take your learning design to the next level by mastering the design of transformational coaching, mentoring, and certification programs.

To apply for acceptance to this certification, check out **get-there-faster.com/xcelerated-training-guru-pathway.**

POWERPACKED KEYNOTES TO YOUR EVENTS

Interested to book me for powerful, insightful, research-backed, revolutionary keynotes and talks that will change your executives's thinking process? Then head on to **get-there-faster.com/speaking** and book me for your next corporate event. Book me and learn the science of acceleration to stay ahead in business!

REFERENCES

REFERENCES

Arnold, V & Collier, P 2013, "Incase: simulating experience to accelerate expertise development by knowledge workers," *Intelligent Systems in Accounting and Financial Management*, vol. 20, no. 1, pp. 1–21, http://dx.doi.org/10.1002/isaf.

Attri, RK 2014, 'Rethinking professional skill development in competitive corporate world: accelerating time-to-expertise of employees at workplace', in J Latzo (ed.), *Proceedings of Conference on Education and Human Development in Asia*, Hiroshima, PRESDA Foundation, Kitanagova, pp. 1–11, http://dx.doi.org/10.13140/RG.2.1.5125.7043.

_____ 2018, 'Modelling accelerated proficiency in organisations: practices and strategies to shorten time-to-proficiency of the workforce', PhD thesis, Southern Cross University, Lismore, Australia.

_____ 2019, *Speed to Proficiency in Organizations: A Research Report on Model, Practices and Strategies to Shorten Time to Proficiency*, Speed To Proficiency Research, Singapore.

Attri, RK & Wu, W 2015, 'Conceptual model of workplace training and learning strategies to shorten time-to-proficiency in complex skills: preliminary findings', *9th International Conference on Researching in Work and Learning (RWL) Conference*, Singapore, Institute for Adult Learning, Singapore, viewed 24 June 2017, <http://www.rwl2015.com/papers/Paper100.pdf>.

ASTD 2014, *2014 State of the Industry*, ASTD, <https://www.td.org/Publications/Research-Reports/2014/2014-State-of-the-Industry?mktcops=c.learning-and-development\textasciitidlec.lt\textasciitidlec.sr-leader\textasciitidlec.learning-and-development>, viewed 24 June 2017.

Beckman, WS, 2013, The Effectiveness of Microsoft Flight Simulator as a Training Aid for Private Pilot Training and Proficiency. *17th International Symposium on Aviation Psychology*, pp. 38-43, viewed 4 Apr 2023, <https://corescholar.libraries.wright.edu/isap_2013/104>

Birnbaum, MS, Kornell, N, Bjork, EL & Bjork, R A 2013, "Why interleaving enhances inductive learning: the roles of discrimination and retrieval," *Memory & Cognition*, vol. 41, no. 3, pp. 392–402, http://dx.doi.org/10.3758/s13421-012-0272-7.

Bjork, RA 2013, Desirable difficulties perspective on learning, in H Pashler (ed.), *Encyclopedia of the mind*, SAGE, Thousand Oaks, pp. 243–245, http://dx.doi.org/10.4135/9781452257044.n88.

Bjork, RA & Linn, M 2006, "The science of learning and the learning of science: introducing desirable difficulties," *APS Observer*, vol. 19, no. 3, pp. 6–7, viewed 24 June 2017, <https://www.researchgate.net/profile/Robert_Bjork/publication/237420547>.

Bower, M, Dalgarno, B, Kennedy, GE, Lee, MJ & Kenney, J 2015, "Design and implementation factors in blended synchronous learning environments:

outcomes from a cross-case analysis," *Computers & Education*, vol. 86, no. 8, pp. 1-17, http://dx.doi.org/10.1016/j.compedu.2015.03.006.

Clark, RC & Mayer, RE 2011, *E-learning and the science of instruction: proven guidelines for consumers and designers of multimedia learning*, 3rd edn, Jossey-Bass, San Francisco, http://dx.doi.org/10.1002/9781118255971.

_____ 2013, *Scenario-based e-learning: evidence-based guidelines for online workforce learning*, Pfeiffer, San Francisco.

Cooper, S., Khatib, F., Treuille, A. et al., 2010, "Predicting protein structures with a multiplayer online game," *Nature*, vol. 466, pp. 756–760, https://doi.org/10.1038/nature09304.

Deloitte 2017, *2017 Deloitte Global Human Capital Trends*, Deloitte University Press, viewed 24 June 2017, <https://www2.deloitte.com/us/en/pages/human-capital/articles/introduction-human-capital-trends.html>.

DiBello, L, Missildine, W & Struttman, M 2009, "Intuitive expertise and empowerment: the long-term impact of simulation training on changing accountabilities in a biotech firm," *Mind, Culture, and Activity*, vol. 16, no. 1, pp. 11–31, http://dx.doi.org/10.1080/10749030802363863.

Dirkx, JM 2001, "The power of feelings: emotion, imagination, and the construction of meaning in adult learning," *New Directions for Adult and Continuing Education*, vol. 2001, no. 89, pp. 63–72.

Dror, IE, Schmidt, P & O'connor, L 2011, "A cognitive perspective on technology enhanced learning in medical training: great opportunities, pitfalls and challenges," *Medical Teacher*, vol. 33, no. 4, pp. 291–6, http://dx.doi.org/10.3109/0142159X.2011.550970.

Eades, J 2014, "Why microlearning is huge and how to be a part of it," viewed 24 June 2018, <http://elearningindustry. com/why-microlearning-is-huge>.

Fadde, PJ & Klein, G 2010, "Deliberate performance: accelerating expertise in natural settings," *Performance Improvement*, vol. 49, no. 9, pp. 5–14, http://dx.doi.org/10.1002/pfi.

_____ 2012, "Accelerating expertise using action learning activities," *Cognitive Technology*, vol. 17, no. 1, pp. 11–18, viewed 24 June 2017, <http://peterfadde.com/Research/cognitivetechnology12.pdf>.

Fred, CL 2002, *Breakaway: deliver value to your customers-fast!*, Jossey-Bass, San Francisco, viewed 24 June 2017, <http://www.wiley.com/WileyCDA/WileyTitle/productCd-0787961647.html>.

Gott, SP & Lesgold, AM 2000, Competence in the workplace: how cognitive performance models and situated instruction can accelerate skill acquisition, in R Glaser (ed.), *Advances in instructional psychology: Educational design and cognitive science, Vol. 5*, Lawrence Erlbaum, Mahwah, pp. 239–327.

REFERENCES

Grovo 2014, "Bite size is the right size: how microlearning shrinks the skills gap," *TechKnowledge 2015*, p. 2105, viewed 24 June 2017, <http://a1.grovo.com/asset/whitepapers/Grovo-BiteSize-Microlearning-whitepaper.pdf>.

Hays, RT, Jacobs, JW, Prince, C, Salas, E, 1992, Flight Simulator Training Effectiveness: A Meta-Analysis, *Military Psychology*, vol 4, no. 2, pp. 63-74, http://dx.doi.org/ 10.1207/s15327876mp0402_1.

Higgins, N 2015, *Gamification: Accelerating Learning*, KBR Kellogg Brown and Root Pty Ltd, Kingston, ACT, Australia.

Hinterberger, H 2011, "Problem-based e-learning in practice: digital laboratories provide pathways from e-science to high schools," in C Ho and M Lin (eds.), *Proceedings of World Conference on E-Learning in Corporate, Government, Healthcare, and Higher Education*, 18 October, Association for the Advancement of Computing in Education (AACE), Chesapeake, pp. 1947–1954, viewed 24 June 2017, < http://www.editlib.org/p/39013/>.

Hug, T 2015, Microlearning and mobile learning, in Z Yan (ed.), *Encyclopedia of Mobile Phone Behavior*, IGI Global, Hersey, pp. 490–505, http://dx.doi.org/10.4018/978-1-4666-8239-9.ch041.

Hug, T, Lindner, M & Bruck, PA (eds) 2006, *Micromedia & E-Learning 2.0: Gaining the Big Picture: Proceedings of Microlearning Conference 2006*, Innsbruck, 25-27 June, Innsbruck University Press, Innsbruck, Austria, viewed 24 June 2017, <https://www.uibk.ac.at/iup/buch_pdfs/microlearning2006-druck.pdf>.

Hutchins, E & Palen, L 1997, Constructing meaning from space, gesture, and speech, in *Discourse, tools and reasoning*, Springer, Berlin, pp. 23–40, viewed 24 October 2018, <http://citeseerx.ist.psu.edu/viewdoc/download?doi=10.1.1.161.1357&rep=rep1&type=pdf>.

Jones, SM, Katyal, P, Xie, X, Nicolas, MP, Leung, EM, Noland, DM, & Montclare, JK, 2019, A 'KAHOOT!' Approach: The Effectiveness of Game-Based Learning for an Advanced Placement Biology Class. *Simulation & Gaming*, vol. 50, no. 6, pp. 832–847. https://doi.org/10.1177/1046878119882048.

Kahiigi Kigozi, E, Ekenberg, L, Hansson, H, Tusubira, F & Danielson, M 2008, "Exploring the e-learning state of art," *Electronic Journal of E-Learning*, vol. 6, no. 2, pp. 77–88, viewed <http://www.diva-portal.org/smash/record.jsf?pid=diva2:185115>.

Karoly, LA 2007, *Forces Shaping the Future Us Workforce and Workplace: Implications for 21st Century Work*, Report No. CT-273, Rand Corporation, Santa Monica, viewed 24 June 2017, <http://www.rand.org/content/dam/rand/pubs/testimonies/2007/RAND_CT273.pdf>

Klein, GA, Hintze, N & Saab, D 2013, "Thinking inside the box: the shadowbox method for cognitive skill development," in H Chaudet, L Pellegrin & N Bonnardel (eds.), *Proceedings of the 11th International Conference on Naturalistic Decision Making*, Marseille, 21-24 May, Aepege Science Publishing, Paris, pp. 121–124, viewed 24 June 2017, <http://arpege-recherche.org/ndm11/papers/ndm11-121.pdf>.

Lingg, D 2014, "Bite-size learning marks the road to workforce efficiency," *MHD Supply Chain Solutions*, vol. 44, no. 5, pp. 1–12, viewed 24 June 2017, <http://search.informit.com.au/documentSummary;dn=740763588509945;res=IELENG>.

Mayer, RE & Moreno, R 2003, "Nine ways to reduce cognitive load in multimedia learning," *Educational Psychologist*, vol. 38, no. 1, pp. 43–52, http://dx.doi.org/10.1207/S15326985EP3801_6.

Michelle, E, 2023, "Use of AI in eLearning," *Elearning Industry*. Viewed 5 Apr 2023, <https://elearningindustry.com/use-of-ai-in-elearning>.

Murtaza, M, Ahmed, Y, Shamsi, JA, Sherwani, F, Usman, M, 2022, "AI-based personalized e-learning systems: Issues, Challenges, and Solutions," *IEEE Access*, vol. 10, pp. 81323-81242, https://doi.dx.org/ 10.1109/ACCESS.2022.3193938.

Pappas, C 2013, "Top 10 e-learning statistics for 2014 you need to know," viewed 24 June 2017, <http://elearningindustry.com/top-10-e-learning-statistics-for-2014-you-need-to-know>.

Phillips, JK, Klein, G & Sieck, WR 2004, Expertise in judgment and decision making: a case for training intuitive decision skills, in D Koehler and N Harvey (eds.), *Blackwell handbook of judgment and decision making*, Blackwell, Malden, pp. 297–315, http://dx.doi.org/10.1002/9780470752937.ch15

RAND (2013). Does an Algebra Course with Tutoring Software Improve Student Learning? RAND Corporation, https://www.rand.org/pubs/research_briefs/RB9746.html

Roberto, MA, & Edmondson, AC, 2008, "Everest Leadership and Team Simulation." Simulation and Teaching Note. Harvard Business School Publishing, Boston. (Product number 2650), viewed 4 Apr 2023, < https://www.hbs.edu/faculty/Pages/item.aspx?num=31990>.

Rosenbaum, S & Williams, J 2004, *Learning paths: increase profits by reducing the time it takes employees to get up to speed*, Jossey-Bass, San Francisco, viewed 24 June 2017, <http://www.wiley.com/WileyCDA/WileyTitle/productCd-0787975346.html>.

Schuwirth, L 2013, "'emotions in learning' is more than merely 'learning of emotions,'" *Medical Education*, vol. 47, no. 1, pp. 3–17, http://dx.doi.org/10.1111/medu.12078.

Shen, L, Wang, M & Shen, R 2009, "Affective e-learning: using 'emotional' data to improve learning in pervasive learning environment related work and the pervasive e-learning platform," *Educational Technology & Society*, vol. 12, no. 2,

REFERENCES

pp. 176–189, viewed 24 June 2017, <http://www.ifets.info/journals/12_2/13.pdf>.

Sims, DE, Burke, CS, Metcalf, DS & Salas, E 2008, "Research-based guidelines for designing blended learning," *Ergonomics in Design: The Quarterly of Human Factors Applications*, vol. 16, no. 1, pp. 23–29, http://dx.doi.org/10.1518/106480408X282764.

Sitzmann, T 2010, "Game on? the effectiveness of game use in the workplace depends on context and design," *T+D*, vol. 20, p. 20, viewed 24 June 2017, <https://www.moresteam.com/whitepapers/download/sitzmann-games2010.pdf>.

Slootmaker, A, Kurvers, H, Hummel, H & Koper, R 2014, "Developing scenario-based serious games for complex cognitive skills acquisition: design, development and evaluation of the emergo platform," *Journal of Universal Computer Science*, vol. 20, no. 4, pp. 561–582, http://dx.doi.org/10.3217/jucs-020-04-0561.

Trigwell, K, Ellis, R a & Han, F 2012, "Relations between students' approaches to learning, experienced emotions and outcomes of learning," *Studies in Higher Education*, vol. 37, no. 7, pp. 811–824, http://dx.doi.org/10.1080/03075079.2010.549220.

Tuomi, I, 2018, "The Impact of Artificial Intelligence on Learning, Teaching, and Education," *Policies for the future*, Eds. Cabrera, M., Vuorikari, R & Punie, Y., EUR 29442 EN, Publications Office of the European Union, Luxembourg, https://doi.dx.org/10.2760/12297.

Van der Meer, J, Berg, D, Smith, J, Gunn, A & Anakin, M 2015, "Shorter is better: findings of a bite-size mobile learning™ pilot project," *Creative Education*, vol. 6, no. 3, pp. 273–282, http://dx.doi.org/10.4236/ce.2015.63026.

Värlander, S 2008, "The role of students' emotions in formal feedback situations," *Teaching in Higher Education*, vol. 13, no. 2, pp. 145–156, http://dx.doi.org/10.1080/13562510801923195.

Whitney, SJ, Tembym P, Stephens, A, 2013, "Evaluating the Effectiveness of Game-Based Training: A Controlled Study with Dismounted Infantry Teams," AR-015-508, Defence Science and Technology Organization, Australia, viewed 4 Apr 2023, < https://apps.dtic.mil/sti/pdfs/ADA585731.pdf>.

Wulf, G & Shea, CH 2002, "Principles derived from the study of simple skills do not generalize to complex skill learning," *Psychonomic Bulletin & Review*, vol. 9, no. 2, pp. 185–211, http://dx.doi.org/10.3758/BF03196276.

Zhang, D 2005, "Interactive multimedia-based e-learning: a study of effectiveness," *The American Journal of Distance Education*, vol. 19, no. 3, pp. 149–162, http://dx.doi.org/10.1207/s15389286ajde1903_3

Zhang, Q, Yu, L, Yu, Z, 2021, "A Content Analysis and Meta-Analysis on the Effects of Classcraft on Gamification Learning Experiences in terms of Learning

Achievement and Motivation," *Education Research International*, vol. 2021, Article ID 9429112, https://doi.org/10.1155/2021/9429112

INDEX

INDEX

A

abilities 28, 30, 39, 48, 56, 61, 73, 124, 147, 197, 204, 232, 256, 294
accelerate 5, 24, 26, 28, 32, 40, 44, 58-60, 73-74, 77, 83-85, 89, 99-100, 102, 107, 113-14, 116-18, 121-22, 128-29, 133, 135, 137, 139, 147, 151-52, 154, 156-57, 160, 167, 169, 171-72, 174-75, 177, 179, 181-82, 202, 204, 207-8, 210, 213, 215, 225, 227, 232, 235, 237, 240, 244, 249-53, 256-58, 266, 292, 294, 299, 310, 321
   accelerate expertise 28, 113
   accelerate learning 59, 147, 232, 252, 257
   accelerate proficiency 28, 99, 113, 117, 121, 204, 253, 292
   accelerate skill 99, 208, 227, 294
   accelerate speed-to-proficiency 151
   accelerate TTP 85, 172, 225
acceleration 97, 127, 151, 169, 173, 209, 228, 235, 256, 258, 308, 310
accomplished 134, 173, 210, 281
accomplishment-based 296
accomplishments 153, 176, 179, 182, 214, 278, 296-97
achievement 124, 129, 150, 308
acquisition 5-6, 15, 28, 32, 99, 103, 115, 117, 127, 169, 208, 219, 228, 232, 250, 255, 258, 263, 265-66, 294
   acquisition journey 263, 265
active 114-15, 117-18, 129, 132, 153, 176-77, 226, 263, 273-74, 276
adaptability 25, 65
adaptable 50
adaptive 21, 29, 39, 169, 172-73, 176, 179, 181, 214, 236, 258, 274, 278, 290, 300, 303-5
   adaptive LMS 290
AI 20, 23-24, 39, 50, 173, 197-98, 233, 300-304

AI-based 192, 197-98, 211, 215, 274, 280, 300, 303-4
   AI-based e-learning 198, 300, 303-4
   AI-based e-learning developments 198
   AI-based e-learning platform 303-4
   AI-based platforms 304
   AI-based search 192, 197, 211, 274
   AI-based search engine 192, 197, 211, 274
   AI-based workflow 215, 280
AI-driven 195, 300, 302-4
   AI-driven content 302
   AI-driven content generation 302
   AI-driven data 195
   AI-driven data insights 195
   AI-driven e-learning 300
   AI-driven solutions 303-4
AI-enabled 302
   AI-enabled e-learning 302
AI-generated 302
   AI-generated automated presentation 302
   AI-generated onboarding videos 302
   AI-generated video 302
AI-powered 23-24, 173, 198, 301-2, 304-5
   AI-powered adaptive learning 305
   AI-powered chatbot 198, 302
   AI-powered chatbots 23-24
   AI-powered content 301
   AI-powered content creation 301
   AI-powered e-learning 302
   AI-powered e-learning tools 302
   AI-powered platform 301
   AI-powered sherlock system 304
   AI-powered system 173
algorithms 21, 191, 215, 258, 280, 290, 302
analysis 56-57, 129, 182, 195-96, 250-51, 273
analyst 120, 171, 202, 251
analytical 48, 230-31

analytics 21, 30, 57, 126–27, 173, 182, 195–96, 215, 230, 237, 280, 291, 305–10
analyze 30, 39, 46, 48, 53, 57, 63, 113, 131–32, 182, 196, 215, 229–30, 237, 265, 301–3, 309
   analyze a real-life scenario 113
   analyze data 30, 48, 57, 63, 196
   analyze data on e-learning 57
   analyze employees' skills 303
   analyze the learner's performance 301
   analyze the problem 131
API 198
applicability 52, 59, 117, 147, 210, 230
application 16, 47, 155, 178, 191, 196–98, 204–6, 262, 266, 291–92, 300–301, 311
AR 9, 11, 13, 16–17, 22–24, 125–26, 136, 158, 198–202, 207, 211, 215, 232–33, 239–40, 254, 264, 277–78, 280, 290, 292
   AR-based 192, 199
artifacts 129, 135, 158, 179, 216, 239, 273, 279
artificial intelligence 20
   artificial intelligence 20
assessment 9–10, 13, 18, 20, 24, 55, 64, 124, 129–30, 132, 136, 152, 157–58, 172, 176–77, 179, 181, 201, 216, 226, 231–32, 236, 239, 273–77, 279–80, 291, 299–301, 307–9
assignment 8, 13, 17–18, 135, 151, 158, 167, 169–70, 178–79, 213, 216, 227, 238–39, 259, 264–65, 276
asynchronous 8, 208, 214, 278
attrition 81–82
audience 45, 146
augmented 9, 199–200, 207
   augmented expert systems 207
   augmented reality 9
   augmented screen 200
   augmented screens 200

B

baseline 77, 88–89, 181, 305, 309
   baseline TTP 309
behavior 60, 207, 230, 237, 294
   behavior-based 229, 237
benefit 32, 48, 50, 52, 56, 61, 63, 84–87, 150, 255, 289
bi-directional 99
bite-size 23, 25, 145, 147, 149, 156, 208
   bite-size learning 145
   bite-size modules 147, 156
Blackboard 13, 19, 290
blueprint 251
businesses 5–6, 20, 39–41, 43–44, 48, 51–52, 55–56, 58, 60, 64, 73–75, 79, 81–87, 101, 103, 119, 121–23, 137, 171, 175, 194–97, 202–3, 252, 297–98, 305, 307, 309, 321
business-relevant 183

C

capability 40, 51, 83, 196, 204, 207, 239, 277
capital-intensive 29, 54, 67
career 44, 65, 311
case-based 113, 172, 202
   case-based contextualized approach 172
   case-based curriculum 113
   case-based e-learning 202
cases 78–79, 101, 113, 115–16, 119–20, 127–28, 132, 137, 169, 172, 174, 202, 225, 251, 263, 273, 275, 292
case-study-based 131, 275
case-study-based lectures 131, 275
certification 174, 183, 307, 309
certified 174
CeLO 29, 34, 41–47, 49–51, 53, 55–58, 60–61, 65, 67, 87, 91, 105, 281, 283, 305
CFOs 29

INDEX

challenging 7, 9, 52, 56–57, 60, 114, 118, 158, 182
    challenging interactions 118
    challenging to build 60
    challenging to compare 57
    challenging to implement 52
chatbots 23–24, 192, 197–98, 300, 302, 304
ChatGPT 300–301
chunk 98, 101–2, 149, 151
chunking 145, 148, 160
chunks 98, 102–3, 139, 145, 148–51, 162, 204, 211, 251, 264–65, 274
classes 298
classroom 5–6, 16, 24, 28, 121–22, 125, 127, 225–26, 251, 265, 289–91
    classroom experiences 290
    classroom instruction 121
    classroom learning 28
    classroom material 127
    classroom settings 251
    classroom training 5, 122, 251, 265
    classroom training design 265
    classroom trend 16
classroom-based 19, 259–60, 262
    classroom-based learning 19
    classroom-based training 259–60
CLO 46–47, 67
closed-loop 99
cloud-based 195–97, 207
cloud-hosted 39
coach 11, 134, 156, 207–8, 214, 241, 277–78, 280, 292, 294, 309
Coach-driven 11
coaching 10, 13, 17–18, 74, 129, 180, 192, 207–9, 214, 226, 232–33, 238, 240–42, 250, 278, 280, 291–92, 307, 309
cognitively complex learning 113
cognitive skills 26–27, 73, 117, 123, 150, 173
collaboration 20, 25, 49, 52, 63, 124, 132, 194–95, 293, 295–96, 298–99
    collaboration function 296

collaboration platforms 293, 299
collaboration skills 25
collaboration technologies 194–95, 296
collaboration tools 194, 296
collaborative 19, 25–26, 207, 225
    collaborative learning 19, 25–26
    collaborative learning activities 25
    collaborative technologies 225
    collaborative troubleshooting 207
collectively 81, 172, 176, 181, 234
communicators 194–95, 240, 278, 293, 295–96, 299–300
community 25, 208, 293, 295–98
competition 40, 43, 61, 82–83, 321
competitive 32, 42–43, 59, 61, 81, 85, 89, 91, 105, 124, 281, 311
    competitive advantages 85
    competitive benefits 32
    competitive edge 59, 81, 281
    competitive e-learning 43
    competitive e-learning initiatives 43
    competitive forces 85
    competitive metrics 105
    competitive weapon 85, 91
    competitive workforce 89
competitiveness 34, 60, 67, 79–82, 85–86, 105
competitors 59, 249
complex 9–11, 13, 17, 24, 26–28, 34, 39, 49, 56–57, 60, 73, 82, 103, 113, 117–18, 121–23, 125–26, 131, 150–51, 168, 171, 178, 180, 199, 202–3, 217, 227–28, 233, 238, 249, 255, 275, 294, 300
    complex cognitive skills 26–27, 73, 117, 123
    complex decision-making 202
    complex decisions 255
    complex hands-on skills 203
    complex knowledge 121
    complex learning 113
    complex next-generation projects 60, 73
    complex organizational structures 49

complex phenomena 125
complex procedures 126
complex scenarios 249
complex skill 28, 117–18, 150–51
complex skill acquisition 117
complex skill learning 28
complex skills 26–28, 73, 82, 103, 113, 118, 122–23, 178, 217, 227, 238, 294
complex tasks 24, 180, 199, 233, 300
complex thinking 9, 13, 228
complex thinking activities 9
complex thinking-based skills 9, 17
complex thinking skills 9, 13, 228
complex workflows 126
complexity 29, 56, 73, 81, 83, 130, 147, 156, 171–72, 175, 179, 182, 227, 251
complex jobs 11, 168, 228
computer-based 16, 19, 119–22
  computer-based scenarios 120–21
  computer-based simulated games 121
  computer-based simulator 122
  computer-based training 19
conferencing 22, 226
connection 20, 280, 294–95
connectivity 133, 135, 155, 158, 178, 213, 239–40, 276, 279, 294, 296, 298
content 7–14, 16–18, 20, 23, 28, 30, 35, 47, 57, 69, 93, 97–98, 102–4, 109, 113, 119, 127–29, 131–32, 134, 137, 141, 145–53, 155–57, 159–63, 173, 176–78, 185, 187, 191–92, 203–4, 206, 211–12, 221, 226–29, 231–38, 240, 245, 251–52, 256–57, 259, 262–64, 266, 269, 273–75, 279–80, 282, 285, 290–92, 297, 300–303, 305
content creation 300–301
content delivery 7, 11–12, 17, 204, 234
content design 97, 232
content development 302
content download 266
content generation 302
content management 204

content on-the-go 157
content practice 301
content research 145
content taxonomies 297
content to learn 231
content to master 231, 238
content to produce 129
content-focused 256, 291
content-heavy 203, 257
content management systems 204
context 7, 21, 79, 83, 113–14, 131–32, 134, 146–47, 156–57, 167–68, 191, 197–98, 206, 210, 212, 256, 260, 265–66, 274, 277, 281, 293, 297, 301, 306
context-based 197
context-light 257
context-sensitive 205
context-sensitive-help 206
contextual 18, 192, 199, 205–6, 211, 266
contextualization 97–98, 113–14, 117–18, 127, 137, 151, 263, 273, 275, 277, 279, 282
contextualize 98, 113, 119, 128–29, 133, 135, 172, 260, 265
corporate 26, 41, 47, 51, 73, 197, 211, 226, 299, 305, 311
  corporate challenge 26
  corporate culture 299
  corporate decisions 305
  corporate innovation 51
  corporate learning 47, 226
  corporate repositories 197, 211
  corporate training 41, 73
corporation 5, 22, 150, 202
cost-effective 6, 39, 44, 74
  cost-effective e-learning 39, 44
  cost-effective solutions 6
cost-effectiveness 58
cost-efficiency 83
Cost-related 84
  cost-related drivers 84

INDEX

courses 11, 17, 19–20, 25, 27, 30, 86, 107, 139, 167, 201, 204, 275, 289, 301, 303, 305
criteria-driven 169, 181
cross-functional 39, 52
cross-functional collaboration 52
curriculum 113, 119, 173, 211, 226, 274, 302
cutting-edge 45, 321

D

dashboard-based 195
dashboard-based analytics 195
dashboards 196, 231
data 21, 30, 39, 46, 48, 53, 57–58, 60, 63, 80, 173, 181–82, 195–97, 211, 230–31, 237, 262, 297, 301–2, 306–10
    data analysis 195
    data analytics 21, 57, 173, 230, 237, 306
    data insights 195, 197, 211
    data related 30
    data security 39
    data visualization 195–96
database 196–97, 207, 251, 297
data collection 57
day-to-day 113
decision 43, 46, 51, 53, 114, 122, 132, 191, 195–97, 211, 251, 255, 274, 305, 309
decision-making 26, 30, 103, 120, 122–23, 191, 202, 205
    decision-making in a simulated business 122
    decision-making skills 103, 122
    decision-making skills in real-world situations 122
    decision-making software 191
decision-support 11, 192, 195, 197, 202, 211, 240, 251, 274, 278
    decision-support software 192, 197, 202, 211

decision-support systems 195, 240, 251, 274, 278
decision-tree 290
deficiencies 81–84
Deficiency-Related 83
deliberate 76, 114, 167
    deliberate difficulties 114
    deliberate efforts 76
deliverables 74, 129–30, 132, 135, 153, 158, 179, 216, 239, 255, 273, 277, 279
demand 26, 29, 47, 83, 133, 155
demand-analysis 45
demonstrate 49, 56, 60–61, 75, 78, 116, 119, 169, 177, 198, 202, 226, 239, 251, 277, 281
    demonstrate capability 239, 277
    demonstrate competence 78
    demonstrate the active involvement 177
    demonstrate the vast potential 202
    demonstrate your commitment 281
designing 5, 16, 113, 115, 127–29, 133, 137, 139, 147, 149, 151–52, 154, 156–57, 169, 174–75, 177, 179, 181, 212, 234, 249–50, 252, 254, 257, 262
    designing and delivering online learning 234
    designing a sequence of cases 115
    designing a training course 257
    designing contextualization 127
    designing contextualization for acceleration 127
    designing contextualized self-guided e-learning 128
    designing e-learning 5, 16, 113, 147, 249–50
    designing e-learning to speed up 16
    designing microlearning 151, 157
    designing programs 147
    designing scenarios 139, 252
    designing training 212, 257
development 5, 16, 19–21, 23–24, 26, 30, 32, 35, 39–47, 50–51, 55, 58–63, 67,

69, 73–75, 77, 79–81, 83, 85, 87–89, 91, 93, 97, 105, 109, 121, 128–29, 133, 135, 141, 145, 152, 154, 156–57, 163, 174–75, 177, 179, 181, 187, 198, 210, 213, 215–16, 221, 235, 237, 240, 244–45, 249, 260, 262, 269, 279, 281, 285, 289–91, 300, 302, 306–7, 309–10, 321
development costs 145
development journey 75, 289, 307
development journeys 321
development of proficiency 73
development opportunities 30
development path 175
development professionals 42
development programs 46, 88
development speed 40, 62, 91, 145, 309
development strategies 281
development strategy 46
device 20, 25, 124, 157, 201, 209, 228, 251, 280, 293
differentiated 39, 47, 65, 105
   differentiated career 65
   differentiated CeLO 47, 105
   differentiated chief e-learning leader 65
differentiator 73
direction-changing 311
directories 207–8, 214, 278, 293, 295–96
disruptions 29
distinguished 321
distribute 14, 129, 150, 153, 162, 195, 212, 251, 259–60, 264–65, 273–74, 292
distribution 307–8
distribution ratings 307
documentation 11, 180, 197–98, 206, 211, 215, 240, 278
documentation repositories 11, 198, 240, 278
documents 12, 134–35, 157–58, 195, 204–6, 211–12, 279
drivers 79, 81–84, 146
duolingo 21, 120, 145–46, 304
dynamically 173, 176, 181, 274

E

easy-to-implement 192
ecosystem 73, 124, 191, 234–35, 255, 264, 275, 283, 311, 321
education 6, 19, 21–24, 26, 29, 80, 117, 125, 200–201, 292, 300, 304, 307–8
education delivery 29
education industry 292
education institutions 19
education service 308
education system 117
effectiveness 6, 26, 46, 48, 50, 56–60, 63, 78, 99, 116, 146, 151, 234, 236, 249, 300, 303
effectiveness scores 57
efficiency 6, 58–60, 87, 195, 202, 206, 249, 300
efficiency and productivity 202
efficiency improvement 60
efficiency of e-learning 300
e-learning 5–35, 39–65, 67, 69, 73–75, 77, 79, 81, 83, 85, 87, 89, 91, 93, 97–103, 105, 107, 109, 113–19, 121–25, 127–29, 131–33, 135, 137, 139, 141, 145, 147–48, 150–51, 157, 160, 162–63, 167, 169–75, 177–83, 185, 187, 191, 198, 202, 209–10, 213–15, 217, 221, 225–28, 230, 235–37, 239, 241–45, 249–67, 269, 273–83, 285, 289, 291, 293–95, 297, 299–307, 309, 311, 321
e-learning channel 17, 102–3
e-learning chunking 148
e-learning classification 7
e-learning content 8–9, 11, 13–14, 18, 30, 47, 57, 157, 160, 263, 301
e-learning contextualization 273, 275, 277, 279
e-learning delivery 11–12, 17
e-learning design 28
e-learning designers 115, 209, 226, 289, 321

INDEX

e-learning development 32
e-learning experiences 23, 44, 50, 321
e-learning expertise 51, 65
e-learning format 127, 242
e-learning goals 54
e-learning guidelines 273, 275, 277, 279, 281, 283
e-learning implementation 58, 91
e-learning industry 20, 23–24, 39, 41
e-learning initiative 34, 43, 46, 48, 50–53, 56–57, 63, 67, 89, 105
e-learning innovations 53
e-learning journey 226
e-learning leader 60–61, 65, 249
e-learning leadership 49
e-learning learning 8, 98
e-learning market 5–6
e-learning model 260
e-learning modes 311
e-learning modules 13, 167, 169, 171, 227
e-learning packages 137, 259
e-learning path 35, 69, 93, 97, 103, 109, 141, 150, 163, 167, 169–75, 177–83, 185, 187, 210, 214–15, 221, 227, 236, 245, 251, 259, 269, 274, 276, 278, 280, 282, 285
e-learning philosophy 217
e-learning platform 19, 25, 242, 294, 302–5
e-learning professionals 44–45, 54, 59
e-learning program 5–6, 30–31, 43–48, 52, 58–60, 62–64, 67, 74, 97, 105, 107, 151, 228, 230, 256–57, 305
e-learning projects 48, 63
e-learning resources 13, 202
e-learning results 5
e-learning revolutions 35, 69, 93, 109, 141, 163, 187, 221, 245, 269, 285, 289, 291, 293, 295, 297, 299, 301, 303, 305, 307, 309, 311
e-learning scores 6
e-learning self-paced 17

e-learning sessions 117, 151
e-learning solutions 27, 44, 49, 258
e-learning strategies 34, 41–42, 44–45, 47, 50, 59, 97–98, 105, 121, 253, 257, 273, 311, 321
e-learning strategist 16, 29, 35, 39, 41–43, 45, 47, 49, 51, 53, 55, 57, 59, 61, 63, 65, 67, 69, 93, 109, 141, 163, 174, 187, 191, 198, 210, 217, 221, 245, 256, 269, 285, 311, 321
e-learning strategists 40, 57, 59, 127, 151, 174, 209, 235, 257, 311, 321
e-learning strategy 39, 45, 55, 64, 103, 122, 217, 254
e-learning system 35, 69, 93, 109, 141, 163, 172, 187, 202, 221, 235, 237, 239, 241, 243, 245, 249, 251, 253, 255, 257, 259, 261, 263, 265, 267, 269, 285, 294
e-learning technologies 28–29, 41, 44, 47–49, 51, 54, 56, 61, 63, 65, 67, 226
e-learning technologists 42, 58
e-learning tool 19, 30, 124, 300, 302–3
e-learning trends 45, 64, 119
e-learning tutor 301
e-learning-based 227, 249
e-learning KPIs 35, 69, 73, 75, 77, 79, 81, 83, 85, 87, 89, 91, 93, 109, 141, 163, 187, 221, 245, 269, 285
emotional 101, 114–18, 126, 130, 147, 228, 256, 260, 263–64, 266, 275
employee 5, 11, 16, 26–27, 32, 35, 39–41, 43–46, 51, 55, 58–62, 67, 69, 73–79, 81–89, 91, 93, 97–98, 105, 107, 109, 113–14, 116, 120, 123–26, 128–29, 133–37, 139, 141, 152, 154, 156–58, 163, 173–75, 177, 179–82, 187, 191–92, 196–200, 203, 205–15, 217, 221, 227, 230, 233–35, 237, 240, 242, 244–45, 249, 255–56, 264–65, 269, 273–74, 277–78, 280–81, 285, 289–92, 295–99, 303–7, 309–10, 321
employee competitiveness 79

337

employee development 5, 16, 26, 35, 40, 43–45, 55, 58–62, 67, 69, 73–75, 77, 79, 81, 83, 85, 87–89, 91, 93, 97, 105, 109, 128–29, 133, 135, 141, 152, 154, 156–57, 163, 174–75, 177, 179, 181, 187, 210, 213, 215, 221, 235, 237, 240, 244–45, 249, 269, 285, 289–91, 306–7, 309–10, 321
employee development journeys 321
employee development programs 88
employee development speed 40, 62, 91, 309
employee engagement 39, 295
employee growth 321
employee learning 41, 44, 61, 89, 126
employee learning curve 44
employee level 309
employee onboarding 199
employee performance 32, 60, 77, 107, 139, 197, 208, 214, 310
employee practices 305
employee proficiency 175, 215, 273, 280, 306
employee proficiency development 175
employee proficiency journey 273, 306
employee progress 203
employee retention 44
employee speed 291
employee training 44
engagement 25, 39, 41–42, 44, 125, 145, 292, 295, 300, 302, 307
engineering 23–24, 79, 119
engineering education 24
enrichment 233
enterprise 195, 208
enterprise systems 195
environment 9, 23–25, 60, 73, 83, 113, 120–22, 126, 129, 199, 201, 294, 298
EPSS (see: PSS)
equipment 24, 119, 199, 201, 207, 232, 292

equipment maintenance 119
equipment repair 207
evaluation 46, 48, 50, 54–55, 63, 237, 296
evaluation criteria 46
expectations 83, 86, 130
experience-building 79
experience-rich 35, 69, 93, 98, 102, 109, 141, 163, 187, 213, 219, 221, 225, 227, 229, 231, 233–34, 238, 242, 244–45, 260, 264, 266, 269, 275, 277, 279–80, 283, 285
experiences 9, 19, 21, 23–24, 44, 50, 120, 139, 169, 198, 202, 214, 250, 260, 264, 274, 278, 280, 290, 292–94, 296, 300, 303–4, 321
experiences for individual 21
experimentation 31–32, 55, 146
expert 11, 26, 44, 78, 82, 85, 120, 129, 153, 176, 195, 201–2, 207–9, 214, 233, 240, 251, 274, 278–79, 292–97, 321
expertise 28, 47–48, 51–52, 65, 78, 80, 113, 116, 122, 202, 207–8, 296–97
expertise locator 297
expertise taxonomy 296

F

fabricated 113, 123, 131
fabricated cases 113
face-to-face 6, 27–28, 73, 117, 150, 195, 257, 259
face-to-face courses 27
face-to-face instructor-led 73
face-to-face instructor-led and on-the-job 73
face-to-face lectures 27
face-to-face lectures or presentations 27
face-to-face meetings 195
face-to-face or classroom-based training 259
face-to-face settings 27, 117, 150

INDEX

face-to-face training 6, 150, 257
facilitation 8, 17, 238, 250
facilitators 23
factors 5, 7, 60, 81–82, 256
failure 31, 114, 117–19, 129–30, 250, 273
faster 9, 27–28, 40, 50, 58–59, 61, 82–86, 127, 162, 171, 180, 191–92, 198–99, 209, 228, 230–31, 234, 249, 256, 263–64, 291–92, 301, 310
fast-paced 25, 29, 42, 53, 60, 73, 87, 91, 321
financial 32, 54, 80–82, 84–85, 116, 120, 202, 205, 251
firefighters 84, 123, 127
forecasts 24
frequent 171
function 40–41, 79–80, 173, 296
function-driven 194

G

gadgets 127, 136, 158, 198, 201, 215, 232, 280
game-based 124
   game-based learning 124
game-like 21, 293
   game-like activities 21
   game-like features 293
games 17, 113, 121, 123–25, 127, 132, 152, 177, 275
   games as e-learning 124
   games in online training 113
gamification (see: gaming)
   gamification learning 124
   gamification methods 293
   gamification technologies 290
gamified 9, 21, 123–24, 201
   gamified assessment 124
   gamified learning 21, 201
   gamified 'virtual world 124
gamify 123
   gamify real-world 123

gamify real-world scenarios 123
gaming 9, 13, 21, 113, 120, 122–26, 200–201, 204, 264, 290, 293
gaming scenarios 124
globalization 39
guidance 24, 46, 48, 208, 210, 294, 304
guideline 9, 15, 28, 30, 35, 63, 69, 88, 93, 103, 109, 141, 158, 163, 182, 187, 210, 221, 245, 269, 273, 275, 277, 279, 281, 283, 285, 321

H

hand-free 199
   hand-free headsets 199
handheld 201
   handheld devices 201
hands-on 9, 13, 17, 23–24, 127, 130, 203, 228, 230, 238, 275
   hands-on activities 130
   hands-on experience 9, 238
   hands-on mastery 230
   hands-on problem-solving 275
   hands-on skill 9, 13, 17, 127, 203
haptic 126–27
hasten 185, 249, 296
hazardous 121, 124
headset 23, 124, 199–200, 207, 211, 254
higher-level 56, 310
   higher-level executives 56
higher-order 9, 41, 113–14, 117, 123, 132, 276
high-frequency 180
   high-frequency events 180
high-quality 301
   high-quality text 301
high-speed 50
hololens 23, 127, 200, 254
homework 175, 178, 227, 238, 251, 263, 274, 277
   homework activities 251
   homework assignments 178, 227

hybrid 16, 22, 234
  hybrid classroom 16
  hybrid learning 22

I

IBM 5, 195, 198, 208, 295–96, 303
ILT 13, 17, 21, 129, 131, 150, 175, 177, 205, 213, 225, 227, 232, 237–38, 251, 257–58, 262–63, 265, 274–75, 277, 291
  ILT phase 129, 154, 177, 213, 227, 237, 258, 263, 265, 275
  ILT session 13, 17, 175, 227, 238, 251, 274, 277
immerse 125–26
immersion 126
immersive 9, 23–24, 123–26, 200–201, 264, 290, 292–93
  immersive e-learning 23
  immersive experience 125–26, 201, 292–93
  immersive gaming 264, 293
  immersive interfaces 123
  immersive learning 23–24
  immersive models 200
  immersive storylines 125
  immersive technologies 124
  immersive technology 293
impactful 52, 60, 199
  impactful metrics 60
impact-making 105
  impact-making metrics 105
implementation 16, 29, 41, 45, 56, 58, 61, 91, 159, 182–83, 194, 244, 257, 261, 283, 297, 305
  implementation framework 159, 182
improvement 15, 46, 48, 50, 57, 59–61, 63, 65, 86–87, 134, 156, 180, 206, 214, 278
in-context 210
individualized 168, 175, 203, 234

information 9, 11, 13–14, 28, 73, 97, 102–3, 113, 118, 125, 128, 132–33, 147, 149, 152, 155, 173, 178, 191, 197, 199–200, 202–4, 206, 208–9, 214, 228, 230, 232–35, 238, 241, 256–57, 259, 264, 266, 276, 290, 292, 297, 305–6
  information access 178
  information content 102, 128, 257
  information content-heavy 203
  information download 256
  information-heavy 257
  information mastery 230
  information retention 28
informational 9–10, 17–18, 127–28, 151, 203–4, 211, 227, 233, 262, 275
information-seeking 257
  information-seeking tasks 257
infrastructure 6, 39, 60–61, 198, 300
  infrastructure investment 6
innovation 23, 31, 40–41, 49–51, 53, 126, 294, 296, 311
instruction 28, 121, 172–73, 192, 199–201, 206, 212, 233, 304
instructional 257, 265
  instructional design 265
  instructional designers 257
instructor 8, 11, 126, 131, 200, 226, 238
  instructor-driven (see: instructor - instructor-led)
    instructor-driven chats 13
    instructor-driven e-learning 8, 17
    instructor-driven sessions 258
    instructor-driven training 225
  instructor-facilitated (see: instructor - instructor-led)
  instructor-led 8, 11, 13–14, 17, 21–22, 73, 119, 129, 131, 133, 149, 154–55, 177, 203, 213, 225, 233, 238, 251, 257–60
  Instructor-pushed 12
  instructor-run (see: instructor - instructor-led)
intelligence 20, 196

INDEX

intensive 9-10, 17, 133
  intensive discussion 133
  intensive hands-on 9, 17
interaction 27-28, 99, 102, 118, 226, 228-29, 231-33, 238-39, 294, 296, 298-99
  interaction matrix 232-33
interaction-intensive 291
interactivity 132-33, 155, 208, 214, 276, 279
  interactivity strategies 208
interconnection 208, 214, 257, 279
interconnectivity (see: interconnection)
interleaving 101, 129, 148, 151, 153-54, 160, 176-77, 265, 274, 276
  interleaving activities 177
  interleaving chunks 148
  interleaving time-spacing 148
internet-based 152, 177
intervention 74, 87, 185, 202-3, 262-63, 265
investment 6, 43-44, 54-56, 235, 249
in-workflow 14, 17
  in-workflow tools 14, 17
isolating 60, 252, 257
isolation 252, 256-57, 298

J

JIT (see: just-in-time)
job-related 132, 135, 158, 216, 275, 279
job-relevant (see: job-related)
jobs 10-11, 13, 26, 46, 62, 73-74, 79, 81, 83, 128, 168, 174, 204, 228, 291
journey 7, 13-17, 34, 67, 73, 75, 91, 101, 107, 139, 162, 168, 172-73, 176, 181-83, 185, 207, 210, 219, 226, 244, 257, 260, 262-63, 265, 273-74, 280, 289, 293, 306-7, 321
just-in-time 25, 102-3, 185, 191-92, 199, 203-4, 207, 209-11, 217, 219, 252, 274, 292
  just-in-time access 203
  just-in-time knowledge access 203
  just-in-time learning 25, 209, 217, 292
  just-in-time learning opportunities 25
  just-in-time learning resources 292
  just-in-time performance support systems 219
  just-in-time PSS 204
  just-in-time resources 191, 209
  just-in-time support 102-3, 210

K

Kirkpatrick 56
know-how 198, 207
knowledge 10, 12-13, 39, 44, 46, 55, 64, 89, 97, 113, 121, 150, 167, 171-73, 176, 182, 191, 198, 202-4, 206, 208, 212, 228, 230, 256-57, 276, 280, 294, 297-99, 303, 305
knowledge-based 191, 229, 237
knowledge-based procedures 191
KPI 30, 35, 41, 53, 55, 58, 65, 67, 69, 73-75, 77, 79, 81, 83, 85, 87, 89, 91, 93, 109, 141, 163, 187, 221, 245, 269, 285, 309

L

large-scale 225
leaders 49-51, 56, 58, 60-61, 79-80, 85, 88, 191, 195, 249, 305
leadership 5, 42, 44, 46, 48-52, 54, 65, 80, 91, 122, 281, 321
  leadership needs 65
  leadership practices 49, 51-52
  leadership roles 50
  leadership skills 48, 321
learner 6, 8-16, 19-28, 31, 44, 49-51, 55, 57, 59, 63, 83-84, 89, 97, 101-4, 113-22, 125-26, 128-32, 134, 136, 145, 147, 150, 153, 157-58, 160, 167-70, 172-74, 176-77, 179-83, 185, 202-4,

208-9, 212, 214–17, 219, 226–28, 231–42, 244, 249–51, 257–60, 262–64, 266, 273–75, 277–80, 290, 292, 294, 300–305
learner-content 229, 231–33
Learner-rich 229
learning 6–9, 11–17, 19–31, 34, 39–44, 46–47, 51–53, 56–61, 63–65, 67, 74, 83–85, 89, 91, 97–98, 101–4, 107, 113–33, 135–37, 139, 145–50, 152–56, 158–60, 162, 167–76, 179–83, 185, 191–92, 198–205, 208–17, 219, 225–30, 232–42, 244, 249–52, 254–60, 262–66, 273–75, 277–80, 289–92, 294, 296, 298–307, 309–11
learning achievement 124
learning activities 25, 103, 167, 169–70, 175–76, 203, 236, 274, 301, 303
learning analytics 57, 305–7, 309
learning approach 225
learning channels 226, 240
learning content 13, 23, 191, 237, 290, 292, 301, 303
learning culture 51, 65
learning curve 28, 44, 296
learning delivery 12, 22, 192
learning department 44, 307
learning design 97, 235, 266, 300, 305
learning designer 147
learning domain 147
learning ecosystem 234–35, 275
learning effectiveness 116
learning environment 294
learning experience 98, 118, 125, 169, 173, 202, 229, 242, 279, 290, 302
learning experiences 19, 23–24, 120, 300, 303
learning expertise 52
learning goals 129, 273
learning initiatives 42, 46–47, 51
learning interventions 262, 265
learning journey 7, 14–15, 34, 67, 91, 107, 139, 162, 173, 185, 219, 226, 244, 262
learning leader 42
learning management 19
learning material 200, 203, 211–12, 227, 292, 302
learning mechanism 22, 254, 264
learning methods 6, 19, 120, 145
learning modalities 234, 250
learning mode 17, 22, 226, 236, 273
learning models 22
learning modules 167, 227, 254
learning networks 299
learning objectives 7, 230
learning on-the-go 204, 251
learning opportunities 24–25, 300
learning organization 40
learning outcomes 41–44, 51, 57, 65, 104, 131, 145, 149–50, 172, 176, 181, 204, 212, 230, 236, 250–51, 262–63, 292, 294
learning path 85, 98, 101–2, 153, 167–76, 180–81, 183, 204, 236, 260, 262, 264–65, 274, 280, 290, 300, 303, 305
learning pathway 21, 167
learning phases 150
learning platform 19, 21, 120, 124, 173, 201, 203, 226, 291, 303–5
learning process 41, 120, 124, 228, 275, 303
learning program 174
learning programs 19, 59, 226
learning requirements 290
learning resources 21, 257, 292
learning routes 234
learning scores 58
learning sequence 168
learning skills 256
learning solutions 24, 26, 29
learning strategies 31, 257
learning strategists 135

INDEX

learning styles 30, 234
learning systems 29
learning techniques 254
learning technologies 21, 39–40, 42, 51–53, 58, 198, 204, 289–90, 292
learning technologist 310–11
learning technologists 59
learning technology 44, 58, 291
learning tools 292
learning transfer 145, 160
learning-based 290
learning-related 305
learning-worthy 149
lecture 8, 13, 27, 130–33, 149, 154–55, 177, 226, 275
linear 128, 133, 151, 155, 178, 273
LMS 19, 168, 173, 183, 192, 203–4, 228, 251, 290–91, 300
long-term 44, 52–53, 64–65
low-complexity 227, 275
low-frequency 180
low-speed 20

M

machinery 24
maintenance 14, 18, 119, 174, 199, 279
maintenance phases 174
management 19, 48–50, 54, 56–57, 63, 65, 80, 121–22, 151, 194, 202–4, 212, 281, 297
  management methodologies 48, 63
  management skills 122
  management staff 281
  management system 19
  management systems 202–4, 212
  management tools 202
  management training 122
manager 183, 208, 255
manufacture 180, 264
meaningful 11, 157, 208, 214, 279–80
measured 76–78, 81–82, 134, 258

measurement 56, 62, 87–88, 174, 231
measuring 46, 53, 56–57, 64–65, 67, 74, 307, 309
media-rich 238
Mentor 134, 156, 277, 294, 307
  mentor-driven 11
mentoring 10, 13, 18, 156, 180, 192, 208, 232, 240, 250, 278, 291–92
metaverse 22, 124
metrics 48, 50, 53, 56–57, 59–64, 67, 75, 77, 79, 81, 85–89, 105, 134, 174, 180, 182, 278, 280, 307, 309–10
micro-assessment 153, 176, 274
microlearning 23, 25, 35, 69, 93, 97–98, 103, 109, 123, 139, 141, 145–57, 159–63, 171, 185, 187, 204, 211, 221, 231, 245, 251, 259–60, 265, 269, 273–74, 276–77, 279, 282, 285
microlearning-based 148
micro-lesson 132, 134, 152–54, 156–58, 175–77, 212, 214, 273–74, 276–77, 279
modalities 233–34, 250, 257
model 100, 125, 131, 191, 201, 252, 254, 260, 292, 300
multichannel 194, 214, 227, 229, 235, 240, 242, 260, 264, 275, 277–80, 295–96, 299–300
  multichannel communicator 300
  multichannel learning 229, 242
  multichannel learning experience 229, 242
multi-content 98
multidisciplinary 255
multi-format 235, 280
multi-mode 235, 240, 280
multi-sensory 28, 102–3, 226, 228, 238
multi-technology 35, 69, 93, 98, 109, 141, 163, 187, 221, 225, 227, 229, 231, 233, 245, 269, 283, 285
multi-technology mix 35, 69, 93, 98, 109, 141, 163, 187, 221, 225, 227, 229, 231, 233, 245, 269, 283, 285

N

nano-coaching 156, 208–9, 232, 277–78
nano-learning 25
nano-mentoring 208, 277–78
need-based 11, 249
need-driven (see: need-based)
new-generation 240, 278
next-generation 60, 73, 105, 127, 254, 300, 311
  next-generation e-learning 300
  next-generation e-learning tool 300
  next-generation gadgets 127
  next-generation projects 60, 73
  next-generation skills 60, 73
  next-generation technology 254
NLP 300, 304
non-contextual 146–47
non-essential 276
non-financial 84
non-game 21, 293
non-linear 26, 114, 117, 132
non-proficiency 84
non-proficient 174
non-routine 26, 73, 134, 156, 180, 214, 277
non-technical 79
non-training 217
non-value-add 157, 174

O

observation 5, 59, 129, 146, 153, 176, 293
obsolescence 41, 53–54, 64, 81, 311
obsolete 82–83
OJT 13, 134, 232, 277, 307
OJT check sheets 134, 277
onboarding 74, 77, 123, 174, 199, 302, 307–8
on-demand 11–12, 14, 17, 21, 35, 69, 93, 98, 103, 109, 141, 163, 187, 191–93, 195, 197, 199, 201, 203–5, 207, 209, 211, 213, 215, 217, 221, 240, 245, 260, 264, 269, 274, 276, 278, 280, 282, 285, 290, 292
on-demand e-learning 11, 17
on-demand informational content 204
on-demand learning 21, 204
on-demand online learning 290
on-demand performance 14, 35, 69, 93, 103, 109, 141, 163, 187, 191, 193, 195, 197, 199, 201, 203, 205, 207, 209, 211, 213, 215, 217, 221, 245, 269, 274, 276, 278, 280, 282, 285
on-demand performance support 14, 35, 69, 93, 103, 109, 141, 163, 187, 191, 193, 195, 197, 199, 201, 203, 205, 207, 209, 211, 213, 215, 217, 221, 245, 269, 274, 276, 278, 280, 282, 285
on-demand PSS 211, 260, 264, 274
on-demand resources 14, 17, 21
on-demand self-guided material 240, 278
on-demand videos 192
one-dimensional 151
on-screen 11, 18, 192, 205–6
on-screen contextual help 18, 205–6
on-screen help 192
on-screen interactive guides 206
on-screen software help 11
on-the-go 12, 14, 18, 20, 25, 136, 157–58, 192, 204, 212, 216, 251, 279, 292
on-the-job 10, 13–14, 17–18, 60, 73–74, 77, 129–30, 133–34, 149–50, 156, 168, 179–80, 182, 191, 209, 213, 215, 230, 232, 250, 257–60, 262, 264–65, 273, 277–78, 307, 309
on-the-job activities 180, 215, 265, 278
on-the-job assessment 130
on-the-job assessment criteria 130
on-the-job assignments 259, 264
on-the-job behaviors 60, 230

INDEX

on-the-job e-learning 13–14, 17, 180, 215, 277
on-the-job e-learning guidelines 277
on-the-job experiences 260, 264
on-the-job learning 150, 182, 257, 262, 264
on-the-job learning resources 257
on-the-job mentored training 73
on-the-job phase 260
on-the-job proficiency 168, 191, 250, 307
on-the-job proficiency orientation 307
on-the-job progress 134
on-the-job results 134
on-the-job success 129, 273
on-the-job support 74, 309
on-the-job training 13, 77, 156, 179, 213
openAI 197, 300–301
optimizing 173, 262
organization 16, 28, 40–44, 47–53, 55, 57–58, 60–61, 63, 77, 83, 88, 114, 120, 192, 259, 281, 296–97, 299–300, 305, 309, 311, 321
organizational 5–6, 29, 34, 40, 47, 49, 52–53, 55, 65, 67, 79, 89, 191, 203, 209, 217, 242, 311
outcome 41–44, 51, 53, 57–58, 65, 74–75, 77, 85, 101, 103–4, 128–29, 131, 133, 137, 145, 149–50, 152–55, 160, 172, 175–77, 180–81, 185, 204, 212, 219, 230, 236–37, 250–52, 255–56, 262–63, 273, 275, 278, 292–94, 296, 300, 302
outcome-driven 250
over-complex 73
over-compress 147, 156

P

pandemic 5–6, 22, 24, 29, 39–40, 76, 80, 83, 191, 225–26, 291
participation 8, 117, 123, 132, 276, 293
participation requirements 8
patterns 196–97, 280, 302
pedagogical 31, 105
peer 26, 43, 132, 208, 226, 232–33, 242, 255, 294, 297
peer-to-peer 132, 226, 276
performance 10–11, 14, 17–18, 21, 27, 32, 35, 45–46, 59–61, 69, 74–75, 77–79, 82–83, 86, 89, 93, 98, 103, 107, 109, 121–22, 126, 134, 139, 141, 147, 156, 163, 179–80, 185, 187, 191, 193, 195, 197, 199, 201, 203, 205, 207–9, 211, 213–15, 217, 219, 221, 245, 255–56, 269, 274, 276, 278, 280–82, 285, 299, 301, 305, 307–10
performance data 301
performance demonstrated 75
performance goals 46, 255–56
performance improvement 61, 134, 156, 180, 214, 278
performance indicators 30
performance issues 82
performance measure 74, 134
performance measures 74
performance of employees 59
performance ratings 308–9
performance retention scores 307
performance review 134
performance reviews 278
performance standards 78, 86
performance support 10–11, 14, 17–18, 35, 69, 93, 98, 103, 109, 141, 163, 185, 187, 191, 193, 195, 197, 199, 201, 203, 205, 207, 209, 211, 213, 215, 217, 219, 221, 245, 269, 274, 276, 278, 280, 282, 285
performance support systems (see: PSS)
performance support technology 199
performance support tool 199
performance systems 98
performance technologies 199

performance thresholds 75
performers 74, 298–99
personalized 21, 23–24, 26, 120, 168, 173, 175, 197–98, 204, 208, 278, 290, 300–304
　personalized e-learning 301
　personalized feedback 24
　personalized guidance 208
　personalized learning 26, 120, 168, 173, 175, 204, 290, 300–303
　personalized learning content 301
　personalized learning experience 173, 290
　personalized learning experiences 120, 303
　personalized learning path 168, 173, 175, 204, 303
　personalized learning recommendations 26, 302
　personalized recommendations 303
　personalized resources 303–4
　personalized search 197–98
　personalized support 278
platforms 13, 19–21, 25–26, 28, 32, 39, 47–49, 51, 57, 63, 105, 120, 123–24, 126, 173, 194–95, 201, 203–4, 206, 209, 225–26, 240, 242, 278, 280, 291–96, 298–305
post-COVID 16, 50, 83
post-ILT 11, 13–14, 17, 134, 156, 179, 181, 213–16, 232, 240–41, 258, 262–65, 277–79
post-pandemic 293
post-work 154, 177, 276
pre-design 251
pre-ILT 14, 128, 152, 175, 210, 232, 235, 258, 260, 262–63, 265, 273
　pre-ILT phase 128, 152, 175, 210, 235, 262, 273
pre-learning 259
preparatory 13, 152
Pre-recorded 11, 17
presentation-based 128

pre-training 150, 227, 237, 275
　pre-training course 227, 237
　pre-training courses 275
　pre-training phase 227
problem-based 113, 118
　problem-based e-learning 113
　problem-based learning 118
problem-solving 25–26, 101, 113, 123–25, 128, 133, 153, 155, 208, 229, 237, 255, 266, 273, 275
problem-solving-focused 255
problem-solving-oriented 136, 158, 216, 279
procedure-based 203
productive 75–76, 83, 199
productivity 5, 78, 86–87, 195, 202, 293, 295, 299, 309
professionals 23, 25–26, 30, 39, 41–42, 44–45, 54, 59, 64, 89, 116, 121, 126, 206, 294
proficiency 13–16, 18, 26, 28, 32, 43–45, 58–59, 61, 73–74, 76–80, 84–85, 88–89, 99–101, 113, 116–18, 120–22, 126–27, 134–35, 139, 150, 152, 157, 162, 167–72, 174–76, 179–83, 185, 191–92, 203–4, 210, 215–17, 219, 227, 239–41, 249–53, 257–58, 260, 262–65, 273–74, 278–81, 291–92, 299, 301, 306–7, 309–10
　proficiency acquisition 15, 32, 169, 258, 263, 265
　proficiency attainment 182
　proficiency curve 76–77, 88
　proficiency cycle 203
　proficiency development 175, 216, 260, 279
　proficiency faster 171, 263, 301
　proficiency goal 167, 169–70, 172, 175, 217, 251
　proficiency growth 76, 258, 260, 262
　proficiency journey 16, 162, 210, 257, 273–74, 306
　proficiency level 76, 181, 258, 262

INDEX

proficiency maintenance 14, 174, 279
proficiency measurements 174
proficiency measures 239
proficiency metrics 134, 180, 182, 278, 280, 310
proficiency on-the-job 18
proficiency path 127, 152
proficiency speed 264
proficiency stage 309
proficiency test 18, 120
proficiency-testing 136, 158, 216, 279
proficiency-time 15, 76
proficient 74–75, 79, 81–82, 84–85, 135, 173, 205, 263, 293
profiling 172, 175, 280, 310
profitability 85
progressively 120
project-driven 194
PSS 10–11, 14, 17–18, 35, 69, 93, 98, 102–3, 109, 128, 134, 136, 141, 156, 158, 163, 167, 172, 178, 180, 185, 187, 191–95, 197, 199, 201, 203–5, 207, 209–17, 219, 221, 231, 233, 238, 240–41, 245, 251–52, 257, 260, 262, 264–65, 269, 274, 276, 278–80, 282, 285, 292, 296, 300
  PSS technologies 194
  PSS technology 209
PSS-enabled 134, 156, 214, 277
purpose-driven 133, 135, 155, 158, 178, 213, 239, 276, 279, 298–99
  purpose-driven conversations 133, 135, 155, 158, 178, 213, 239, 276, 279
  purpose-driven discussions 299
  purpose-driven networks 298
  purpose-driven social connectivity 298
purposeful 133, 155, 208, 214, 279

Q

qualified 82, 174, 239, 277, 290–91
qualified or certified 174

qualified workforce 82
qualitative 59, 195, 310
quantifiably 310
questions 12, 132, 191, 194, 197, 203, 205, 232, 250, 252–53, 294, 299, 301–5, 310
quizzes 9, 12–13, 17–18, 120, 124, 129–30, 153, 204, 236, 273, 301

R

ramp-up 82
rapidly 20, 30, 44, 120, 197, 211, 300
rate 32, 39–40, 53, 58–59, 61, 82–84, 87, 228, 258, 260, 266, 307
readiness 59, 82, 84–86, 174, 192, 234, 249
  readiness of staff 86
  readiness of the workforce 85
  readiness of your teams 192
realistic 114, 124, 126–28, 130, 153, 181, 255, 263–64, 266, 273, 278
  realistic assignments 264
  realistic cases 128, 273
  realistic challenges 266
  realistic games 127
  realistic goals 181, 278
  realistic problems 263
  realistic situations 124
real-life 9, 113, 117, 120–25, 132, 202
  real-life cases 132
  real-life experiences 202
  real-life fire 124
  real-life scenario 113, 132
  real-life scenarios 9, 117, 121, 125
  real-life situations 120–22
real-time 8, 11, 22–23, 194–97, 199, 205, 207, 211, 294–96, 300, 303–4
  real-time activities 8
  real-time answers 303–4
  real-time collaboration 194–95, 296

347

real-time collaboration technologies 194–95, 296
real-time collaboration tools 296
real-time community 295
real-time conversations 207, 304
real-time data 196–97, 211
real-time data insights 197, 211
real-time data visualizations 196
real-time face-to-face meetings 195
real-time feedback 23, 300, 304
real-time insights 196
real-time participation 8
real-time support 205
real-time text communication 194
real-time information 199
real-world 9, 13, 23–24, 98, 103, 113–15, 120, 122–23, 125, 279
    real-world cases 113
    real-world environments 9, 23
    real-world experience 115
    real-world problem 103
    real-world problems 98, 114
    real-world problem-solving 103
    real-world projects 120
    real-world scenarios 23–24, 123, 279
    real-world scientific problems 125
    real-world situations 13, 122
reflection 32–33, 65–66, 89–90, 101, 103, 105–6, 131, 137–38, 151, 155, 160–61, 183–84, 217–18, 227, 239, 242–43, 251, 255, 266–67, 276, 284, 312
reinforcement 13–14, 28, 103, 134–36, 145–46, 150, 157–58, 160, 204, 215, 240, 280
    reinforcement activities 160
    reinforcement learning 136, 158, 215, 280
    reinforcement training 240, 280
    reinforcement training content 240, 280
remote 11, 13–14, 16–17, 22, 26, 29, 39, 129, 132, 154–55, 177–78, 194–95, 201, 207, 213, 225–26, 232–33, 239–40, 258, 275–77, 291
remote assist 11, 207
remote assistance 207, 240
remote assist technologies 207
remote classrooms 225
remote e-learning 13–14, 17, 275
remote e-learning delivery 17
remote e-learning guidelines 275
remote experts 201
remote learners 22
remote learning 16, 22
remote lectures 132, 154, 177
remote session 13, 132, 154–55, 177–78, 233, 276
remote session content 178
remote sharing 239, 277
remote teaching 22
remote teams 194–95
remote training 17, 258, 291
remote training technologies 291
remote troubleshooting 194
remote working 39
remotely 207, 231
repeatability 80
repeatable 75, 78, 215, 280
representative 16–17, 130, 208
research-based 321
resources 11, 13–14, 17, 21, 44–45, 50–52, 63, 73, 122, 126, 167, 169–72, 175, 191, 200, 202–3, 209–10, 212, 217, 227, 233, 235, 242, 249, 254, 257, 266, 291–92, 294, 303–4, 306
result-driven 134, 277
revolution 5, 7, 9, 11, 13, 15, 17, 19, 21, 23, 25, 27, 29–31, 33–35, 69, 89, 93, 109, 141, 163, 187, 221, 245, 269, 285, 289, 291, 293, 295, 297, 299, 301, 303, 305, 307, 309, 311, 321
revolutionary 19, 50, 61, 197, 254, 311
    revolutionary approach 61
    revolutionary e-learning 19
    revolutionary products 61

INDEX

revolutionary technologies 50
revolutionary tool 197
rules-based 215, 280, 290

S

sales 74, 76, 79–80, 86, 119, 194, 307
scalability 6, 39, 59
scenario 9, 13, 17, 23–24, 101–3, 113–17, 119–25, 127–37, 139, 151, 153–56, 158, 214, 216, 231, 249, 251–52, 260, 263, 265, 273, 275–77, 279
  scenario-driven 134, 157, 277
  scenario-solving 210
scenario-based 9, 35, 69, 93, 97–98, 103, 107, 109, 113, 115–17, 119, 121–23, 125, 127, 129, 131–33, 135, 137, 139, 141, 151, 163, 185, 187, 203, 212, 221, 231, 245, 251, 263, 269, 273, 275, 277, 279, 282, 285
  scenario-based app 231
  scenario-based contextualization 97, 151, 282
  scenario-based e-learning 35, 69, 93, 107, 109, 113, 115–17, 119, 121, 123, 125, 127, 129, 131–33, 135, 137, 139, 141, 163, 187, 221, 245, 269, 273, 275, 277, 279, 285
  scenario-based e-learning contextualization 273, 275, 277, 279
  scenario-based e-learning courses 107, 139
  scenario-based e-learning design 127
  scenario-based e-learning gamification 123
  scenario-based e-learning reflection 137
  scenario-based e-learning variables 127
  scenario-based learning 9, 103, 212, 263

scenario-based questions 203
scenario-based short sessions 251
scenario-based simulation 113, 122
search-based 257
segmentation 9, 229–33, 260, 262
segmentation by category 230
segmentation of skills 229, 232
self-assessments 192
self-directed 6, 145, 249–50
self-driven 150
self-filled 297
self-guided 9, 13–14, 17, 128, 152, 175–76, 178, 203, 211–12, 227, 238, 240, 249, 260, 262, 273, 278
  self-guided e-learning 13–14, 17, 128, 273
  self-guided e-learning guidelines 273
  self-guided homework 178, 227, 238
  self-guided informational content 211
  self-guided learning 9, 175, 249
  self-guided learning activities 175
  self-guided material 212, 240, 278
  self-guided microlearning 152
  self-guided micro-lesson 152, 176
  self-guided pre-work 260, 262
self-learning 13, 17, 21, 128, 226, 228, 250
self-paced 6, 8–9, 11, 13, 17–18, 28, 119, 192, 203, 225, 231–32, 251, 258, 262, 292
  self-paced content 13
  self-paced e-learning 8, 17–18
  self-paced homework 251
  self-paced homework activities 251
  self-paced learning 6, 28, 203, 225, 258, 292
  self-paced learning activities 203
  self-paced learning technologies 292
  self-paced material 9
  self-paced mode 231, 262
  self-paced online courses 11, 17
sequence 35, 69, 93, 97–98, 101, 103, 109, 115–16, 141, 150, 162–63, 167–73, 175, 177, 179–81, 183, 185, 187, 215,

221, 227, 245, 251, 258, 260, 262, 264–65, 269, 274, 276, 278, 280, 282, 285
shelf-life 53
shortened 32, 77, 83, 86–87, 91, 98, 114, 118, 126–27, 147, 152, 169, 171–72, 174, 176, 181, 202, 207, 227, 235, 257, 259, 274, 291, 295, 305
shortening 81, 84–85, 105, 107, 119, 199, 206, 209–10, 227, 232, 249, 256, 289, 301
   shortening training 227
   shortening training duration 227
   shortening TTP 81, 84–85, 105, 107, 119, 199, 206, 209–10, 232, 249, 256, 289, 301
shorter 25, 32, 77–78, 81, 84, 86–87, 98, 101, 114–16, 120, 136, 145, 147, 150–52, 158, 160, 162, 167, 182, 203, 216–17, 227, 235, 251–52, 258, 260, 273, 279
   shorter chunk 98
   shorter chunk of content 98
   shorter content 147
   shorter courses 86
   shorter e-learning 101, 151, 160
   shorter e-learning sessions 151
   shorter e-learning units 101
   shorter learning 252
   shorter micro-lessons 152, 273
   shorter on-the-go assessments 136, 158, 216
   shorter sales cycle 86
   shorter segments 158, 279
   shorter sessions 145, 150–51
   shorter training 84, 87, 203, 217
   shorter TTP 81, 86–87, 162, 235, 258, 260
sign-off 134, 156
simulated 9, 23–24, 113, 120–25, 131, 152, 177, 264
   simulated business environment 122
   simulated challenges 264

simulated games 121
simulated scenarios 113
simulated virtual worlds 124
simulation 9, 24–25, 113, 119–22, 125–26, 132, 201, 204, 274–75
simulator 13, 17, 121–22, 232, 264
skill-deficiency-related 83
skill-related 81–82
skills 5, 7, 9–10, 13–14, 17–18, 20, 25–28, 44, 46–49, 51–52, 55, 60, 65, 73, 76–86, 97, 101–3, 113, 116–18, 120–24, 126, 128, 131, 137, 146–47, 149–50, 153, 156, 167, 172, 178–79, 201, 203–4, 208, 217, 227–32, 237–39, 242, 244, 252, 254, 256–57, 262, 266, 273, 275, 280–81, 290–91, 294, 296–97, 303–5, 310, 321
skills on-demand 17
skills on-the-job 10
SmartGlasses 200
smartphone-based 201
smartphones 20, 25, 201–2, 204, 212
S-OJT 134
specialist 44–45, 146
speed-enabling 35, 69, 93, 109, 141, 163, 187, 221, 245, 269, 285, 321
   speed-enabling e-learning 35, 69, 93, 109, 141, 163, 187, 221, 245, 269, 285, 321
   speed-enabling e-learning ecosystem 321
   speed-enabling e-learning systems 35, 69, 93, 109, 141, 163, 187, 221, 245, 269, 285
speed-related 81–82
   speed-related competitiveness 81
   speed-related drivers 82
speed-to-proficiency 84–85, 116, 149–51, 160, 172, 289
stage 7, 13–17, 75, 162, 307–9
start-to-end 101, 168, 174
step-by-step 120, 199–200, 233, 254
story-telling 114, 134, 157, 277

INDEX

strategic 29, 34–35, 41–44, 46, 48–49, 52–56, 63, 65, 69, 80, 87, 91, 93, 97, 99, 101, 103, 105, 107, 109, 113, 141, 163, 187, 221, 245, 258–59, 269, 281, 285, 310–11, 321
   strategic decisions 53
   strategic e-learning 35, 69, 93, 97, 99, 101, 103, 105, 107, 109, 141, 163, 187, 221, 245, 269, 285
   strategic e-learning design 97, 99, 101, 103, 105, 107
   strategic framework 87
   strategic goals 43
   strategic leadership 42, 91
   strategic management 80
   strategic objectives 42
   strategic plans 281
   strategic questions 310
   strategic recommendations 48, 63
   strategic rehearsal 113
   strategic role 29
   strategic skills 65
   strategic success 42
   strategic technological investment 43–44
   strategic technological thinking 41
   strategic technology 46
   strategic technology decisions 46
   strategic thinker 53
   strategic thinking 41, 48–49, 52, 54, 65, 258, 321
   strategic thinking skills 49
strategically 40, 47–48, 126, 192, 202, 210, 227, 238, 258–60, 277, 295, 306, 310
strategies 5, 7, 11, 16, 27, 31–32, 34, 41–42, 44–45, 47, 50–51, 53, 59, 64, 87, 97–99, 105, 107, 113, 121, 127, 137, 151, 208, 244, 250, 252–55, 257–58, 273, 281, 289, 309, 311, 321
strategist 16, 29, 35, 39–43, 45, 47, 49, 51, 53, 55, 57, 59, 61, 63, 65, 67, 69, 93, 109, 127, 135, 141, 151, 163, 174, 187, 191, 198, 209–10, 217, 221, 235, 242, 245, 256–57, 269, 285, 311, 321
strategy 6, 39, 45–46, 55, 64, 89, 99, 101–3, 107, 118, 122–23, 137, 139, 145, 147–48, 151, 162, 167–68, 172, 185, 203, 210, 217, 219, 225, 228, 244, 250, 252, 254, 258, 262–65, 282–83, 289, 293
structured 15, 117, 232, 260, 264
student-generated 239, 277
students 22, 28, 120, 124–26, 149, 173, 201, 225–26, 292, 302–4
subscription-based 198
systematically 176, 182, 252
systems 10–11, 14, 17–18, 22, 24, 29, 35, 57, 69, 87, 93, 98, 102–3, 109, 141, 163, 168, 185, 187, 191, 193–95, 197, 199, 201–5, 207, 209, 211–13, 215, 217, 219, 221, 226, 235, 237, 239–41, 243, 245, 249, 251, 253, 255, 257, 259, 261, 263, 265, 267, 269, 274, 276, 278, 280, 282, 285, 290

T

talent 46, 73, 303, 305–8
   talent analytics 305
   talent development 46
   talent distribution 308
   talent frameworks 303
   talent profiles 307–8
targeted 27, 88, 208, 214, 217, 251, 278–79, 299, 303–4
   targeted employee 88
   targeted group 88
   targeted instruction 304
   targeted knowledge 299
   targeted learning 303
task-driven 134, 277
   task-driven OJT 134, 277
task-focused 134
taxonomies 7, 9, 16, 230, 296–97

team-driven 194
teams 22, 48, 60, 75, 124, 192, 194-95, 208, 293, 296-97, 299
technical 25-26, 48, 56, 79-80, 125, 199, 228
  technical expertise 48
  technical jobs 79
  technical material 125
  technical skills 25-26, 228
  technical support 199
  technical training 56
technicians 122, 199, 207, 230-31, 304
techniques 30, 117, 121-22, 130, 162, 254, 278, 289, 293
technological 23, 40-41, 43-44, 50, 52, 61, 87, 89, 125, 198, 225, 321
  technological advances 125, 225
  technological challenges 23
  technological infrastructure 61, 198
  technological innovations 40
  technological investment 43-44
  technological investment decisions 43
  technological organizations 87
  technological space 50
  technological thinking 41
technologies 9, 16, 19-24, 26, 28-29, 31, 39-42, 44-45, 47-54, 56, 58, 60-61, 63, 65, 67, 73, 76, 83, 86, 91, 98, 102-3, 119, 124-26, 137, 172, 176, 182, 191, 194-95, 198-200, 202, 204, 207-9, 211, 213, 215-16, 219, 225-26, 229, 233, 235, 237-42, 244, 264, 277-80, 289-93, 295-96, 298-300, 306, 311
Technologist 42, 58-59, 310-11
technology 5, 19-20, 23-24, 39, 42, 44, 46-47, 49-50, 52, 54-55, 57-58, 60-61, 64, 82, 98, 102, 126-27, 150, 191, 199-203, 205, 209, 227, 242, 252, 254, 275, 277, 279-81, 290-91, 293, 295-97, 299-300, 311
technology-backed 40
technology-based 5, 40
technology-driven 6, 40, 145, 240, 279

technology-enabled 238
thinking-based 9, 17, 132, 229, 237
thinking-intensive 154
thinking-oriented 231
time-distributed 259
time-related 81
time-spaced 35, 69, 93, 97-98, 103, 109, 139, 141, 145-49, 151, 153, 155, 157-63, 176, 187, 212, 221, 231, 245, 259-60, 264-65, 269, 273-74, 276-77, 279, 282, 285
time-to-market 50, 53, 81-83
  time-to-market competitiveness 81
  time-to-market of products 83
  time-to-market performance 83
  time-to-market pressure 82
  time-to-market pressures 82
time-to-proficiency (see: TTP)
  time-to-proficiency(TTP) metrics 75
  time-to-proficiency of training 79
  time-to-proficiency of training cases 79
tracking 226, 292, 307
training 5-6, 11, 13, 16-20, 22-23, 26-28, 40-41, 44, 46, 56, 59, 73-74, 77-82, 84-87, 97, 113, 118-23, 125-27, 137, 145, 150-52, 156, 160, 167, 169-72, 174, 179, 185, 191, 194, 199-207, 209-13, 217, 219, 225-28, 232, 240, 250-52, 257-60, 262-63, 265, 274, 280, 289-91, 294, 298, 307-9
  training activities 167
  training and development 44
  training and education 23
  training and e-learning 41
  training and learning 118, 258, 289
  training capacity 86
  training cases 79
  training certification 307
  training classes 298
  training content 240, 280
  training costs 307
  training course 171, 257
  training curriculum 211, 274

INDEX

training data 308
training delivery 202, 290–91
training department 40
training design 6, 97, 113, 137, 258, 263, 265
training designers 127, 174
training duration 59, 81, 84, 87, 127, 151, 227
training event 191, 207, 209, 217
training experts 44, 294
training function 41
training intervention 185, 202–3, 262
training method 5, 28
training modalities 257
training modules 123, 152, 203, 309
training organization 28
training program 28, 46, 78, 174, 209
training requirement 174, 217
training session 11, 13, 16–17, 22, 145, 212, 225–26, 260
training simulations 121, 125
training solutions 6, 40
training staff 46
training stages 13
training technologies 291
training-focused 217
training-related 59, 174
training-related metrics 59, 174
transformation 6, 56, 65, 67, 321
   transformation experts 321
   transformation strategy 6
transformative 321
troubleshooting 26, 118, 123, 194, 199, 207
TTP 27–28, 50, 53, 60–62, 64, 75–79, 81, 83–89, 91, 98, 105, 107, 114, 116, 118–19, 126–27, 137, 147, 151–52, 162, 167, 169, 171–72, 174, 199, 202, 205–7, 209–10, 225, 227, 232, 234–35, 244, 249, 256, 258–60, 263, 281, 289–90, 295, 298, 301, 305–9, 321
   TTP benefit 86
   TTP durations 79

TTP impact 88
TTP in technical jobs 79
TTP in the workplace 81
TTP measurement 88
TTP metrics 53, 61–62, 64, 75, 77, 79, 87, 89
TTP of the workforce 91
TTP of your employees 295
TTP of your workforce 259
TTP or proficiency measurements 174

U

understand 7, 13, 47–48, 51–52, 64–65, 79, 125, 128, 198, 209, 230, 233, 262, 300, 306, 309–10
unpredictable 81, 134, 156, 180, 214, 277
unpredictable challenges 81
unproductive 185, 219
unproductive time 185
unproductive training 219
upfront 11, 128, 203, 256
upskilling 30
up-to-date 12, 14, 30, 41–42, 44–45, 54, 64, 296
   up-to-date information 14
   up-to-date on e-learning trends 45, 64
   up-to-date on emerging e-learning 54
   up-to-date on industry 54
   up-to-date on industry trends 54
   up-to-date with compliance 12
   up-to-date with compliance requirements 12
   up-to-date with industry 30
   up-to-date with industry developments 30
   up-to-date with the latest e-learning 41, 44

V

variations 113–14, 118, 132, 226, 275

video 9, 11-12, 14, 17-18, 22, 28, 128, 134-35, 137, 149-50, 152, 157-58, 174, 177, 192, 194-95, 197-201, 204, 211-13, 225-26, 228, 232-33, 238-39, 258, 264, 274-75, 277, 279-80, 302
- video conference 239, 277
- video conferencing 22, 226
- video conferencing tools 22
- video generation 302
- video libraries 198
- video tutorials 9, 11, 17

video-based 13, 127, 150, 152, 177
- video-based chunks 150
- video-based content 152, 177
- video-based informational content 127
- video-based tutorials 13

virtual 8-9, 11, 13-14, 17, 22, 24-25, 97, 120, 122-25, 129, 132, 145, 149, 151, 154-55, 177-78, 201-2, 213, 225-26, 228, 232, 234, 237, 257-59, 275-76, 291
- meeting 8, 46, 195
- virtual and remote classrooms 225
- virtual battlespace 122
- virtual classrooms 24, 226
- virtual environment 24, 122
- virtual immersive universes 123
- virtual instructor-driven e-learning 17
- virtual instructor-led session 149
- virtual interactions 226
- virtual labs environment 9
- virtual learning 22, 228, 258, 291
- virtual learning delivery 22
- virtual learning platforms 291
- virtual lecture 226
- virtual lectures 226
- virtual meetings 8
- virtual mode 225, 291
- virtual reality (see: VR)
- virtual session 11, 17, 129, 145, 149, 151, 154-55, 177, 213, 228, 258-59, 276

virtual simulations 24, 120
virtual situation 125
virtual team 25
virtual training 22, 145, 226, 291
virtual training delivery 291
virtual training sessions 22, 145, 226
virtual world 124, 226
virtual world-based games 124
virtually 98, 124, 127, 213, 238, 254
visualization 195-96
- visualization platform 195
- visualization tool 195-96

VR 9, 13, 17, 19, 22-24, 125-26, 132, 136, 158, 198-99, 201-2, 204, 211, 215, 232-34, 239-40, 264, 275, 277-78, 280, 290, 292
- VR-based 16
- VR devices 201
- VR gadgets 136, 158, 198, 201, 215, 232, 280
- VR headsets 211
- VR learning 290
- VR models 233
- VR platform 126
- VR-simulated 126
- VR simulations 126
- VR technologies 9, 125-26, 202, 292
- VR technology 199

W

walkthroughs 206, 232
well-accounted 42
well-contained 133, 155
- well-contained scenarios 133, 155
well-defined 116
- well-defined sequence 116
- well-defined sequence of cases 116
well-designed 137, 227, 262
- well-designed blended 227
- well-designed pre-work 262
- well-designed scenarios 137

INDEX

well-established 124
well-known 19, 21
well-managed 207
well-scoped 128, 134, 151, 153–54, 156, 183, 214, 276–77
  well-scoped realistic case 153
  well-scoped realistic cases 128
  well-scoped scenario 154, 276
  well-scoped scenarios 128
  well-scoped sequence 183
well-sequenced 262
well-suited 23, 25
workflow 10–11, 14, 18, 126, 136, 158, 185, 191, 199, 209–12, 215, 217, 219, 233, 274, 280, 292, 296, 311
  workflow tools 11, 14, 18
workflow-based 11–12, 17, 233
  workflow-based automation 233
  workflow-based automation tools 233
  workflow-based e-learning 11, 17
  workflow-based e-learning delivery 11
workforce 53, 60–61, 73, 80–85, 89, 91, 105, 139, 191–92, 234, 259, 281, 291, 305–6, 309–10, 321
workplace 10, 17–18, 25–26, 41, 60, 73, 81, 84–85, 98, 116, 121, 167, 195, 255, 257, 264–65, 306–7, 310
  workplace analytics 306–7, 310
  workplace ecosystem 264
  workplace learning 84–85, 257, 265
  workplace learning expert 85
  workplace learning strategies 257
  workplace learning strategy 265
  workplace problems 255
  workplace skills 10, 17–18
work-related 136, 158, 215, 280, 297
work-related content 297
world-class 206

FROM THE SAME AUTHOR

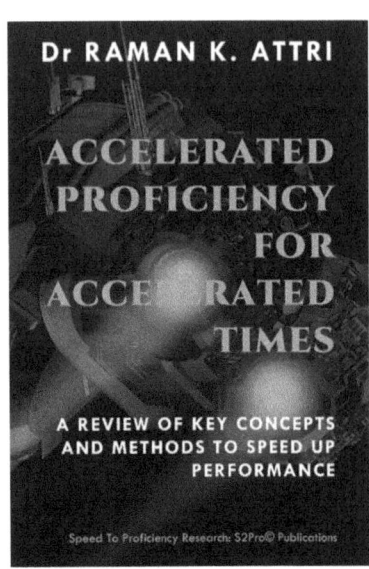

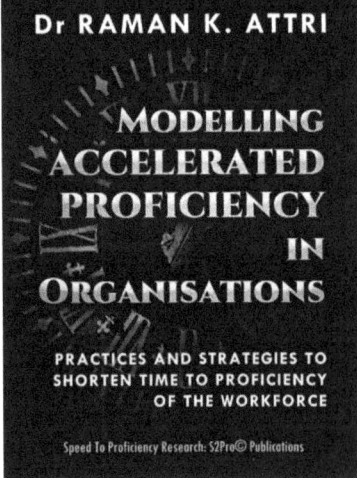

FROM THE COVER

In the midst of an unparalleled technological and digital revolution, thriving as a distinguished Chief e-learning Officer demands a unique set of strategies to conquer the fast-paced business landscape. This all-encompassing guide is tailored for e-learning strategists, digital transformation experts, and e-learning designers who are eager to unravel the core principles and emerging trends that propel success in today's dynamic digital realm.

Dive into *Chief e-learning Officer in the Era of Speed* and unveil the transformative e-learning approaches that will redefine the way you empower your workforce in this era of rapid change. Learn to stay ahead of the competition by reducing time-to-proficiency and enhancing employee development journeys. Confidently traverse the digital revolution as you delve into groundbreaking, research-based e-learning tactics.

Master the design of a speed-enabling e-learning ecosystem that swiftly prepares your employees for success. With the tools, insights, and guidelines provided in this book, you'll be able to craft compelling, future-proof e-learning experiences that expedite employee growth. Embrace the potential of cutting-edge e-learning strategies and unlock the secrets to accelerated triumph in our fast-paced world.

More than just a guide, this book imparts the strategic thinking essential to navigating e-learning strategies in the era of speed. Elevate your leadership skills and shine as a global Chief e-learning Officer, leaving your indelible mark on the digital revolution within your organization.

Do you want to be a speed-savvy CLO or Training Leader with an edge?

Find out about science-backed strategies and corporate training transformation with **GetThereFaster L&D Leaders Academy**. To match the speed with time, you need to master the art and science of speed. Learn the latest and greatest research-backed frameworks and models to accelerate your workforce's performance ahead of time. Develop your managers to stay prepared for the era of AI. Reach out today for a no-obligation call to discuss a Chief Learning Officers' workshop or learning executive coaching session. Book Dr Raman K Attri and get coached by a leading expert on the science of organizational learning speed.

Becoming a top L&D thought Leader in the era of speed has never been this fast!!

Email: contact@get-there-faster.com
Socials: https://nue.bio/chief
Website: https://get-there-faster.com

www.ingramcontent.com/pod-product-compliance
Lightning Source LLC
LaVergne TN
LVHW061539070526
838199LV00077B/6834